Francisco Moises is currently living in Canada. He was educated in Portuguese, English, and French in Mozambique, Kenya, and Canada. He holds a diploma in Fiction Writing and Journalism and three university degrees from the University of Victoria in British Columbia. He reads in English, French, and Portuguese. He intends to dedicate himself to full time writing.

I dedicate to Moises, my paternal grandfather.

My special thoughts go to my late parents and my late aunt Albertina and my late uncle Lino, the parents of my cousin Zefina and Zefina herself, who supported and loved me, each one of them in his or her own unique way.

Remembering the details of the episodes of my early life as I do and portraying them in the book as I did, meant that most of the people who came into my life, particularly my loving cousin Zefina and the missionaries in Mozambique, became very special to me because of the talents that each one of them had and demonstrated in their relationships with me. Their loving care, tolerance, and patience played a major role in moulding my character; I learnt much from them.

Zobue Seminary in Mozambique in particular played a major role in my moral and spiritual transformation and in physically preparing me for the future challenges that have been the lot of my life after leaving Mozambique. Because of that, I stood firm in my convictions when facing the tyrannical politicians I met and confronted on the way, and morally triumphed over them.

Life in the relatively free atmosphere of Kenya enabled me to acquire in-depth knowledge pertaining to different fields. I wish to pay tribute to the teachers of my time at Eastleigh Secondary School in Nairobi who inculcated in me the importance of reading which has become my personal culture and heritage, so much so that in my subsequent efforts to acquire further education at college and university, learning became easier because I had read a great deal on what I later came to study. My wide-ranging reading enabled me to write my memoir in which the influences from the many books and classics I have read come to the surface.

I wish to express my gratitude to the staff at Austin Macauley publishers in London who showed much interest in my memoir and who readily accepted it for publication. I am also pleased that the work is being published in London, the world centre of culture and the epicentre from which information radiates to the world. From London, my work stands a better chance of being more known and of reaching many parts of the world.

Francisco Moises

DARING TO SURVIVE

AUSTIN MACAULEY
PUBLISHERS LTD.

A CIP catalogue record for this title is available from the British Library.

ISBN 9781785548802 (Paperback)
ISBN 9781785548819 (Hardback)
ISBN 9781785548826 (eBook)

www.austinmacauley.com

First Published (2016)
Austin Macauley Publishers Ltd.
25 Canada Square
Canary Wharf
London
E14 5LQ

Part One: Early Days
Chapter 1

Adventures have been part of me and my early life. When difficult situations confronted me, I boldly faced them in order to survive, triumph, and carry on with life. I faced the challenges that have been the lot of my younger days from my birth place in central Mozambique through to Kenya with fortitude, and sometimes with mindless courage. I lived in Kenya longer than in other African countries I went through including Malawi and Tanzania, before leaving for Canada, a dreamland of plenty and unparalleled freedoms. In my younger days, I discovered Canada quite accidentally on a bottle that someone had dumped by a footpath after drinking its contents. The bottle said Canada Dry on it, which I read then as Canada Dree because the letter y, epsilon in Portuguese; k, kappa in Portuguese; and w, are not part of the Portuguese alphabet of 23 letters. In Portuguese y has the sound of e and not y as in English. I did not know then what Canada was until a father Yvon Chouinard, a Catholic priest from Quebec belonging to the Congregation of the White Fathers, which has now switched its name to Missionaries of Africa, came along, and said that he was from Canada.

Then I realized that Canada was the name of a place or of a distant village and village is what the word Canada is supposed to mean from the word *Kanata* of the Native

Iroquois Indian Language. It is said that Jacques Cartier, the Frenchman who is reported to have been the first European explorer of Canada, chanced upon an Iroquois settlement where he met and talked with an Iroquois chief. He is reported to have asked the Iroquois potentate what was the name of his place while expansively waving his arm towards the village. The Indian chief who did not understand French but guessed that the stranger wanted to know the name of the place said Kanata, meaning village or settlement. There is a variation to this story I read in a book many years ago. The Languages Portal website of the Canadian Government called Kanata says that Jacques Cartier heard the word from two Iroquois boys who told him about a village called Kanata. He transliterated the word as Canada and his version was accepted and adopted by the governments of Canada which followed the historical encounter between the Frenchman and the two Iroquois boys.

Father Chouinard told us about Canada and its cold, having himself come close to death at one time after getting frostbitten. He told us many things about Canada and I began to visualize Canada as a place of intense cold, snow and ice, Eskimos and their igloos and of proud Indians who are also known as the First Nations because they were there first before other people joined them. Incidentally, many years later, the first delicious apples I ever ate in my life even before I had imagined that I would one day wind up living in Canada, were Canadian. I bought them in a grocery store at Westlands, the posh western suburb of Nairobi which is dubbed as *The Green City in the Sun* and Nairobi is indeed a city in the sun. And then Kenya began producing its own apples in the cool Limuru region to the north of Nairobi, but its apples were not as good or sweet-smelling as the Canadian ones.

Canada, however, will not be part of my adventures in this narration but will be referred to from time to time when need arises as a shining example of what I will want to illustrate. My life in Canada has been without major bumps or earth-shaking incidents and will be dealt with in another narration that I will write in the near future. My story now will confine itself to the places where my early adventures, some of which were hair-raising and a few somewhat mysterious, took place.

The earliest events I can remember date back to the 1950s after I was born on an unknown date of an unknown month of an unknown year. Predominantly illiterate, villagers had no calendars and most people were born in the villages away from hospitals where doctors and nurses could not record their births. I was one of those who were born in a hut with the traditional or bush matrons in attendance. It is different with people being born now in the age of computers, cell phones, rapid communication, and greater literacy. We not only know the dates of birth of our kids as they are born but we also know the exact time they are born because there are people who can record events on paper or on computers before reporting them to governments for the official population census.

My memory retains patches of the earliest events of my life. It usually retains the beginning and the end with the courses of the events patchy or obliterated from my brain with the passage of time and unforgiving advancing age, the lot of all humans who are lucky enough as to live for a long time. Then what is the earliest event my memory can recollect? Of the events I barely recall them; I cannot say which one took place first.

I will take a gamble and begin with the one when I was with my mom who had my younger brother as a baby strapped on her back and a load of grain or flour on her head. We were coming from visiting my aunt Albertina who was my mom's older sister and the mother of Zefina, my genetically linked lover and cousin, who tugged along with me for quite a long way in my younger days before we parted company.

My mother and brother on her back and I were returning to our village. We had been walking for some time in an area covered with grass with a few scattered short trees when mom decided to visit or see a woman before reaching our village. She did not tell me that we were going to see someone she knew. The person she took us to was not a mere commoner and was not an acquaintance of my mother either because I had never seen her before. She was a healer or a spirit medium or a witchdoctor, if you like; although the term witchdoctor vexes modern African thinkers who regard the name that the West, particularly its missionaries in Africa, coined and gave to our traditional healers, as mean and belittling and a great insult to one of the pillar institutions of African societies. No matter where one goes to in Africa, there are healers to attend to the physical and the spiritual needs of the people. The intention of the missionaries was to make us look bad about ourselves and feel ashamed of what they regarded as our barbaric or savage ways.

I can, however, say with authority that Africans do not discard their millenary ways and secrets. Those who accept alien cultures and religions to the point of rejecting their identities and discarding things they have known all their lives, are few. Even those who do so, do it hypocritically. They will shout hoarsely, denouncing the so-called uncultured African ways in public and later, in the dead of the night within the walls of their huts or residences, they practice the traditional ways of their peoples, for the fear of the unknown is more powerful than the brainwashing power of westernization and of alien religions, be it Christianity or Islam.

It is never easy to wipe out the cultural identity of a people or to obliterate that aspect of their lives that is intrinsically imbedded in their bodies and souls. I can

4

illustrate what I am saying by referring to our ancestors who were taken in chains wearing nothing but rags or the barks of trees or even while naked, who their chiefs and other powerful villagers sold for trinkets to white men at sea ports for export to the New World. They did not forget Mother Africa's cultural values and secrets. Before being shipped away, they were not allowed to take anything. They went to the New World with no belongings and on journeys of no return to Mother Africa.

More often than not the jujus around their necks and around their arms or their waists were removed from them and thrown away, in order to make them feel deprived of their protective charms on which they so much depended. The chiefs and warriors who sold their own people to white men or to Arabs, believed in the power of those charms and that was why they discarded them from their owners. White men probably also feared those charms or did they tear them from their captives and throw them away to show their owners that those things were useless now because they had failed to protect them from being captured and being sold in the first place? Perhaps that was what the western Christian men told them before telling them that Jesus was the saviour of their souls and not of their bodies because they were slaves who belonged to them.

The slaves did not go to the Americas with manuscripts containing formulas on how to make protection charms or on how to practice traditional healing. All knowledge was in the minds and souls of the slaves. Those who were already witchdoctors in Africa found it easier to re-invent themselves in alien lands where wildlife and vegetation were different from those found in Africa. Other slaves who became healers learned things by themselves. Their African ancestral spirits went with them and the slaves prayed to their ancestors to help and protect them and their ancestors revealed secrets to them in their new lands.

The beauty of it is that despite the deprivation of material goods, the slaves revived African healing ways as *curandeiros* or *macumbas* in Brazil, in the form of voodoo mixed with the elements of Catholicism in Haiti, the Caribbean and Louisiana in the United States, and as obeah, a word from a west African language of Ghana to mean witchcraft, in Trinidad and Tobago and other regions of South America and the Caribbean.

The spirit medium mom took us to see lived in a cluster of huts by the small and shallow Lake Chidzime. She was one of the three or four wives of a man who was called Nzungu Dimingu, a name that literally means "Whiteman Dominic," although he had no traces of the white race in him. Why the man was called Nzungu Dimingu, I do not know and I never asked to know. For me it was just a name; an amusing and funny name though.

He was not the only African who had that rather strange name. Another native I later came to know by the name of Nzungu Dimingu that had been given to him as a nickname, was a literate man who worked as an interpreter for the colonial administration. He helped natives who could not speak Portuguese to communicate with the Portuguese colonial authorities. His name was Domingos, Dominic in English and his fellow Africans nicknamed him Nzungu Dimingu perhaps because he was mostly in the company of white colonial administrators, spoke Portuguese, the language of the colonizers, fraternized with them, behaved like them and treated his fellow natives with much contempt and generally acted like the white colonial officers did.

Did I believe in the powers of African healers then and do I still believe in them now? That is a tricky question. As a little boy immersed in the beliefs, fears and apprehension of the only world I knew then, I implicitly believed in all the superstitions of my people. What choice did I have?

Could I fight and win against the apparently all menacing dark world we lived in?

To start with, mom did not even tell me that we were veering off the path to our village to see a healer halfway between the village we had left behind and our village we were going back to. I do not even think that it crossed her mind that she should tell me. In her mind she knew, or so she thought, that what was good for her was also good for me and my baby brother on her back. She thought it was imperative that we were checked for protection from malign forces. As an illiterate woman, she believed in all the superstitions of our tribe and nothing could detract her from that. The question I now have is why did she decide to see another witchdoctor when her own older sister at whose house we had stayed at for a few days was a renowned witchdoctor? Why did she not seek help from her sister? If she did whilst we were with her, I do not remember her sister treating her, my younger brother and me.

As I grew up, went to school, and, willy-nilly, became a Catholic, I entered a new world that was different from ours. This new world was the world of a distorted religion called Christianity that had been adulterated with the empirical and scientific aspects of industrialized Europe or of the Western world. The missionaries told us that whatever we believed in was hogwash and a path to eternal damnation, doom, and hell for all eternity without end, as if the word eternity in itself did not imply endlessness. They had to emphasize it with the words "without end" so as to scare us stiff so that we converted to their religion. The missionaries told us that evil spirits did not exist, ignoring the fact that the Gospels they taught us as the word of God said that Jesus Christ went about casting off evil spirits from the possessed, and that Jesus himself was tested and tempted by an evil spirit they called Satan. The entire Bible is replete with mention of evil spirits misleading and hurting humans, starting with that evil spirit in the form of a serpent who hoodwinked Eve and Adam into eating the forbidden fruit of the Garden of Eden.

I must say however, that despite what I may say about still believing in the ways of my people, education has somehow dented my hard core beliefs. It makes me at times doubt things that I had unquestionably believed in because I tend to question things in order to find empirical answers. I know there will never be answers to some things that take place by following their own logic or without rhyme or reason. Even the Catholic Church believes in the inexplicable phenomena it prefers to refer to as mysteries, like the mystery of the Holy Trinity, that is of three gods in one and yet those three gods are not regarded as three distinct gods but one omnipotent and omnipresent entity called God with a capital g, to mean that there is no other god but him. It also talks about the mystery of the Immaculate Conception whereby the Virgin Mary got pregnant without making love with Joseph but through the power of the Holy Ghost or the Holy Spirit. Note the mention of the words ghost and spirit in a religion that said that we were heathens and that there were no ghosts or spirits, and that our belief in impalpable and unseen entities was an obscurantist ignorance and stupidity. In the face of such misleading teachings that contradict what is to be found in the Bible, the best I can do is to remain sceptical and be open-minded toward some of the inexplicable happenings or events I will report in my narration.

I must state that I have seen or heard of enough things that defy empirical understanding which could not have taken place without some forces behind them, as I will demonstrate in the course of this narrative. So, reader, stay on board so that you may know what some of the events were, where they took place and you will be amazed to know about them. You are not duty-bound to believe in them, but I am not inventing them for my story. I the narrator believe in the right of people to enjoy the freedom of choice to believe or not to believe, or to question what I say. I will call no one names, as it is not nice to do so because it is disrespectful to other people.

I do not remember whether I saw the husband of the healer woman who welcomed us coldly with a grave voice and a stern face, as if my mom, by baby brother and I were thieves or just unwanted intruders. Her demeanour was typical of the behaviour of healers and of their seriousness and lack of humour. It appeared that mom and the healer knew each other from earlier days. I do not remember what mom and the woman discussed or what mom told her about her fears and concerns. I remember the woman spraying magical water on us from an earthen pot with the branch of a tree as she mumbled words to exorcize evil spirits or curses from us that witches might have projected against us or to protect us from evil spirits or witches who could cast evil spells on us.

That was the first of the very few encounters I had with spirit mediums in my early days. They all happened by accident and I never regretted that they took place. Whether that exorcism done to us when we were not manifestly showing signs of demonic possession, did us any good or not, I cannot say. I am sure that my mom and the healer were convinced that it liberated us from some nasty demonic influences which had not yet begun to manifest themselves in us and make us sick, suffer, scream, and contort our bodies with anguish and pain. Perhaps, she was right to have done what she did to us. I do not know. I think that everything happened for the best in the best of all possible worlds.

The husband of the healer died a few years after our impromptu visit to his healer wife. What of, I never came to know. I never inquired. Inquiring is not in our nature, but blind belief is. Inquiring is in the nature of the cat and its curiosity killed it in the end and we did not want to be like the unfortunate feline. After his death, his small harem—I say small because I knew of men who had upwards of ten wives like an uncle of mine called Andrade who had ten or even more concubines—left his homestead as usually happened and went elsewhere to join their relatives or to get new husbands, except one of them called Palibe, a woman from the *Anyungwe* tribe of the region of Tete, about 300 kilometres to the north of our region.

After her husband's demise, Palibe was the only one of his widows who stayed in the village, perhaps because she had lost track of the way to her home village or because there was no need for her to return to her home village because there was no relative back home to return to. So she stayed put around a son of one of the widows of her husband who did not like her. He and his wife did not care a jot for her. She lived miserably and later died after a short illness that crippled her already malnourished body. Her death saddened me greatly and I was angry with the way the step-son and his wife, whose younger sister my older brother later married, had been callous to her. They made no secret of their dislike of her. They did not mourn her passing away after they buried her like a valueless dog, because they felt that her death had liberated them from the burden she had been to them.

In my opinion, old Palibe had been a great humorous dame who spoke our Sena language with the affectations of her *Chinyungwe* mother tongue. Her accent made us think that she was speaking our language with mocking intonations as her own mother tongue is spoken. I and the other boys in our village used to make fun of her name by saying *palibepo*, adding the suffix *po* for no other reason than because our word for *palibe* was *nkhabepo*. *Palibe* in the Nyungwe language and *nkhabepo* in Sena means "nothing" or "there is nothing" or it means something is missing. It was also a word that was said when a girl was found not to be a virgin on her first intercourse with her husband, which was a serious situation because our girls had to be virgins at marriage.

Non virgin or prematurely deflowered girls were rejected and sent packing to their parents with no hope of them ever becoming the first wives of men looking for wives for the first time, as their not having been found as virgins was announced to the four winds for everyone to hear and know. Girls found deflowered or with lost virginity were automatically regarded as damaged goods and were rejected, dishonoured, and considered as valueless and as a source of great shame and embarrassment to their parents and the community. They could only expect to be the third or fourth wives of men looking to increase their harems or for more wives with whom to make more children, but not for their honour. And such wives were ill-treated and their husbands constantly reminded them that they were not virgins when they gave them the favour of adding them to their harems.

An inglorious case in point was a cousin of mine by the name of Chanazi who lost her virginity to a crass married man who became mad, or, at least, pretended to have gone mad after he deflowered her. The man went about wild with an axe in hand, howling so that he could be heard as far as his voice could reach in our village and beyond. He stood on top of an anthill by a footpath close to his residence waving the axe at passers-by whilst shouting incomprehensible words without ever attacking any one because he knew he would be arrested and deported from our village to some little island off the coast of Mozambique or to the Portuguese Devil's Island of Sao Tomé in the Atlantic, off the coast of West Africa, to work there as a slave in the sugar cane, coffee or cocoa plantations, never to return to the village again, if he hurt or killed someone. I think that the man behaved in that manner out of fear, fear of the male relatives of the girl who could have descended on him to wring his neck or to whack him until he passed out, to punish him for what he had done with and to my cousin. He had not really become insane as such; he was just play acting and fooling around with us to amuse himself.

He reportedly recovered from his insanity after a shaman treated him. I knew that he would never be forced to take Chanazi to be his second wife because he was much older than my cousin and her parents did not like him because they knew that he smoked hashish and that he had possibly killed someone or people in Salisbury, now Harare in Zimbabwe when it was the British colony of Southern Rhodesia; he had lived and worked there as either a domestic servant or a farm labourer and his wife was suspected of being a bad witch from a family of feared witches.

The morning following the night Chanazi lost her virginity, a sense of irremediable sadness descended on her home as if someone had died there or as if lightning had struck it, which is regarded as an ominous event following which homesteads that are visited by lightning are cleansed by shamans. Lightning did actually crash land on her home a couple of years later. Her mother ran berserk with grief; she cried and howled after severely beating her several times. Chanazi remained indoors, locked up, as it were, and was not seen for a week. A delegation from her family went to the home of her fiancé to inform them of her loss of virginity and to return the money that the fiancé had paid as bride price because with her defloration by someone else, her engagement was rendered null and void.

Her family acted swiftly in order to prevent the fiancé's family from learning about her defloration from other sources, which would force them to go to demand the return of the bride price. That would be a greater shame than the shame they felt when they went to report the event to the boy and his parents. As a result of her defloration, Chanazi had no chance of getting married to a man looking for a wife for the first time. The loss of her virginity had sealed her fate as unworthy of being married, and it was rather unfortunate for a pretty girl like her.

She ended up marrying a leper. It was too bad. But it was the fate of girls who lost their virginity before being married. Lepers found it difficult to get women who would accept them and marry them and girls who lost their virginity prematurely, were the only girls they could hope to marry, if the girls did not mind it and preferred to have a husband than to have none at all.

Chanazi was the victim of our tradition and its obsession with the purity of girls and virginity. She was the victim of her libido that found no outlet or physical expression outside of marriage and marriage did not come easily to her. Girls were always under stress because of the tyranny of the rule requiring the preservation of virginity which was placed on them. We were different from peoples of other tribes whose girls slept with men and sometimes had kids with them before getting married to other men for whom virginity was not important or did not matter a jot in the scheme of things. In a few tribes, girls who were virgins at marriage were sent back to their parents to lose their virginity to other men before returning to be wives of their husbands. But not so with us Sena people, who would not take, as our wives, scrapes that other people had played with and did not marry.

One day well before Chanazi involved herself in the sexual act which destroyed her purity and virginity, I was with her in a field of my maternal uncle Bulande, who was her biological paternal uncle and who later became her stepfather. Her father had died when she was a small girl. Aunt Sebastiana, her mother, remarried a man of mixed Portuguese and African blood by the name of Barros who looked very much like a white man. When that man also died, Sebastiana became the second wife to Bulande who had been her brother-in-law from her first marriage. So there ran some traces of common blood between her and me on my maternal side because her father and my mother had been brother and sister from the same womb and the same father.

We were in the middle of the field, well sheltered and concealed by tall maize stalks and a few scattered trees with birds chirping and crickets singing. I found it difficult to understand what she did. She undressed herself and told me to play with her. She pulled my shorts down. She seemed to have derived some pleasure from it because it pleased her fantasy with a real boy although I did not come off into her because I did not penetrate her and my body had not begun to manufacture the liquid of procreation. And it seemed that the pleasure she got from playing with me was unlike the pleasure she got from wanking herself. The experience caused me much discomfort and even pain after that. She was lucky that I was a little boy who could not deflower her. It is possible that she might have done the same thing with other little boys.

"Don't talk about what we have done here," she said. "If you do, I will wring your neck like a chicken." I never said anything to anyone about it until now, writing about it in this narrative.

"I won't talk about it because I want to play with you again," I reassured her. I felt proud that I had played the little game with her, although I did not enjoy it because I was little and we were related by blood.

I kept my promise and never bragged about it because she was a relative and it would have been a shame to her if I had disclosed the secret. If I had talked about it and my uncle's family had come to know about it, she would have been in real trouble especially from her waspish mother who would have whacked her until she got tired of beating her for having played the dirty game with a boy who was under age and a blood relation whilst she was engaged to someone else and was a grown up. But her mother would not have made a public fuss about it for fear of jeopardizing her marital arrangement and bringing shame to her and to my uncle's family. As long as I did not penetrate and deflower her, she was still a virgin because she would be found difficult to penetrate and would bleed when her hymen was broken by her future husband.

My adventure with Chanazi was not in fact the first one. A couple of years before it, I had another one with another maternal cousin. I had gone to visit her family and stayed with them for several days before returning home. Her mother was aunt Albertina who my mom with my baby brother and I had visited when on our return home we found ourselves stopping over to see the healer wife at Nzungu Dimingu's homestead.

Being the little kid that I was, her parents sent me to sleep in the same one room cottage with my cousin Zefina. Zefina was as beautiful as her mother, if not more beautiful. She was so beautiful that I sometimes thought that she was a fairy and not a real human girl at all. She loved me intensely and I adored her but I never thought of it then in terms of sexuality because she was my elder sister and in our language, a cousin is a sister and we even have no word for cousin. It never seemed to have crossed her parents' minds that their daughter with burgeoning boobs almost near full size and who was older than me by some years, had then started to have libidinous impulses and would like to release them with someone like me. They thought that their daughter would treat me as a little young brother. They discounted that I would initiate a sexual activity or do something funny with their daughter, which I was not going to do because I was so young that I never even thought of sex then. And at that time, I never dreamed that my cousin would act in a funny manner.

As soon as we were in bed, Zefina began to breathe heavily as if nervous and reaching for me to undress me whilst telling me that she loved me so much after she had

15

undressed herself. She told me to be quiet and made me go on top of her and directed my little erect member to her sexual region. I was so young that I did not know what to do and Zefina got really frustrated with me because no matter what she did to help me, I could simply not perform to her expectation. I was simply not of the age to be able to involve myself in sexual activities and please a girl of her age. She never gave up despite my poor performance. She kept doing the same thing every night after we were in bed. Perhaps she drew some pleasure when my member rubbed on her soft valley of pleasure. I think she did, but she would not have liked me to penetrate and deflower her, if I could, because that would doom her from ever getting a husband. She was aware of the consequences of being deflowered.

She never told me not to tell people about it as Chanazi had asked me not to, and I never thought of telling anyone about it because we were first cousins and I loved her and she adored me. I did not want to bring disgrace to her and force her parents to make us sleep in different huts. In fact, I derived much pleasure sleeping in the same bed with her whilst covered in the same blanket and coiled about her body like a baby about a mother. Zefina was not a fool. She knew what she was doing. She never played the game she played with me with any bigger boy who could mess up her virginity before marriage or with boys who could not marry her after messing up with her purity.

Years after our little misadventures when I was an adolescent with virility flourishing in me, we found ourselves in spots secluded from other people where we could have done, as we would have pleased. But Zefina was not reckless like Chanazi. As we sat talking or silently in those places, I could see that she was suffering much as she was caught between her love for me, her libido and her resolve to overcome temptation in order to uphold her dignity because her parents were people of great dignity. Her libidinous impulses were immense and I could see her anguish and my impulses were great too. She would look at me with tears running down her face and confess her love for me and regret that we could not do things, as we might have liked because of our consanguineous links.

She once said, "I love you Chico but you are my brother and I'm your sister. If we make love and you deflower me, we will be in trouble, as we can't marry after that. We will become pariahs. We'll be thrown out of the village to live in the bush with snakes and wild animals and perish ignominiously out there. And no one will bury and mourn us."

"I know. There isn't much we can do," I agreed with her. I was horrified of committing incest because it was taboo amongst the Sena people and was not concerned with genetic implications of incest I did not know about at the time, if we did things and she became pregnant by me. I said to her, "Love me all your life more than you'll ever love another boy, and I will also love you more than I will any other girl, although we won't engage in sexual activity."

"You sure you won't hate me for not doing things with you that we would if we were not related by blood?" she asked.

"Hell, no," I said. "And why should I? It's not your or my fault that we are related by blood. It's the accident of circumstances. Furthermore, incest will anger our ancestral spirits or God and will bring us deadly consequences." Carnal love between cousins, and first cousins at that, was regarded as incest in our tribe, although it would not be incest in some other tribes in which cousins do marry. But that was the way of other tribes and not ours that the two of us could not change. And we were scornful of such tribes we regarded as impure and barbaric.

"You're right," she said. She reached for me, grabbed me and held me firmly in her arms with her firm breasts against my chest and her eyes wide open staring at my face with an infectious smile playing on her lips. She giggled to root me where I stood and prevent me from pushing her away and telling her that what she was doing was inappropriate because I was her brother. Her breath was warm and sweet. She planted a full kiss with her tongue into my mouth and our tongues met. I felt a great sensation of pleasure taking hold of my body. It was the devil winning the battle of temptation against us but we did not eat of the forbidden fruit which was our victory over the devil.

"This is the furthest I can go with you," she said dryly after she had disengaged herself from me and began to laugh like a mischievous girl. "What we did in my cottage as children, was infantile and is over. And that's that." What she said was easier said than done and she knew it. She was not ready to drop the pleasure of flirting with me as yet, as I was also not prepared to give up the idea that she was my lover, at least a platonic one, rather than my cousin or sister.

I agreed with her reluctantly because what she had just done had whipped my virility into readiness for sex with her, but the thought of consanguinity prevailed over my impulses. I preferred not to argue with her as the idea of carnal experimentation with her horrified me because I regarded her as a girl from almost the same womb as myself because our moms were sisters from the same parents.

"We've sinned," I said to her with a Christian mind set to me. Although we had not yet been baptized in the Catholic Church, she and I regarded ourselves pretty much as members of the Catholic religion. I was later baptized by father Jean Ribeau at midnight on Easter Sunday on 28 March 1964 whils she had been baptized in 1962. Father Ribeau, who would be my first teacher of Latin at Zobue Seminary two years later, was a very pious Swiss priest of the Congregation of the White Fathers. He spoke Portuguese with his dragging French Swiss accent that made many a boy laugh at him. He did not take kindly to anyone who poked fun at his accent, saying that he was not a Portuguese. He was in fact very critical of Portuguese rule in Mozambique but he did not make his feelings public because the Salazar regime would throw him out of Mozambique and he would not be allowed to set foot in Portugal or any of its colonies again. One evening, he slapped a fat boy for laughing at his accent. He later joked about it, saying, "I've confirmed Gordinho" which was the name of the boy and also incidentally the Portuguese word to mean *a little fat male*.

His use of the word confirmed was also dramatic as it referred to the slight slap a bishop gives on the cheeks of believers getting the Sacrament of Confirmation as the final act to confirm that the believers have become soldiers or militants of Jesus Christ as per the doctrine of the Catholic Church of Rome.

That kiss with my cousin Zefina was the last thing we did before we began to treat each other as brother and sister and avoided facial expressions and behaviour that could excite and incite us into amorous feelings and possible incest. We also minimized instances of just the two of us being together at secluded spots because we knew that temptation would come naturally to us and force us to start our fight against temptation all over again. And, in fact, subsequent temptations did revisit us and we had to fight the demon all over again.

Principled as she was then, she never said to hell with the tradition and let's just do it regardless of the consequences. She and I knew that making love was inappropriate and we would make our families very sad if they came to know about it. She knew then that I could deflower her, as I was no longer the little boy she had played with in her cottage many years previously. She was

19

determined to overcome the sexual impulses she was experiencing in order to remain a virgin for that day when she would be happily married to become the proud wife of someone and have children with him. I do not even think that she would have accepted if I asked her to make love with me after saying to hell with the stupid tradition. When Zefina was later married while I was at Zobue Seminary; she was to all intents and purposes, a virgin girl, but unfortunately, she married a man who took another wife and my poor cousin had to put up with that because she would not abandon him to marry another man as she believed that she was meant to have sex with only one man in her life and not to sleep with other men even if she had divorced him or he had died. That was how serious my poor cousin Zefina was.

My third adventure of early sexual encounter as a little boy was rather funny and it makes me laugh each time I recall it. It was late afternoon and the sun was just setting and darkness was approaching fast as I walked by three mango trees belonging to the family of my playmate Macie with whom I had just been playing in the bush earlier on. I saw ripe mangos on the trees. I was tempted to get one or two of them to please my taste buds. I picked up stones and began to throw them at the fruit the way we usually did to bring ripe mangoes down when Macie's adolescent half-sister saw me throwing stones at the fruit. She started to run to me and I began to run away, fearing that she would catch me and drag me to her father to accuse me of stealing their mangos.

I was terrified at the thought of being accused of theft and being regarded as and live with the infamy of being a little thief in the village, because other kids would later steal things and the villagers would blame only me for their thieving without proof that I was the one who stole the things. She ran as fast as the wind and in no time she was gaining on me because she had longer legs than me and she was determined to get me before I could approach my home and be in the safety of my family's compound. And, half-way, at a valley between their homestead and mine, which was usually flooded when it rained heavily or when there was flooding, I tripped on something and fell and in no time at all, the girl was on top of me saying, "You stole our mangos. You little thief! " she howled. Instead of beating me which she could do because I could not fight her as she was grown up, or dragging me to her home to hand me over to her father as a little thief, something she could have easily done, she dragged me to a clump of grass by the footpath in the valley.

"You've to play with me, if you don't want me to beat you up or accuse you of stealing our mangos," she said whilst breathing heavily after her hard run, with the intention of raping me. I was crying and pleading with her to forgive me and let me go because, after all, I had only tried to steal their mangos and had not actually stolen any. I was also tired after the short hard run and was panting and sweating.

I could not believe what she did next. I had never guessed that she was infatuated with me and was dying to express her libidinous impulses with me. Now she had really trapped me and I had no way out except to surrender to her wish. I found myself at her mercy and in a real quandary of either having to succumb to her crazed sexuality or of her dragging me to her father to accuse me of being a petty thief who had stolen their mangos which I did not because my stones had not hit and brought down any mangos, and I had not run away with any mangos at all or I had not thrown away any after I saw her running to me.

As I did not want her to accuse me of stealing their mangos, I submitted to her desire. She undressed herself and forcibly undressed me. She lay on the grass and made me go on top of her, which I did whilst hardly believing what she was doing with me. It was like a dream and a

21

fantasy coming true and my member was stirred to life, although I could not deflower her. For me it was a better fate than if she had accused me of stealing their mangos. I knew that after that game, she would not accuse me of stealing their mangos, as I would disclose that she had raped me and she would find herself in a most unenviable situation with her parents who could have beaten her until she passed out.

So, the situation she created was a well-balanced see-saw for both of us. She had provided me with some deterrent power against her. It was like a win-win situation because she won over me and I won by playing with her sexually or, a lose-lose situation because she lost her dignity and she had humiliated me by forcing me to do as she wanted with me.

I in fact felt great about it afterwards, as it was a sign that I was a handsome little boy as women in the village never tired of telling me that I was a very attractive boy. In fact, my cousins Chanazi and Zefina had played their games with me not only because of their libidinous urges but also because I was a handsome young boy. They did not go about playing their games as they did with me with other little boys in village who would have talked about it in public.

The girl was rather pleased with the whole game, although I could not deflower her for lack of strength to accomplish such a mammoth task at that time, but I fared much better with her than I had done with Chanazi and Zefina before her. Despite her silly behaviour, I do not think that she wanted me to mess up her virginity. She just wanted to play and have her way with me, to please her fantasies and transform me into her toy, a toy who would do her bidding.

After the incident in the grass at the valley, I had thought that the episode would be the beginning and the end of her adventure with me. No. For her it was just the beginning and she had no intention of ever stopping. She was intent on doing it all the time, every evening if possible. She was so infatuated with me to the point of not being able to control her impulses, although I could not marry her because I was young whilst she was nubile. And as long as I did not deflower her, the little games were okay for her and for me too who came to like them. Under the cover of darkness in the evenings, she would surreptitiously creep to my cottage with two other adolescent girls to engage in sexual activities with me. Her adolescent friends played with two other under age playmates of mine who were my next door neighbours.

In the end, someone, either one of the girls or one of my little next door friends, talked about what the girls did with us. When her mother found out about it, she railed against her and she probably beat her daily for many days in order to drive some sense of dignity into her. One morning, her mother made the point of dressing her down about what she had done with me when she saw me walk past her hut where she was with her daughter on my way to Macie's hut whose mom was the second wife of her husband.

There was some distant family connection but no consanguinity links between my rapist and me, as was the case with Chanazi and Zefina. Although what she forced me into was inappropriate because of my age, there was no stigma of incest in our relationship. My playmate's mother was the sister of the husband of my great aunt Chanazi who was the younger sister of Nsasa, my paternal grandmother. My great uncle and my great aunt lived in a distant village from ours.

The girl's mother, who might in fact have been proud of her daughter's sexual exploits with me as they demonstrated her active sexuality, was concerned over the whole thing only because it would ruin her daughter's reputation and bring shame to her family in the village, if the incident was known, but it never became public knowledge. I would have been devastated with shame if my little affairs with Chanazi and Zefina were known like the one with this girl was known to her mother and perhaps to her father. Her mother wanted her to stop what she was doing with me and be serious whilst waiting for a Mister Right who could marry her, as I could not because I was a little boy. Her mother probably feared that the girl could be tempted to play the same game she was playing with me, with an adolescent or grown up boy who could destroy her virginity and not marry her and make her not worthy of marriage.

The sexual adventures I was involved in as a kid were initiated by the girls who were all older than me and were all I had experienced as a little boy, although I was much admired by other adolescent girls who never had the opportunity to force me into little games like the three girls indulged in with me. I never had any other adventures with girls in Mozambique until well past the age of seventeen in Nairobi, Kenya, where moral exigencies were not as tight as had been in my tribal homeland. I never accused my early lovers of being lousy. They were just sex-starved adolescent girls who went after small boys like me then who could not mess up their virginity, in order to please their sexual fantasies and impulses whilst awaiting marriage when they would present themselves as virgins physically but not morally, because their purity had been tainted with their little games with me.

The same sex-starved girls, who played games with little boys, would resist men attempting to rape them to the death in order to protect their virginity, particularly if the rapists were men they did not like or hated or they would not like them to be their husbands because the men were ugly or for some other reason. There was the incident of a girl in our village who bit half of a rapist's tongue off. The rapist, a leper and a well-known murderer with a string of murders behind him, was called Gwedje. Gwedje, a man of unpredictable moods and a heavy smoker of hashish, was a friend of mine although he was much, much, older than me. One of his younger sisters called Chasasa married a maternal cousin of mine. Gwedje ambushed the girl along a footpath with tall grass, and raped her at knife point. The girl resisted heroically but Gwedje was able to overcome her, pin her down on the ground and rape her. While he was forcing himself into her and his tongue was hanging out with excitement, the girl bit it with so much anger and hate that she tore it off and Gwedje remained with half a tongue, which affected his speech, and thereafter he could not speak without lisping and his words came out pretty much inaudibly.

I retain a good memory of an incident with Gwedje which took place before his rape of the girl. We teased each other with no holds barred. His pitiless sense of humour annoyed me at times, particularly after I had decided to attend the Catholic seminary at Zobue to become a priest. He did not understand much about what a Catholic priest was supposed to be. A Catholic priest was supposed to be the perfect pure image of Jesus without moral or physical defects unless the physical defect happened after becoming a priest. Then the Church could no longer withdraw the Sacrament of Priesthood from such a person because priesthood is one of the seven sacraments regarded as holy that the Church cannot annul without a strong spiritual reason. Although priests are supposed to be celibate, it does not necessarily mean that they are impotent or that they are castrated so as to deprive them of their manhood and desire for sex, as the people in my village thought.

Gwedje convinced himself that priests had no desire for sex because they were either castrated or were given injections that killed their virility and libido. One day while on holiday from the seminary, I happened to be in the same big canoe with him whils crossing the Zambezi to the other side of the river in Sofala. He had his bundle of sugar cane he was going to sell at a market at Magagade shopping centre across the river so that he could have some money. With us there were also a good number of women taking farm produce for sale to the Indian storekeepers, when he began to tease me in a pitiless manner.

"Hey, you, my priest friend," he said derisively.

"What's up, Gwedje?" I asked him.

"Do you really mean to say that you feel nothing when you see or look at women like these ones with us in the canoe? Your thing doesn't really stir up to life? For you women are just like moving pictures in a film?"

His question amused the women who burst out laughing. Some of the women even clapped their hands to support him for saying what they could not say to me. A lot of them had daughters waiting for boys who could marry them. Each one of those women with daughters would be only too pleased if I gave up my idea of wanting to become a priest and took their daughter, if I could function as a man with a woman. I could take as many of the girls as I would like, upward of ten or even more to be my wives or concubines, since polygamy was our way of life. I could not imagine myself having more than one wife though. Two would be the most I could have, provided they were hard working and slaved out in the fields to produce food for me because I would not want to work with my hands in a field, which I regarded as a job people with the status of natives did. Manual labour would be degrading to me, an assimilado with the status of Portuguese citizen.

Gwedje's teasing was the best joke the women were having at my expense because they strongly believed that I was sexually impaired and useless to women, which in their minds explained why I wanted to be a priest, but none of them would say it to me for fear of provoking me and of me ordering the chief to arrest them and have them mercilessly caned. They needed a crazy man like Gwedje to say it in order for them to have a good laugh at me.

Gwedje was not a madman as such, as some people believed. He behaved like one because he was dependent on hashish to give him relief from the affliction of his leprosy when the condition worsened during the full moon. I was told that the disease does in fact wax during full moon and wanes when the moon began to lose its fullness. His dependence on hashish made him impulsive and dangerous, which explained why he had murdered a number of men and raped or attempted to rape scores of girls without ever really being arrested, tried, and imprisoned because he was regarded as an out and out lunatic. There was a score of public songs that celebrated his strange and infamous behaviour or slandered him. In his mind dominated by the effects of hashish and a little bit of insanity but not much, the songs about him glorified him, even if they contained words that disgraced his name.

I told him that his joke was hurting me and asked him to stop. He would not stop. He in fact stepped up his provocative remarks to the amusement of the women who did not want him to stop. As I could no longer tolerate his teasing, I threw a bet to him, which surprised the women who were convinced that I had no sexual desire.

"Hey, friend Gwedje," I said to him, "I'm ready to prove to you and to everyone else in the village that I'm not the impotent man you think I am. Send me your sister Maria this evening so that I can prove to you that I'm not impotent. I will dig her proper and good. She won't be disappointed. I can assure you." I was determined to prove to them that I was as active sexually as anyone else, if even more active as I had been suppressing my virility by being at a seminary where we were cloistered and never saw women and only fantasized about them without telling other fellow students because we did not talk about sex out there, and it could be cause for rustication from the school. It was a sin to think and talk about girls.

"I accept the bet," he said. "I will send Maria. If she refuses, I will beat her until she comes to you, crying and running." He was serious about forcing his younger sister to me to test my manhood.

"Bring her by the scruff of her neck, kicking and screaming, if needs be. I will show her and she will confirm to you and the whole village that I am a functioning individual," I said to the amusement of the women who laughed at the tops of their voices hearing a priest, as they were already calling me that, talk about his desire to fuck Gwedje's sister. Gwedje, who would kill any other man talking about ploughing his sister like I did to him that day, was very excited about the idea of putting me to the test so that he could laugh more at me if I failed to dig her for lack of virility. Because we were great friends, any nonsensical chat between the two of us, no matter what we talked about and how we conversed, was great talk, worthy of laughter, light chat. I did not doubt that Gwedje wanted to force his sister onto me. I did not think that the crazy man was joking either. I was ready to take her to bed which would have grave consequences for me because, if that happened, I would not be able to stay at the seminary as the priests would send me back home after learning that I had deflowered a girl during the vacation, with the order that I return home to marry the girl, failing which they would ask the Vatican to excommunicate me from the Church. And the Pope would have excommunicated me too because by the early 1960s, the Church was still kicking non-conformists out of the Catholic Faith but no longer ordering them to be burnt at the stake as happened in the Middle Ages.

I later learned that Gwedje beat up his sister for refusing to meet me just for casual sex, which was not the way of our people, without me immediately taking her as my wife after the sexual encounter. Casual sex was unheard of amongst the Sena people. And also young people did not marry without prior courtship or before parents arranged their marriages. His sister who was more sensible than him, knew that it would be a shame to meet me just for sex, to lose her virginity for the sake of pleasure and not for marriage. The shame of it all would be greater because her older sister was married to a maternal cousin of mine, although there was no bar against sex between me and Maria, as we were not related by blood, close or distant, for such an act to be regarded as incestuous and a taboo.

Gwedje's own father and mother had to stop him beating his sister and they were not amused when they learned the reason why he was beating her that time around. He used to beat his sisters and younger brothers all the time. He tied up young boys he caught stealing fruit from his family's orchard, with ropes to trees before smoking hashish prior to beating them, releasing and warning them that if he caught them again, he would kill them with his knife he brandished before their eyes.

Gwedje was the sad and tragic comedian of our village and the villages beyond. He was known everywhere. No one blamed him for the wrongs he committed. Everyone liked him and everyone feared him. Apart from his tendency to rape virgin girls and none of those he raped wanting to become his wife because of his leprosy and unsteady character, preferring to remain spinsters all their lives, good old Gwedje was never cross with anyone who did not cross his path. He was full of humour which in a way explained why he wanted to force his sister into having an affair with me; a priest, as he thought I was one of virtue because I was studying at seminary.

Although bets were taken very seriously among the Sena people and he could even have betted on having his sister to be my wife and the sister would have no say about it and his parents would have welcomed it, this bet of his, for me to have gratuitous sex with his sister, was more than his parents could take. They took him to task and made him feel ashamed of himself.

I heard later from Maria herself that her parents were also not amused with me for betting with an immoral intent. She stressed that she would indeed have liked me to be her husband, if I gave up my crazy idea of being a priest. She said that the bet would have been more than welcome if it was for me to court her prior to marriage, in which case I would have to go to her home and not her to come to me. As per tradition, it was always the boys who went to court girls at their homes and never the other way round.

"For me to come for you to just to fuck me as if I was a whore?" she said. She added that I had been as crazy as her brother for betting the way we had betted. "You should have been ashamed of yourself, you who are more sensible than my brother and are a priest."

I explained to her that I had thrown the bet in anger against her brother for teasing me in the presence of women. I told her that for me, the challenge was an adventure which was still valid, if she wanted to take it albeit belatedly. "Your brother wants proof for me to demonstrate that I can dig women. If you're ready, I'll plough you straight away." She laughed before saying that she did not want that kind of relationship. I stressed to her that I attached no moral considerations when provoked the way her brother had provoked me. "The idea of having you come to me was mine and not from the brother who took the bait and swallowed it because he thought it was a good challenge for me. You did well by refusing to come," I said. "If you'd come, I would have desecrated you to please your brother's curiosity because he wants evidence to demonstrate that I can function with a girl."

She fell silent before giggling because our antics had amused her. "If you want to marry me, I'm there waiting for you, but I'm not for casual pleasure that you and my brother wanted to use me as your guinea pig."

The moral standards of the Sena tribe were strict, so much so that there were older women known as counsellors whose task was to ensure that girls remained virgins before marriage. Such elderly dames frequently physically checked girls to ensure that they had not lost their virginity; such was the tyranny of the importance of the preservation of virginity in unmarried girls amongst the Sena people.

Chapter 2

I knew Moises, my paternal grandfather, when I was a small boy, when I was a puny, and at times sickly, little boy. He was a short and strong man, brave and slender. He feared nothing. He carried a sharp knife in a sheath he himself had made with palm leaves which was secured by a string he tied around his waist. Work in the field to produce food for his family had made him tough and rough in appearance but not in his manner and demeanour where he was a gentleman, great and serene.

He had been a hunter too before I was born, I was told. He culled rhinos and buffalos with a powerful homemade firearm. He did that in the days when such animals were so abundant in Africa that they could be seen everywhere and they killed more people than the number of people who died of illnesses and other causes. Shooting such critters was never an easy task with a primitive gun using homemade gun powder. It required a lot of ability, and stealth and agility to climb trees quickly like a little monkey, because those animals are very dangerous and can charge if they spot the man who intends to kill or who wounds them. Rhinos are practically blind but have a very sharp sense of smell whilst buffaloes have a sharp eyesight and a sharp sense of smell that are many times more sensitive than those of humans and are highly aggressive, so much so that they charge because of sounds around them without investigating or checking out what they are first.

And what is more about the African buffalo? The critter can be very vindictive. If wounded, any human it will encounter, is guilty of the offence that has been committed against it and it will attack anyone not only the offender.

When I knew him as my grandfather, he was just an old peasant who also laid traps to ensnare francolins and guinea fowls which his traps caught in large numbers every day and people went to buy them from him. He gave some of the birds he caught to my mother, saying, "Cook and eat them with your husband and children." My mom would thank him and he would say "my pleasure" to her before stressing, "Your kids are the source of my joy." But my older brother and I were not always kind to him. We would go to his hut and refuse his entreaties to get onto his veranda to sit down and chat with him. We would say nasty words to him. Mom would rush to rebuke us but grandfather would tell her not to worry because he enjoyed seeing us teasing him. I do not think that we were teasing him. We were simply being mean and nasty to him for no apparent reason. We were just naughty to him and he did not take offence. He in fact enjoyed our tomfoolery.

My grandfather, who appeared to have had no other wives in his life, which was unusual with Africans of his time, lived next to us with his wife Nsasa, a tall woman with a lighter complexion than him. It is possible that he never had more than one wife because of the influence of Scottish missionaries in Nyasaland where he had lived and where all his sons, including my father and his daughter were born. This explains why all of them had British names, Jim, John, Ben for my father, Tony, and Patience, the only paternal aunt I knew. The Scottish missionaries in Nyasaland gave him the Biblical name of Moses. We later rendered it as Moises, which is the Portuguese form of the name Moses.

Grandmother Nsasa wore copper rings over her ankles. She was sweet and forever tolerant. She spoilt me and my brother because she never reprimanded us for anything we did wrong. She and my grandfather lived with aunt Patience, who was older than my father. Aunt Patience was hard of hearing and had a goiter. She loved me and my brother and was very protective of us. She refused to get married in her life for a reason no one ever understood. In her younger days, she had received proposals from men she turned down. She lived with her mother as a spinster until she died.

My grandfather made us the first bows and arrows my older brother and I ever used. The bows he made us were small for our age. As we grew up, my brother and I made our own bows and arrows. No one ever taught us how to make bows and arrows nor did we ever watch people making arrows. To make bows and arrows is simple. All one needs is spindly stems of hard wood plants and strings or ropes of sisal for them. As for arrows, we used the rays from bicycles' wheels, sharpened and inserted them into reed stems; we tied them at the points of insertion to keep them tightly in place. As we grew up, we made bows and arrows that were fit for our size, to kill what we wanted to kill with them. The bows and arrows that grandfather made and those we ourselves made after we started making them for ourselves, were rather small. We used them to hunt, shoot, and kill grasshoppers and small birds for us to eat and for the fun of having and carrying bows and arrows like the other kids did.

Grandfather died while my brother and I were growing fast and doing many things to help our family and his family. It was painful for us not to seen him anymore. We began to miss his wisdom and good advice. He was a man with some psychic abilities, although he was no healer or a witchdoctor. He was all the same, a man with an amazing intuition.

Before we became adolescents, we made bigger bows and arrows which we used to kill big birds and rabbits for food. We also used our weapons to harass mongoose that invaded our compounds to snatch chickens and ducks. They were annoying pests, the little burglars, and we hated them with undying passion. With time, we made even bigger bows and arrows which we used against little animals and also for protection against some bad people we called *mapanga* who were sent to our region to abduct people who were allegedly used as slave labour in coffee, tea, and tobacco farms in Nyasaland, belonging to a British farmer who was known to us as Henzi.

Henzi was also said to be a cannibal, which was doubtful because the British colonial rulers in Nyasaland would not have allowed one of them to kill and eat Africans. It is impossible to believe that he would have his black henchmen slaughter people for food without the colonial rulers ever finding out about it or anyone knowing about it not informing the government. I can see though that the colonial rulers in Nyasaland could ignore his enslaving activities; after all the British administrators in the neighbouring territory and the Portuguese colonial rulers in Mozambique, implemented *thangata* which was forced labour Africans did without being paid, except the bad food they were given of stale maize meal flour and rotten beans or dried fish.

The men Henzi sent to abduct people from our region in Zambezia, Tete, Manica, and Sofala were on his payroll, although they were very poorly paid or not even paid at all. He did not insure them and their families. His terrorists died of diseases in the bush. And at times the mapanga were killed when those they intended to capture resisted and fought back with lances or spears or even bashed them to death with hoes. Villagers also killed them in hunting mounted parties in the bush to stamp them out from the bush to which women went to collect firewood and where boys also played.

Villagers decided to take the matter into their own hands instead of involving the army of the colonial regime, which did not understand the situation. The one time people asked the army to hunt and neutralize the mapanga for them, the soldiers with rifles and machine guns went wild, stopping, arresting and beating up pretty much everyone they saw along footpaths or found hunting in the bush or laying traps for birds and animals. They thought of the mapanga as anti-government rebels, which was not what they were. They were not fighters struggling to free Mozambique from colonial rule but just criminals who were not motivated by political ideals. They were just apolitical thugs, gangsters, and abductors.

Regardless of whether the gangsters were sent by one bad colonial settler in Nyasaland or not, one thing was undeniably true; the terrorists were for real. It was not a laughing matter that was to be dismissed as a funny joke. They existed and were wild men, usually in rags and full of lice with unkempt hair because they stayed and hid in the bush where they did not wash. From time to time, some of them were captured and paraded in the villages for villagers to see, spit at or swear at, jeer at them and beat them with sticks or punches, not to the extent of killing them before letting them limp back to wherever they came from, hoping that once back in their regions, they would tell other would be mapanga that they would be playing with fire if they dared go and predate in our regions. Once as prisoners in our villages, they were never killed or lynched as we Sena people were not a horde of barbarous and mindless individuals despite the cruelty of the terrorists when they caught some of us. We did not make them pay for their barbarity with their lives.

Sometimes the evil doers were handed over to the authorities who never told us what they did with them. It was possible that the Portuguese regime sent them to do slave labour in the sugar cane, cocoa, and coffee plantations of their Devil's Island colony of Sao Tome e Principe in the Atlantic to which they also sent prisoners from Mozambique, Angola, Guinea-Bissau, and political agitators from Portugal itself. The mapanga usually appeared in the bush around our areas in the rainy season when vegetation blossomed, with trees and tall grass provided them with shelter, concealing them; it helped them to waylay and seize people who fell to their ambushes.

Many years later while living in Nairobi and working for the BBC Monitoring Service Unit there as a radio news monitor for the Portuguese and French, I happened to work with a Mr. John Bamber, a slender and intelligent Englishman who was one of our editors; for the news we translated into English from other languages, had to be edited before being wired to the BBC in London. From there, a line sent it directly to Washington DC for the American government which was interested in what was happening in Africa and which also passed to the BBC information from West African radio stations its own monitoring station in Abidjan, Ivory Coast, obtained.

He told me that he had heard of cases of cannibalism in Malawi. Bamber had worked in Malawi as a BBC news monitor covering radio transmissions from Salisbury, now Harare in Zimbabwe, Lusaka, Zambia, and Blantyre in Malawi, in a small one-person monitoring station which later closed as the unit in Nairobi was able to cover those stations. Reception was rather poor because of the distance and the radio stations of those countries relied on antiquated equipment the colonial regimes had installed instead of installing new transmitters.

"There are constant reports of children disappearing in Malawi," he said. "It's claimed that the children are eaten, although the government of Malawi denies the rumours whenever they're heard. And people know that when the Malawian Government denies it, it means it's true."

"Do you really think that the missing children are eaten?" I asked him rather sceptically. I had expected him to say something about Henzi, he did not seem to have heard about while in Malawi, or did Henzi close shop before or immediately after Nyasaland's independence in 1964 and return to Britain to live quietly on the proceeds of his farming enterprises in Malawi and without Africans to eat as he had done in Africa? Obviously, in Britain, he would not have bands of mapanga to go into the shires to kidnap people for him to enslave and eat as he was reportedly won't to do in Nyasaland.

"Despite denials from the Malawian government, people know that the missing children are eaten," he stressed without hesitation.

"Who eats the children?" I asked.

"I don't know because no cannibals are ever arrested and tried in courts of law, perhaps the government of Malawi does not want to get embarrassed with cases of cannibalism and come under pressure to suppress it."

I was saddened, profoundly disturbed to the core of my innermost human feelings, and found it difficult to believe that by the end of the twentieth century, there could still be people out there eating other human beings. It is a historical fact though that the descendants of a marauding tribe of the Zambezi Valley called Zimbas whose ancestors were feared in central and east Africa for their cannibalism, were to be found straddling the border area of north-western Mozambique with central Malawi. The once powerful Zimbas had been reduced to a handful that now call themselves Nyanja people and do not take kindly to being called Zimbas because the word Zimba means cavemen or savages or, perhaps because they know that their ancestors were cannibals and they do not want to be tainted with the infamy of the actions of their ancestors.

The Zimbas defeated the Portuguese and overran Sena and Tete in the Zambezi Valley. Later in 1587, the ferocious cannibals overran Kilwa in what is today mainland Tanzania where they killed 3,000 people. In 1590, the Zimbas entered Mombasa where they reached an agreement with the Portuguese who let them kill Moslems whilst they watched because the cannibals were killing and eating Moslems who were the sworn enemies of their Christian faith. In 1593, the Sena chief Kalonga Mzura of Lower Zambezi, fielded 4,000 warriors and made an alliance with the Portuguese in 1608 to fight and defeat the Zimbas who were led by their Chief Lundi.

I later lived in the land of the Zimba people at the Catholic Seminary at Zobue for four years before I left Mozambique. While there, I never heard that the tribesmen there were practicing cannibalism.

I did not ask Bamber whether he had heard people speak of a British cannibal called Henzi, which was probably a distortion of the name Haynes. There was no need to ask him about it because close to twenty years had passed after I had heard people talk about the *Ngerezi* (English or British) cannibal in Nyasaland which became Malawi upon attaining independence in 1964.

Sometimes no matter where one goes to in Africa, one is bound to hear talks of cannibalism, most of it being lazy talk about some tribes by members of other tribes who hate them. That could be the case of the rumours in Malawi and even in Mozambique, where, as a young boy, I was told that the Lomue people to the east of us in Zambezia were cannibals. The belief was exacerbated by the Portuguese colonial policy of divide and rule. They said that it was true that the Lomue practiced cannibalism. But why didn't the Portuguese suppress their cannibalism since they had the power to do so? We ended up believing it because the allegation was repeated. Our minds bought it. We accepted it. The colonial policy prevailed over us because we were disorganized and our disorganization enabled the imperial power to maintain its grip and rule us.

It was no surprise for me that many years after Bamber had told me about children being eaten in Malawi, I was to hear a similar claim being made in Nairobi about children disappearing and being eaten by people who were known as Wanubi in Swahili or Nubians in English. I never really cared to know who the Nubians were until I had to do some research on Google after beginning to write this story.

Who are the Nubians the old witchdoctor in Nairobi told me ate children who went missing in Nairobi and where did they reside in the Kenyan capital, with its predominantly black population with Indian, Arab, Somali, and white minorities in the mix? And why were incidents of missing children being eaten never once reported in the Kenyan press, in *The Standard* and *Daily Nation* or *Taifa Leo*, the humorous Swahili Language edition of the *Daily Nation*, which took much pleasure in sensationalizing events and caricaturing individuals?

Nubians are an ethnic group of southern Egypt and northern Sudan who speak various forms of Nilotic-Sahelian dialects and who appear to be a mixture of Arab and African blood. It is probable that the old Kenya witchdoctor in Nairobi was referring to the Sudanese people of the Nile region of the southern Sudan when he talked about Nubians. I wonder whether he knew who the Nubians were, who had their own black pharaohs and built their own civilization with pyramids in southern Egypt and northern Sudan.

As children, my brother and I lived with our parents. And because we were of the age to do nothing and did not go to school, we spent our time playing around with other kids of our age who also did not go to school. We ran about, shot lizards and geckos on the walls of our huts with our bows and arrows and went to the bush close by our huts to shoot grasshoppers and small birds which we roasted on fires we made and sometimes ate them on their own or with roasted sweet potatoes.

We got much excitement when we heard the sound of a plane flying over us. We would look at it, listen to its droning sound, jumped, and waved to it in salutation. Although we lived like people in pre-historic times, the symbols of technology were round and about us. It was not before long we began to see helicopters we called *nyandjeti*, the word in our language for dragonfly because the aerial vehicle resembled dragonflies but with moving rotors. Those metallic dragonflies were really interesting because, unlike the planes, they could land anywhere. Out of them came white men and occasionally white women who talked to themselves while our women danced around them in excitement and to welcome them while our men stood around watching the amazing dragonflies on the ground. The aerial travellers liked to see such spectacles glorifying them and their expertise.

Cars and trucks mainly carrying cotton from markets where native cotton growers sold their produce to the government or carrying food the villagers sold to the government or private enterprises, trundled by us along the unpaved road through our village, raising dust behind them. Sometimes natives walking on the roads or by the roadside were run over, crippled, or killed by vehicles that did not stop because the villagers they smashed were of no importance. We never thought that we mattered a bit in the scheme of things for the colonial regime, except as producers of goods for their comfort or as their worshippers.

Accidents in which people were run over became problematical for African drivers. Not that they got into trouble legally for running over and killing their fellow natives. No, far from it. The drivers were overwhelmed with their superstitions because in their minds, nothing happened by itself or accidentally. They made post haste visits to witchdoctors who made divinations to discover the cause of the accident before administering the required treatment like spiritual exorcism as if the force that had made them run over persons were evil spirits, or the healers treated them against the pernicious effects of witchcraft and gave them protective jujus against evil spells from witches and other bad people.

Colonial administrators and settlers, who did not entertain superstitions like ours, hardly thought of what happened after running over our villagers. They would usually blame the crushed villagers for having been stupid for walking in the middle of the road or very close to the road. To them it was like nothing was the matter. They brushed aside what took place and later at home, opened bottles of wine or beer and drank it as if to celebrate what took place.

But not all white people were as heartless as all that. Some of them, although few and far between, were nagged by their consciences which forced them to feel sorry for the pain they inflicted on the families of the persons they ran over, even if it was the fault of the villagers who were run over and killed. They would come around contrite and express their regrets, and would pay some compensation to the relatives of the victims, and go to church after that to seek some relief for their minds and souls.

The families of the deceased persons were left with the crushed corpses to bury after which they went to see witchdoctors who would tell them whether evil spirits were responsible for the accidents or not or, who in the villages were responsible for what happened as a result of witchcraft. The persons named after divination were usually women because witchcraft is a female province, although rarely some men were also known to practice witchcraft and such male witches were considered to be even more dangerous than their female counterparts. The unfortunate souls would later be confronted with having done the black magic that cost the lives of the people who had been crushed in the accidents.

If confronted and the supposed witches insisted on denying they were the cause of the mortal accidents, they were challenged or were forcibly taken to witchdoctors specializing in the administration of a poison called *mwavi*, a potent magical trial by poison, or of *thale* which required that the accused place one of their palms on a red hot magical metal or piece of broken pottery. The *mwavi* would not kill innocent people but only guilty ones. Likewise, the thale only burnt the palms of guilty people and not those of innocent ones.

I must hasten to state that I have never witnessed instances of *mwavi* or *thale* being administered so as to speak with any authority about what I might have seen or what happened. I cannot vouch as to the veracity of the effectiveness or non-effectiveness of such practices. I cannot also dismiss them, for there are many things that defy logic and scientific approach not only with my Sena people but also with other people. I prefer to remain sceptical about the ability of mwavi or thale to discriminate between guilty and innocent people because in my opinion both mwavi and thale have no organic minds or brains.

I personally would not accept the challenge of drinking a cupful of mwavi nor place the palm of my hand on the thale, regardless of whether I know that I am guilty or innocent of what I am being accused of because for me a poison is a poison and thale is a really hot metal that can burn and char the palm of my hand. I would not be reassured by the claim that the poison and the red hot thale can know whether I am guilty or innocent. I would not uphold the tribal side of my mind that tells and reassures me that mwavi and thale are magical and have a mind and the ability to know whether I am guilty as charged or innocent. More often than not, the mwavi poison was administered to animals like dogs or cats rather than forcing the accused to drink it, if he did not want to take chances.

People standing up and resisting drinking mwavi or having an animal subjected to it for them, had the right to do so or, refuse to place their hand on the red hot metal or piece of pottery, but they would automatically be regarded as guilty as charged. For their fear was regarded as evidence that they were guilty. They would live with the stigma of guilt and suffer from moral consequences as feared and evil people without being physically punished or lynched or regarded as pariahs, as now happens in many places in Africa where alleged witches are beaten up, rusticated from villages, and even sometimes killed or burnt alive. Our witches were feared and even called grandpas or grannies and rarely treated with violence. Sometimes, some fearful people would give bribes to the witches while saying, "Oh, the cruel one, oh the evil one, take this money or this dress here for yourself but spare me the curse of your evil spells."

With dour faces, the purported witches would always receive the gifts without thanking because gratitude was not part of their evil nature and say, "Good. You did well to remember me. Behave yourself, now that you know who I am and what I can do."

Most people thought that attempts to please witches with bribes could actually encourage the witches to engage in more of their evil deeds in the hope of getting more bribes and that the best approach was to denounce them to their faces as witches and despicable characters. And some people even threatened the witches with daggers or machetes in their hands and told them to undo their black magic against them or their relatives or, that if they did not stop pestering them with their evil practices, they would kill them. But never in my days in the villages of the land of the Sena people did I ever hear of alleged witches being killed.

Chapter 3

Another major adventure of my early days I can clearly remember was that of a hunting party. I joined out of fun or because the big boys and the men who participated in it did not forbid or discourage me from joining them despite the dangers inherent in the manner they hunted. When I recall the episode, I think that it must have been the way our pre-historic ancestors hunted in groups for there is safety of numbers.

Decisions to go on hunting forays were never spontaneous. They were always pre-arranged. A few people thought of going to hunt at a particular time on a particular day starting from a particular place in the village. The information was relayed by word of mouth to generate enough interest for the event. When the day and the time arrived, people would begin to assemble at the chosen site with their unbreakable hide-stringed bows made of *ntalala* or *thendjwa* trees; bows for adults were not made of the stems of any trees like those children made for themselves.

I was with the other kids playing about the village when we heard a kudu horn blowing to summon hunters to the assembly place. Shortly afterwards, we saw men converging to a place in the village with bows and quivers full of arrows slung on their shoulders or armed with spears, followed by their hunting dogs or their dogs were running ahead of them without barking or howling but excited and whining with their tails wagging and at times gambolling, eager to burst out into the bush to seek out animals.

I joined the group while my friends decided not to and went home instead after warning me that hunting parties were not for little boys like me. I was so excited to be in the group and did not even think about what might happen to me because I wanted to be adventurous and courageous and fear had no space in me. I had always accepted that I was expendable and could die or be killed at any time. The thought of death did not scare me nor did I welcome it. I just did not care, but I would never expose myself to danger in order to risk my life and be killed. For me life was an interesting adventure. My belief has been to endeavour to live as long as possible to stay alive, despite being reckless and the risks that recklessness engendered. But I did not live in fear of death.

After about twenty men had gathered, the most experienced hunter addressed the gathering to tell the men which direction to take from the gathering spot. The leader, a sinewy man of medium height turned to me and said, "You kid over there," he said pointing to me with an arrow in his hand, "You know hunting parties are not kid's stuff. You're not tough enough to join us. Hunting is fraught with many dangers like falls, thorns, snake bites, and wild animals charging against hunters. If you come and a warthog or a wild pig hurts or kills you, you will blame yourself and not us."

"I agree. I will blame myself and not you if I'm hurt or I fall down or smash my toes," I said defiantly. "If I get killed, I will not blame myself or you because I will be dead and will never come back to this world to blame you or anyone else for that matter. Dead men tell no stories or accuse no one of causing their death."

"But your parents will blame us, if you get hurt or die while hunting. They'll make trouble for me as the leader of this hunting party."

"Don't worry about my parents. I call on all of you not to fear death. Whether we fear it or not, we will end up at its gate and getting into its house one day never to return to the earth to hunt again."

The adults laughed at my wit and for asserting our hard core belief in a one-term lifetime on earth because we did not conceive that people could return to earth as reincarnated beings, although it is believed that in rare cases, a few people had resuscitated after dying and before burial. If it is true, that is another matter and not reincarnation. We believe in the afterlife whereby the souls of those who had been good people on earth become our eternal ancestral spirits, and the guardians of the post generations of their families on earth, and the souls of bad people become eternal evil spirits who could pester the generations of those of their families on earth.

Gwedje, my great leper friend, was one such person who was reported to have come back to life after dying. When I tried to express my doubt or scepticism to Kabulunge, my maternal grandmother who was talking about it to me and other people one day, she did not take kindly to my attitude. Although a kind old woman at the best of times, she was unlike my paternal grandmother who was forever smiling and tolerant and who never ever sprang on me to trash me. Kabu, as we called her, was a tyrant who brooked no opposition from anyone to what she said. She looked at me ramrod stiff like a cape buffalo about to charge and waved her finger at me. That was a warning and a sign that she could charge at me without further warning as she had done before for contradicting what she had said. She had rained blows and slaps on me for doubting the legend about the monster n*thonga* which, according to folklore, is a huge serpent lying low underground somewhere in the world and whose movements in the past had caused rivers and lakes to appear. So Kabu was not a dame to trifle with. She was a tough and aggressive woman.

"What do you little slave who came to this world from the womb of my own daughter know?" she said. "Try again to contradict me and I will show you who I am."

I fell silent because I knew that one more word from my mouth would make her jump on me and trash me severely in the presence of other people. As to whether Gwedje had died and resuscitated, I still have my doubts, although I had swallowed it out of fear when I was a young boy after my grandmother had threatened to turn me into a sorry sight. As for my grandmother, she spoke with authority because she claimed that Gwedje had once been married to a younger sister of hers who had died after giving birth to a stillborn child. Her sister had died before Gwedje became a leper, something which, according to her, had happened after Gwedje had violated rules governing the use of a powerful juju a witchdoctor had given him.

Whether he became a leper for the reason my grandmother gave us or not, I have my doubts there as well. I know though that many witchdoctors attach conditions to the use of the charms they give to their clients. If the clients violate the conditions, it is believed that something terrible happens like becoming a leper or it could lead to the violator becoming a lion or some fearsome animal.

After warning me of the dangers of joining the hunting party, the leader waved the group on and the barefoot men began to move, walking in a disorderly but silent fashion whilst in the village in order not to make unnecessary noises that could disturb people conversing on the verandas of their huts or snoozing or having a siesta after eating heavy meals. It was only when the hunters were well outside of the village before plunging into the bush that they began to howl and excite the dogs which began to bark and run sideways or ahead of the hunters to startle animals so that the hunters could chase them while inciting the dogs to bite the animals and also whilst shooting their arrows at the fleeing beasts. Hunting parties were not only meant to kill animals for meat but they were also a form of sport and entertainment.

The hunters were usually tireless runners. The barefoot men were immune to thorns, stones, logs, grass, and shrubs. They and their dogs could chase animals big like waterbucks, wildebeests, or zebras for hours on end until the animals were completely exhausted and foamed at the mouth and were unable to run any further or to charge at the hunters or the dogs. Whether the animals were struck with arrows or not, the men with axes would give *coups de grâce* with blows on their heads with the backs of their axes. The animals would be carved and the meat distributed. The more animals they killed in one foray, the more meat each hunter took home. If they killed only one animal and the meat was not enough for all the hunters, some of them got the meat and others went home empty handed and they would be the ones to get meat next time around if again only one animal was killed and not enough meat was available for everyone.

The hunting party I joined on that day was not very successful. The hunters were able to kill a wild boar though. Unlike most herbivores that run to escape from hunters and dogs or from carnivores and keep running until they are exhausted and unable to run anymore until they are killed, wild pigs and warthogs are slower runners and can charge to turn hunters into the hunted or to turn the tables on the hunters. And on a few occasions they hurt or killed hunters.

As we went deeper into the bush with grass and scattered trees, we startled a wild boar which began to squeal in terror as it fled, with us and the dogs in hot pursuit. As its speed was no match for the dogs and the hunters, it turned around and began to charge at us with much ferocity, scattering dogs, and men, who ran helter-skelter while howling with fear. Some men jumped into trees to escape from its vengeance. It was not possible for the hunters to stand their ground so as to shoot their arrows at it while they themselves were forced to run for their lives from the animal.

In that *sauve qui peut,* I also ran about blindly before chancing on an anthill. I ended up on top of the anthill about three to four meters high without even knowing how I got up there. It seemed that some force or some wind had just hurled me to the top of the anthill. I climbed so fast before the animal could get me, plunge its teeth into my body, and trample me with its hooves with the fury of a devil. It appeared to have singled me out perhaps because I was the smallest and only unarmed person in the group. The animal grunted to me while looking at me with its mandible foaming as if to say that I would be dead, which certainly I would be as it would have made a mess of me, if it had got me. My courage faltered at the sight of the fearsome beast down below but I did not scream in fear. I trembled but reassured myself that as long as I did not fall, I was safe from it and its malice. I was not going to fall. I was shouting courageously to scare it off and force it to go away from me.

As dogs came to harass it from behind, an idea crossed my mind. I scratched the soft earth around where I was perched and threw it into its eyes in order to blind it, even if temporarily in order to get some reprieve and allow more dogs and men to come to save me. I got so much of the dusty earth into its eyes that the beast was unable to see before some of the hunters aimed arrows at it which overwhelmed it. It collapsed and a hunter gave it a *coup de grâce* on the head with an ebony rod. The beast squealed as he continued to batter it to death.

Seeing the animal lifeless, I jumped down, feeling victorious and praising myself for my bravery and drumming my chest with the palms of my hands like a gorilla. In no time, men were all about me congratulating me on my courage and on a job well done. I was given a whole leg of the animal after it was carved because I was the hero of the day. The hunting party dispersed with most hunters without much meat but with some having enough for dinner that day.

My parents were very happy and mom cooked the meat I was given and we invited my grandfather, grandmother, and aunt Patience for dinner that evening so as to celebrate my great achievement. My heroic deed was reported to the whole village. The event made me feel great. I earned a lot of respect from older folks and admiration from young girls. I walked with pride. A hunter who had a number of bows and arrays of deadly arrows he had accumulated over many years, gave me one of his bows with a leather string and a quiver with ten arrows. I was very grateful to him. For me, his gift was the best prize I could have earned in my younger days.

The incident with the wild boar graduated me overnight into an adult although I must have been around ten years old or so. Although the bow I received from the hunter was too big for me, I handled it with dexterity like an experienced adult who had manipulated big bows and arrows for a long time. I could shoot arrows with deadly accuracy against rabbits and mongooses. Thus armed, I felt I could go anywhere on my own in good or bad times, on journeys even at times when alarms were sounded about the reported presence of mapanga in the bush.

I did not intend to use the arrows anyhow and lose them. They were too precious as they had been made by the local blacksmith and the man who had given them to me had paid dearly for them. I would have no money to have the blacksmith make new ones for me if I lost them. I decided to use them only against big animals if I encountered them or in self defence against the abductors when they were reported to be in our area and I chanced on them or we went to hunt them down in the bush.

As I intended to make good use of the bow to kill birds like francolins and guinea fowls when I saw them on the ground and not when they took to the air so as not to lose the arrows, I made a type of arrow we call *mphina* which consist of a conical wooden warhead shaped with knives and inserted into the stems of reeds and securely tied at the area around the insertion so as to prevent the warheads from coming out when the arrows were fired. I flighted them with guinea fowl feathers in order to embellish them and for better balance when in the air or when fired at a target. Those I could afford to shoot against big birds in the air and lose, if I could not find them when I went to look for them after shooting them. I could make more of them myself. Wooden-headed arrows were better and more powerful than the catapults that most boys or even men used to kill big birds and carried around their necks when out of the village, and even when they had their bows and arrows with them. Some people added nails with their sharp ends driven into the wooden warheads and the circular ends on the outside to enhance the stinging power of such arrows. In my opinion, the nails were pointless as they reduced the overall impact of the wooden warheads. The nails would sting yes but their overall effect would be negligible.

I was going to use the wooden-headed arrows against big birds, if I chanced on them as they scurried on the ground along paths as francolins and guinea fowl usually did. Francolins and guinea fowl were abundant in the bush and they liked to stray onto footpaths, perhaps to have some fun. A wooden-headed arrow striking a guinea fowl anywhere on its body would kill the bird instantly or immobilize it. If struck on the head, the bird would die instantly.

A wooden-headed arrow could be deadly even against humans as well if aimed at the head. Uncle Lino, the father of my cousin Zefina, had once killed two foreign terrorists with his wooden-headed arrows which he aimed at their heads. He had fallen into an ambush the terrorists had mounted to trap and capture people. As the men were about seven to ten meters from him and were urging him to surrender to them, he was quick to draw and place a wooden-headed arrow to his bow, stretched it with much fury and hate of the men before letting it fly against one of the men who he hit on the head. The evildoer howled with pain and died almost instantly after falling down. He quickly placed another wooden-headed arrow to his bow. As he stretched his bow, the evildoers, seeing one of them had fallen and died, took to their heels terror-stricken whilst screaming with fear like little monkeys. My uncle sent the arrow after one of them and hit the miscreant on the back of his head. The evildoer staggered and died upon hitting the ground.

The other three terrorists ran on as hard as their legs could carry them and disappeared into the bush. As he was alone, my uncle did not chase them for fear that the fleeing men could decide to stop and mount an ambush against him again and surprise him as he pursued them. Other men arrived at the scene and helped him to dig holes a short distance away from where he had killed the evil men. They dumped the bodies of the two evildoers into the holes before filling them up with earth and planting shrubs and grass on the graves so that when the plants and grass grew, they would cover and conceal the graves and people would not recognize the places as graves. My uncle and the other men saw no need to pursue the other terrorists, as by the time they had finished burying the dead men, the escapees must have been a long way away and heading for a much denser forest or on the way to their place of origin.

My uncle and the men who helped him bury the dead evildoers could not bury them in the village's cemetery. The cemetery was for the villagers regardless of whether they were good or bad people and not for terrorists from a foreign land who came to disturb our peace and abduct our people, even killing villagers who resisted being kidnapped. Their activities were regarded as unfair to us as we did not do likewise to them in their areas or in their country.

I made five wooden-headed arrows to add to the pack of my ten metal arrows and kept making more so that I could have a quiver full of them. Whenever I went out, I was armed with five wooden-headed arrows and five arrows with metal heads, leaving five metal-headed ones at home. I would then feel that I was armed and deadly. I felt ready for any adventure against wild animals or even evil-minded men alike.

Chapter 4

The year of 1958 was the hardest period in the life of thousands of people in the lower valley of the Zambezi because of the floods that inundated whole regions, swept to death many people and domestic and wild animals. Our Island region of Inhangoma, which is below sea level, got the worst deal possible. I somehow managed to survive the catastrophe. Hardly any patches of land in the region escaped inundation or remained dry for a long time. As the water rose, the very few spots that were dry would be submerged in no time. There was no Noah implementing God's plan of building a huge boat to save one pair of each species and leaving the rest to face their doom. I would not have liked such a fate because it would simply be a bad thing as everyone else would have perished, leaving only one man and one woman alive and the same would have happened to each species of beings.

Even before the Zambezi and the Chire, its tributary to the east, began to rise, we knew that flooding was on the way without knowing how bad it was going to be because people had seen and heard the rain birds which are onomatopoeically called *mbachuche* in our language, meaning *let it pour*.

Rain birds are somehow mysterious. In dry seasons they are neither seen nor heard singing the word mbachuche. They appear only shortly before the rains.

Where do they hide during the dry season, what do they do and eat and how do they survive? Do they hibernate during the dry season or do they live in some non-physical dimension, or are they spirit birds that only appear just to warn us of the impending rains and then disappear soon after not to be seen or heard of again before the next rains begin. And how do they know that the sky is about to open up and let the rain fall? No one can give answers to these questions. Nature alone knows the answers but nature is mute and we cannot force her to speak to us.

It was around midday of a day in 1958 with some fair sunshine and a few scattered clouds in the sky when I was going from my village to a neighbouring village with my playmates Nsali and Macie, the stepbrother of the girl who had raped me after I attempted to steal their mangoes. We were going to meet our friends who we sometimes played with in another village when we saw two birds the size of turtle doves fly ahead of us to a little forested area, singing the word *mbachuche* as they went by. It was the first time I had seen the rain birds, although I had heard them before prior to previous downpours. I do not remember their colour because I only saw them for a few seconds. I was excited to see them, albeit fleetingly. It seems that they don't like to be seen, as if fearing that humans could curse them. They do not mind being heard, it appears, because being heard is what they want so that people know that there is rain coming with possible flooding.

"Mbachuche!" said Nsali rather unnecessarily because the birds had already sung the word mbachuche repeatedly as they crossed ahead of us. He took a wooden-headed arrow from his quiver and placed it on the string of his bow, but the two birds had disappeared into the trees by the time he raised his bow and arrow and had aimed it in the direction in which the birds were flying. The birds flew as fast as turtle doves and there is no way Nsali could kill any of them, even if he was ready to shoot as they flew over us.

"Why would you shoot and kill a rain bird?" I asked Nsali. "You wouldn't eat it. I doubt whether anybody has ever eaten rain birds." We laughed because I sounded funny and provocative to Nsali and he took my joke in good humour and laughed with Macie and me.

Nsali had primed his bow and arrow simply because it was what we did when we saw birds, rabbits, and even snakes sometimes, which we did against the advice of the elders because some snakes, particularly the mambas, could react with aggressive anger to provocation and deliver lethal bites. A bite from the mamba, the most feared of all the snakes in Africa, is a death sentence and legends have been spun about the mamba which has transformed it into a living devil incarnate.

We continued to walk after Nsali had returned the arrow to his quiver but with the bow in his hand still raised in the air. We had our bows in our left hands at the ready so that anytime we could take arrows from our quivers to kill birds and bad men, although the mapanga were not around most of the time. With the rains in the offing as the two rain birds had heralded, we knew that grass and trees would blossom after the rains started to fall and the evildoers would appear in our area to strike terror into our hearts.

One day after we saw and heard the rain birds, the rain began to fall with great intensity. The sky reverberated with thunder and the earth shook as lightning bolts fell incessantly without hitting residences and claiming human victims, at least not in our village. Perhaps it did kill some unfortunate people somewhere else. We did not know. In the bush, lightning felled many trees and seared the grass which did not catch fire because everything was so wet; the ground was waterlogged and water was knee deep with people running everywhere, bubbling as it encountered clumps of grass, stones and trees. People stopped going to the fields to stay indoors and we boys stopped going to school because we studied under a big *nsau* tree close to a lake that was the domain of a fierce and feared crocodile which lazy tongues in the village claimed to be the familiar of the mother of Chief Marikano who was described as a dangerous witch.

I also believed that the toothless mother of Chief Marikano was the commander of the creature which attacked people for her sake. The crocodile was even known by the strange name of Man'dhangira. How did the villagers know what its name was? It is probable that the woman was overheard whispering about it and saying its name to a fellow female witch or, someone in the village made up the story and spread it around and people believed it without questioning its veracity. The Man'dhangira saga was one of the mysteries people talked about and no one doubted what was said about it. Despite the fantastic things that were being said, the fact was that there was a dangerous croc in that little lake because people had seen it and it had attacked many people trying to draw water from the lake or even passers-by who stopped to quench their thirst with cupped hands.

Before long the rain water began to rise and go past our knees and reach our waists. We hoped that it would not rise any further but it continued to rise and forced us to move to higher ground which in no time also became flooded before the water stopped to rise for some time. We were happy that it had stopped and expected it to subside and the land to dry up, as we had had enough of the water.

One evening after the flood had begun to recede, many of us were still congregated on a slightly drier patch of land with water all around us. We were there because the water had invaded our residences and rendered them unliveable. Some of us including me heard the distant song of another bird which at that time I did not know existed. An elder who heard it shushed us to silence. After we had all fallen silent, he said, "Khurea." Khurea is the flood bird. "More flooding is on the way, boys," he said ominously. We remained quiet as the bird went on chanting the word khurea meaning flooding. We were resigned to the incoming fate with no one making the slightest noise or coughing or burping. No one commented on what the elder had said because we knew that the mysterious bird which was hardly ever seen, but only heard, was right because its foresight was infallible. And flood birds were only heard at night. Why only at night? It is a mystery only those birds knew and understood. And nature maintained her muteness and refused to tell us why the bird was only heard at night.

The mysterious flood bird can stay for years on end without being heard until floods begin to inundate the land. Why and where does it hide? Is it a spirit bird existing perhaps in a non-physical dimension and only coming down to earth to announce that we are in for a hard time with floods? Nature has mysteries that cannot be explained.

No sooner did the flood bird sing its ominous word khurea which gave it its onomatopoeic name than water began to rise again and dry patches of land started to disappear. Many people moved away from our village to higher villages which in no time were also flooded, forcing many people to move away to higher areas further away and others to cross the Zambezi to further areas of Sofala to be away from the flooding that was dubbed *Nsasira*, meaning the hunter or the pursuer as, no matter what we did or where we went, the water just followed us to punish us mercilessly, as if for some wrongdoing we might have done. We struggled to remain alive.

It was not unusual for me perched on trees, to see grass huts that the floods had uprooted upstream, with people on top of them, crying and moaning hopelessly and goats bleating, dogs barking or growling and the cats purring, float by to doom and death, as we watched helplessly, unable to rescue them because we ourselves needed to be rescued. We did not find it funny and we did not laugh or cry at their fate because our own fate was no better than theirs.

Suffering had desensitized me. It had transformed me into a man of steel without pitying myself or pitying others because everyone was struggling to survive the flooding. I did not think of death whilst in the water. We just lived and suffered in the water. Repeatedly I was swept by the water and I clung to some tree floating by until people in canoes came to pluck me out and place me in their boats after which I did not even feel overjoyed because it was a reprieve and not the end of my suffering or our troubles.

We were hungry most of the time. We had lost all our food when the granaries were flooded and swept away and ripening food was lost in the fields before being harvested. Water kept us alive and we could live for as long as we could by drinking water and the fast flowing water was not dirty. As long as our bodies were hydrated, we lived on. We were never dirty nor were we infested with germs or worms. Sometime we had some wild fruit and ate fish if we could roast it on some tall and still dry anthill that had not yet been swept away.

With so much water around and us moving and living in water chest deep or neck deep or, in dug-out canoes or on trees, there were other dangers including snakes and wild animals like wild pigs and warthogs trying to find places that were dry and where humans had congregated. Humans and animals competed for dry spaces in order to survive. Fortunately, there were a few enormously big elevated mounds around which people stayed or squeezed onto while hungry and shivering with cold, particularly in the evenings or at night because there was no firewood to make fires to keep us warm. We only got warm from sunshine in the day. We were a marooned people and only wished that the water did not get higher, as we would have no other places to go to from the elevated mounds. If it had risen any further, we would all have perished.

My father and uncle Lino, Zefina's father, were indefatigable with my father's enormous canoe, helping people out of the water and sending them to drier mounds where no one rejected those being brought despite the lack of space. People just squeezed in with some over the others. I was at one of these places one evening when I heard men shouting and telling people to put out the only fire that was burning and ordering us to keep quiet. Why were they ordering that the fire be extinguished and telling us to keep quiet? I asked myself silently, without directing the question to anyone around me.

The answer was not long in coming and I understood why. I heard hippos, perhaps two grunting brutes coming up from downstream. We could not see them as it was a dark moonless night and we did not want to see the monsters. Unlike other animals that were blinded by fire or feared fire, hippos like rhinos, their land cousins, are attracted to fire. They like to investigate when they see fires at night and even to put it out with their enormous feet. They act as self-appointed fire fighters.

I could only imagine what might have happened to us, if the two monsters had come out of the water to the place sheltering us. A disaster of immense proportions would have ensued with the brutes moving about, trampling us to death, pushing us, biting us into pieces and panicking people falling into the swift moving water down below to certain death in that moonless night. The animals passed us by without coming ashore to make trouble for us. The fire was not re-ignited that evening, as we did not know whether the monsters had gone away from the area or they were still around and a fire could attract them to us. But the brutes had gone away. From that day on, no fire was made in the evening even if there was some firewood, to prevent hippos sneaking up on us and causing us troubles of apocalyptic proportions.

Hippos and crocodiles, which are usually confined to rivers and lakes during the dry seasons, come out of the rivers to roam everywhere in time of big floods. They would return to their usual abodes when water began to recede and no hippos or crocs ever get stranded on land, unable to return to their usual homes as the water begins to subside, as happened to fish of various kinds which remained trapped in pools of water to be caught by people or to become food for vultures and scavengers. I and my brother caught a great deal of fish from pools of water after the flood of that year. We caught so much fish that we could not eat it all. We cut them open and salted them before drying them in the hot sun for our subsequent consumption. We even gave away some of it to neighbours and relatives.

There was an episode that took place when I was with my father and uncle Lino during the flood of 1958. It is hard to believe what happened, although I believed it without any shadow of a doubt when the event took place.

One day when the three of us roamed everywhere in my father's canoe with the two of them paddling, or polling it to rescue people from water, trees and anthills from being submerged, we chanced upon an anthill where an old toothless woman was perched with an unusually big earthen pot by her side. We could not tell who the old woman was, as we had never seen her before. She did not belong to our village. She was a total stranger. She had just arrived on the anthill because my father and uncle had seen the anthill without her the previous day. We did not know where she had come from and how she had got there in the first place as the land had been completely flooded and people, no matter how tall, could disappear in the water completely. She could not have swum from wherever she had come from to that anthill. Had someone placed her there from a canoe as punishment for being a bad person, for being evil or a witch? Cruelty of that magnitude was not part of our collective customs or behaviour. Some very few individuals could be hard-hearted and commit ignoble crimes like marooning, but not drowning, old hags on anthills during flooding because they thought that they had caused them many troubles in the village. That way the culprits would not be blamed, if water swept away the old women to her death as they would claim that they had tried to help the hags. If the rising water swept them away and they died, it was acts of God and not their fault. And no one would blame God we did not even think of or pray to in our hour of dire need when everything seemed to be against us.

We stopped by the anthill and uncle Lino spoke to the woman after greeting her with smiles and calling her granny; as the canoe bobbed in the water, my father stilling it with a bamboo pole he had planted in the ground under the water so that it could not be swept by the moving water. I watched my uncle talk to her.

"Granny," uncle Lino said, as he gawked at the strange woman, "we're here to help you. We can take you to a better, drier, and safer place, to a bigger anthill because your anthill will disappear soon. The water is still rising."

"Much as I would like to be rescued, my son, I can't leave this place."

"How so, granny? The water will sweep the anthill before the day is over. You don't want to die, do you, grandma?"

"It better sweep me away than me leave this place with you," she said dryly.

My uncle, my father, and I were surprised to see that the old woman did not want to be rescued while everywhere else people called out to us to be rescued when they saw our boat. Men whistled, women ululated or sang, boys and girls shouted while dogs barked for us to go and rescue them. And there was that dour and wrinkled old hag refusing to be rescued so that she could to continue to live. What were her reasons? I asked myself.

"You can't be serious, granny. Don't be so hard on yourself like that. We your grandsons won't be happy to see you die. "

"How many times do you want me to tell you that I can't leave this place, you naughty boy?" she said with an aggressive voice while contorting her ugly face with anger and impatience towards my uncle.

"But, granny, tell us why you can't abandon this spot and come into our canoe to a safer place?"

"I have got a son with me I can't abandon."

"But we see no son of yours with you."

"Do you want to see him?" asked the woman.

Better judgment told my uncle that we should leave the witch alone and go away. His worst judgment compelled by his well-meaning humanitarian concern to rescue the old lady, made him curious while my father who had perceived the evil aura of the hag, which I had not, discouraged my uncle from continuing to entertain her. My father told him that we should leave her alone and go away to find people to rescue because she had refused to be rescued and we should not feel guilty about it because we did not refuse to rescue her.

"I'd like to see your son," uncle Lino said.

"Open the lid of the earthen pot here and you will see him in there."

"Don't do it, Lino," my father shouted to my uncle. "You could get a terrible curse." But my uncle would not listen to him because his wife was a healer and she had rendered him harm proof against curses, black magic, and evil spirits.

My uncle removed the lid and saw a hyena coiled in it. He went into total shock as he put back the lid on the earthen pot and jumped from the anthill into the canoe, which bobbed and swayed violently from the impact of his landing, or falling rather than landing. As he got up, he began to spit and swear at the hag to avert any evil consequences from opening the pot and seeing the creature in it. My father and I also spat out and said words to avert evil from the old woman from affecting us before my father and my uncle paddled the canoe furiously so as to be away from that place with its evil aura as soon as possible. It was well after we were at a considerable distance from the anthill that my uncle told us what he had seen.

"I'd told you that we should leave her alone and you didn't listen, Lino. See what you saw? It's total evil," my father said.

For me it was not surprising that the old woman might have had a hyena, or perhaps it was a dog or a cat or a rabbit my uncle mistook for a hyena. We believe that hyenas are the forefront familiars of witches or that witches consort with them during their nightly evil runs and forays. We the Sena people are not the only tribe which believes in the ability of witches to consort with hyenas. The Shona and the Ndebele of Zimbabwe believe that witches ride on the backs of hyenas which take them to places where they want to go to at night.

For the scientifically minded person, this may sound like utter nonsense. Westerners tend to forget that in the Middle Ages, it was believed that witches adopted or consorted with cats which became their familiars. That belief compelled the Catholic Church to order the extermination of cats then. The elimination of cats led to the unchecked proliferation of rats and the rats caused the Black Death which claimed about half of the European population.

My uncle was still in shock as we moved away. After recovering, he admitted that he had been foolish not to have listened to my father despite the fact that he was older than my father and was married to my mother's older sister. In our custom, uncle Lino was an older brother to my father, which explains why Zefina and I would not be encouraged to be in love or marry, although we could marry because my father was no blood brother of uncle Lino and Zefina's mother was the daughter of another wife of my uncle's who was not related to my aunt and my mom.

The following day, I was eager to know what had happened to the old hag. My father and my uncle roared with me in the boat to the area to see whether the anthill was still there with the old woman on top of it with her earthen pot with her strange son in it or whether it had disappeared. We found that the anthill had disappeared and the woman had probably been swept away to her death with her earthen pot containing her unusual son or, she had mysteriously moved on to another place, but not in our village because we never saw her anywhere in our village or in the neighbouring villages after the flooding.

As the flood began to recede, we began to breathe with ease as more and more land emerged from under the water and began to dry up. We prayed hard so that the water did not return again, at least not that year and not with the surging force of that year. We had plenty of fish but nothing else to eat it with, except wild grain from tall grass that resisted flooding and its grain remained in it. We harvested such grain. The grain was edible and nutritious. In times of plenty, no one ever harvested it for food. It was left for birds to gorge on.

When most of the water had dried up but the land was still wet, we began to receive relief food that had been donated by the Americans including yellow maize flour, beans, powdered milk and we got it in large quantities. There was plenty of fish to eat that food with. Missionaries and colonial officers saw to it that the people got the food at centres that had been established to distribute it to us.

Although it is hard for a formerly colonized person like me to say something positive about colonialists, I must all the same say, that the colonial officers were dutiful and efficient administrators. When we went to the distribution centres, we received the food in quantities we could hardly carry home on our heads. The administrators were our oppressors alright, but they did not hoard or misuse the foods or sell it to shopkeepers to be sold to us as happens in independent African countries getting food assistance after natural disasters, and where those in power steal the food for themselves or sell it to those to whom it is donated who should receive it free of charge or who have to scratch their backs to get money to buy it.

That gesture from America and the Americans in our time of great need convinced me that the Americans were the best people in the world and nothing could ever convince me to believe that they were not. That belief is stuck with me even today and will never quite leave me, no matter what.

Even as a secondary school student in Nairobi many years later when the Cold War was in full swing, when I began to regard the Americans as ordinary as any other people, and I even tended to bend to leftist ideas including Mao's fantasies, I could never accept Soviet and Chinese propaganda that the American were evil. If the Americans were bad people, where were the Soviets and the Chinese in our hour of need? Why didn't they give us food and were only eager later to give those they supported amongst us instruments of war, destruction and death to fight the colonial regime, which they did for their own sake because they wanted to use them as surrogates in their confrontation with the West

They indoctrinated those they supported amongst us with the hateful ideology of communism. And those they armed were called freedom fighters, which was a misnomer, for those people did not fight for freedom or at least their leaders wanted to implant their own tyrannical regime, which they did following the departure of the Portuguese colonialists and this story will show why independence that should have been a great thing, turned out to be a sour grape in Mozambique. In some places, Portuguese flags were reported being seen on flag posts after being hoisted at night by people who would rather prefer to see the colonialists back than endure the Calvary of living under the new tyrants.

As the struggle for independence was taking place, I was critical of the Americans and of their Western allies, particularly the French who supplied 150 sturdy and highly manoeuvrable Alouette III helicopters to the Portuguese armed forces who used them with deadly effect against guerrillas in the wars of independence in their African colonies. Former guerrillas who faced helicopters and helicopter gunships confirmed that helicopters were more dangerous that fixed wing planes.

As we began to pick up the threads of our lives after the flooding, people began to work the land which the flood had fertilized and in no time they had bumper harvests, as if nature had wanted us to forget our previous suffering. We began to forget about it but the grim vestiges of it were everywhere. We could see human skeletons and bones of people who had died elsewhere after being swept away in the flood and their osseous remains ended up in our area. None of us thought of opening holes to bury the bones in them for fear of picking up evil. With time, the skeleton or bones just disappeared, perhaps picked up by hyenas which could still crunch on them and swallow them.

The flood of 1958 was a test of my will to live and see another era dawn and be able to recount the episode. It was an extraordinary adventure for me, although a grim one. It was hard to survive but I do not regret that it happened despite all the bad things that the flooding caused. Our human lives are just like that and nothing is ever always plain or smooth sailing.

Chapter 5

After 1958, annual floods came and went. They were a blessing to water our fields for us to produce food and to provide us with plenty of fish without inundating our region so brutally and causing death and suffering of epic proportions as had happened in 1958 or, in some earlier floods before my birth which older people who had lived through them still remembered and talked about.

The curse of mapanga who invaded our area every year also returned almost every year. Unlike the flood that tended to be a blessing, the presence of the foreign assassins was always a curse for bringing and sowing fear and causing sleeplessness, terror, and death. Despite the danger they presented to us, the abductors were not as worrisome as the big floods were because we could not fight the water. As for the abductors, as soon as the red alert swept the villages reporting their presence in our bush and forests, everyone went about armed to the teeth with home-made guns, bow and arrows in hand, machetes, wooden clubs, spears, axes and big hard wood rods or clubs, the kind of weapons the mapanga, who were usually armed with daggers and knives, could not match. People carried any tools they could use to fight the criminals.

At times when the foreign terrorists were reported to be in our region, women and children moved about in groups with armed men accompanying them. As soon as the presence of the evildoers was reported, hunting parties were organized to go into bush, grasslands, and forests with hunting dogs to seek them out and eradicate them from there so as to render the countryside free and safe for the villagers, particularly men who went to tend traps for birds and hunt wild animals, and women who went to pick up firewood and boys like myself who used to take to the woods with playmates to play there and have fun.

In the days when we had no school, particularly on Sundays, I liked nothing better than to team up with my friends and go into the woods and set up see-saws with ropes attached to wooden boards on which to sit or stand after tying up the ropes to branches of trees. We would play slowly or leisurely most of the time and energetically sometimes, moving back and forth as fast and as hard as we could do, bending our knees and stretching our legs as we did so.

We took sweet potatoes and dry fish and gourds with water. We roasted the potatoes and the fish before sitting down to eat slowly after playing on our see-saws. We would return to play on the see-saws after eating before returning home as the sun dipped onto the horizon. We always made sure that we returned home before darkness to avoid encounters with nocturnal marauders like hyenas. Playing on seesaws was one of the best exercises I liked followed by fighting other boys in the village and wrestling.

Fighting other boys was not frowned upon by our parents. It was in fact regarded as character-forming and good for fitness as it toughened us up and made us fearless. Fighting other boys made me strong as I always won so much so that some boys, particularly those I had defeated, took to their heels while screaming with terror when they saw me approach them with clenched fists to intimidate them. I also liked to wrestle which we did as a sport and no one felt bad when thrown down unlike in fist fighting which we did in anger to establish supremacy and to strike fear into the hearts of other boys.

If we did not go into the woods, we went to swim in the Zambezi where we swam in large numbers while completely naked. We hollered and splashed in the water so much that it seemed to intimidate and keep crocodiles at bay. Nobody was ever snatched in the jaws of crocodiles when we plunged into the river in large numbers.

Only those who attempted to swim alone could fall prey to the predators. Few were the people who went to wash alone in the river, anyway. Those who did went to wash in sections of the river that were so shallow in dry seasons with water knee deep that no crocodiles would attempt to move in those waters without exposing themselves to danger, of being attacked and killed and ending up on the plates of villagers as a delicacy.

Many years would pass without ever anybody being caught in crocodile attacks. The crocs were happy staying away from villagers who killed them for meat and their skins white men later bought from them. They fed mainly on fish in forested areas of reeds and bulrushes. People and canoes hardly went to those areas because of the hippos which took shelter from the hot sun there. People in canoes were no match for hippos. So, we felt that it was better to leave them alone where they took refuge. Hippos only go out of the river to feed on land at night and return to the river before daybreak. They avoid coming ashore in heavily populated areas for fear of people with guns.

Chapter 6

The red alert reporting the presence of mapanga in the bush around our villages had been sounded after a woman with a baby on her had escaped by a hair's breadth from being abducted by a gang of three terrorists and taken to Henzi in Nyasaland. She and her baby were saved just in time. She screamed as the abductors were dragging her from the footpath to disappear with her and her baby into the bush. Her distressed screams attracted two men who were armed with bows and arrows and who were coming behind her. They rushed to the place where she was screaming, with arrows on their bowstrings and ready to shoot.

When the terrorists saw the men, they panicked and left the woman in order to save their own lives. The men were more interested in consoling her and her baby and taking them to the village to ensure their safety than mounting a search operation to either kill or capture the evil doers. After the incident that left the woman completely shaken and numb with fear for many days, our village, and the neighbouring villages, changed gear to a war footing. Men went about their usual business or travelled in groups whilst fully armed to deter the miscreants from taking them by surprise and to enable them to fight back, capture, or kill the terrorists.

I myself went about always fully armed from the day I had acquired the powerful bow and arrows from the hunter who gave them to me after the day of the hunt when I did my bit in the killing a wild boar. I loved my new weapons and used them to kill birds and animals to feed my family and my grandparents and aunt Patience. I felt that my grandparents had done much to feed my parents and my brothers and me when I was much younger and that it was my turn to repay them for their goodwill with my own good deeds, to help them survive as they grew older.

Hardly a day went by without me bringing home one or two or more guinea fowl or francolins from the bush. I passed by my grandparents' hut to drop one or more birds off to them. When I went to angle for fish, I would give part of the fish - I caught mainly tilapia, cat fish or tiger fish - to my grandparents. Grandmother thanked me each time while grandfather thanked the ancestors, as if it was the ancestors who had killed the birds or caught the fish. He implored the spirits to protect and keep me safe from evil wherever I went and would be.

As a Christian convert of the Scottish missionaries in Nyasaland, he would also say a prayer in our language to the Christian God. One day after praying to the Christian God, he asked me to sit down and he began to reminisce about his days as boy with the Scottish missionaries in Nyasaland. He remembered one of the missionaries by the name of Hastings.

"Pastor Hastings," he said, "was a good man like all the Scottish missionaries but he was very hard on our beliefs. He would never be happy with me if he knew that I also prayed to our ancestors he called evil gods."

"But our ancestral spirits are not gods and are not evil," I said to him. "We don't have gods except Mulungu, we don't worship. It's your Scottish missionaries who forced you to worship Him and my Catholic missionaries who are doing the same with me forcing me to worship Him."

"It's not fair that they do that with us," grandfather said.

"I know it's not, but what do we do?" I asked him.

We were silent for a while as if to think about what to say to each other before my grandfather began to speak again, to deplore what the European missionaries had done to him and were doing to me. "Grandson, do what you think is best for you. If you want to stick with the missionaries and forget the ways of our people, go on, but know that there could be a heavy price for you to pay."

"Grandpa," I said in alarm. I was scared because my grandfather had lived through four generations while I was only in the teens of my generation, "what do you mean by a heavy price to pay and what do I have to buy to pay a price?"

Grandfather laughed at my naivety because we were talking at cross purposes.

"I don't mean it that way. You don't have to buy anything and pay money for it."

"What do you mean then?"

'I'll give you an example. You and Zefina, your maternal cousin, have strong feelings towards each other but have decided not to entertain the feelings for fear of your relatives and incurring the wrath of the ancestors."

I was shocked and shuddered as I could not figure out how my grandfather had known about Zefina and me. I suspected that Zefina might have told her mother about it while seeking her advice and her mother had spoken to my mother about it and she, in turn, had told my grandfather so that he could warn me about an amorous relationship with my cousin. I boiled with anger against Zefina for letting the cat out of the bag that would destroy us psychologically with shame. I felt shame overwhelming me as I thought how I would look my aunt in the eye when I met her next. How was she going to regard me: as her nephew or her would be son-in-law? I hoped that uncle Lino did not know about it and prayed that he should not know anything about it, although he would do nothing against me and he would forgive his daughter and me. He was a man with an immense capacity to forgive and let things go.

"Who told you about Zefina and me, grandpa?" I asked him with a desperate voice.

"No one, but I know," he said before adding, "I can be beyond time and space if I want and see secrets about people. That's how your secret with the beautiful Zefina was revealed to me. Everything comes to me in a state of trance or even as dreams whose details I can remember."

I had known that my grandfather was psychic but I did not know that his soul could regress to the past, see the present, and peer into the future.

"I love Zefina. A pity we can't come together and marry when I'm older."

"Love Zefina as your sister," he said, "and don't both of you be tempted into anything silly. If you succumb to temptation and you have carnal knowledge of her, both of you will not live long. That will be the price both of you will pay for offending our ancestors and trampling our customs underfoot." I did not quite believe that we could die prematurely after Zefina and I had sex, but I felt that it was better to pay heed to the warning and also because having sex with a close cousin would disgrace our families.

I told my grandfather that I would not tread the path of evil and be punished with rejection by our families and by the ancestral spirits or by God. I told him that Zefina and I wanted to go to heaven and be with God. I did not however ask him what he knew about my future, as I was not interested in prophecies about me and my life. I did not want to worry my head off with prophecies. Furthermore, in our culture, people do not concern themselves with what will happen in future as happens with many other people, although at times our healers will warn people if they foresee imminent danger for them in order to help them avert catastrophes. As happened with everyone else in the tribe, my interest was the past and the present and how the evils of the past and the present could affect me in the present. The future did not concern me because God had endowed me with eyes in front of me and did not place another pair of eyes at the back of my head to see the past. This belief in part explains why no prophets, great seers, and astrologers emerged in the tribe where astrology is totally unknown.

Astrology is alien to the Sena people because it never occurred to us that planets had influence on our lives like bad or evil spirits and witches did. Those are the ones I would fear, if I did not have protective juju against them. The only heavenly bodies we thought or knew affected us was the sun which is the source of all life on earth and also the cause of much suffering and death when it dried up the land and water to cause drought, and the moon which affected lepers and lunatics and influenced the menstrual cycles of women. That explains why menstruation is called *kumwezi* in my language literally meaning *being in the moon.*

The moon is important. We can see it. It is very much a part of our beliefs, fears, and superstitions. The brightness of the full moon enables us to walk at night and see what is ahead of us like snakes and other lethal creatures whereas the dark moon is portentous, concealing many dangers and people avoid walking at night when the moon is dark because they cannot see around and ahead of them.

As for the stars we see at night, they are far away and do not affect us or influence our lives. Why worry about such things which appear to have no minds and lives of their own, shining brighter when the moon is bright and dimming when the moon is dark and not at all being seen during cloudy and dark nights. We are not aware of the existence of the planets of our solar system which in the superstitions of other peoples who know about their existence are of vital importance to their lives because they believe that the planets exert influence on their affairs.

The anger I had felt against Zefina vanished from my heart after my grandfather had told me how he had come to know about me and her. I began to feel greater affection for her as my sister and nothing beyond that after knowing that she was not the one who had disclosed our secret.

Chapter 7

A couple of days had gone by after the red alert about the mapanga and the alarm had sunk and settled in our hearts and made us conscious and aware of the existing danger. One morning my parents left home for the field very early in the morning while I was still sleeping. After I got up, ate something I found, I decided to follow them, which was against the advice that we had been given after the red alert about the presence of the foreign terrorists was sounded. No one was to walk alone because one person alone, even if armed, could be overcome by a gang of terrorists. I felt so reassured with my bow and arrows that the thought of going through an area that was densely covered with grass did not intimidate me. I was not going to be scared like a chicken. I had conquered the ferocity of a wild boar and I was not to let foreign terrorists frighten me in my own territory.

I was born to defy odds and play my part in the fight against evil, even alone, if need be. I thought that staying put at home for fear of the terrorists would be tantamount to cowardice and handing victory to them on a silver platter. I told my elder brother that I was going to join our parents but he was too sleepy to grasp the full meaning of what I was telling him. He just murmured a few words like "ah, okay, I want to sleep" and he slid into sleep.

I did not have much patience with him to take more time to see to it that he understood what I was saying. I always thought that he was a lazy bum and that was why our father sometimes got him to leave his bed in the mornings by lashing him with a stick. I left with my oversized bow in hand and an arrow with a metal warhead in the bowstring and my quiver with nine arrows slung on my shoulder, ready to act at a moment's notice. I walked steadily past residences until I reached the perimeter of the village before walking along the path bounded by tall elephant grass, shrubs and small trees while looking on the sides and in front so as to deter evildoers from springing on me and taking me by surprise. I knew that surprise could beat the strongest, as an African saying stresses.

As I approached an abandoned homestead with mango trees and overgrown with tall grass, which had been the homestead of my maternal great uncle Sande Meya, I heard some rough and roguish voices ahead of me speaking our language, ungrammatically and with a strange accent or the people were speaking their language which was similar to ours. I steeled myself for action, as I suspected that it was a gang of evildoers. I held my breath and stood still for a while before continuing to walk to where the men were instead of turning tail and running back to the village whilst screaming with fear. I held my bow with the arrow before me in a shooting position whilst walking very slowly when I saw about five ragged men with unkempt hair on the left side of the path. I knew they were abductors. There was no doubt about it. I edged towards them whilst walking like a chameleon with shaking legs in the air before putting down every foot when one of them spoke to me in our language with his heavy accent.

"Come here, you little guy. Don't be afraid. We'll not harm you. We're good people. We're your uncles and have candy for you."

"See," one of them said. He showed me candy.

"Fuck you," I screamed to them, "Keep your candy to yourselves. You motherfuckers are in deep trouble with me today," I shouted to them so that if there were other people close by, they could rush to join me in combat. I began to stretch the string of the bow with an arrow on it and began to swing the arrow to them, pointing at each one of them in turn. "I'll kill you all, you bastards."

My cockiness surprised the criminals whose bodies were convulsing with extreme fear as they stared death in the face. They looked at one another without speaking as I took some steps backwards to give myself more distance which would enable me to take arrows from the quiver and rapidly shoot and kill them all. I had trained for it and I could do it in quick succession and with amazing speed. I guessed they were silently conferring about what to do to me without speaking—to dare to rush and spring on me or to bolt for it and save their lives.

Before I realized it, the panicking men began to run into the tall grass. I put back the metal arrow and placed a wooden-headed one on the bowstring and trained it at the man behind and the conical head of the arrow hit him on the shoulder with such force that I heard him howl with pain, stagger, and collapse and fall with a heavy thud. I knew that he would not stand up immediately and continue to run with his friends because the arrow I fired at close range with much fury had momentarily paralyzed him and it would be sometime before he could recover and resume running which he would hardly do in the state of dizziness he was in and also because of the extreme pain the wooden-headed arrow had inflicted on him. He was lucky that I did not hit him on the head which would have killed him instantly. His companions kept running, not perhaps knowing that one of them had fallen and was going to be taken prisoner, rushing through tall grass as they went.

I knew they would not turn around and return to challenge me and free their colleague when they realized he was not with them. The sight of my arrow had done its job of filling their hearts with terror and they knew that I would not hesitate to use my arrows to kill them all. I was not only determined to do so but I was also dying to do it. I later regretted not having killed some of them as they themselves would not have hesitated to kill me if they had caught me I had tried to resist them or screamed for help. They would have strangled me with their rough hands. They had strangled young boys before who had tried to resist being captured.

I concentrated on their fallen colleague, striking him with my unbreakable bow before tying up his hands behind his back with a rope from my quiver and forcing him to stand up with kicks, which he did with much difficulty while grunting like a drunken man as I toted the arrow I had hit him with in his face. He knew that if I used it again against him from a distance of less than one meter, the arrow would make a total mess of his face and kill him. In fact, I would have to step back to have more distance before shooting the arrow at him. I frog marched him to the field of my parents where there were many people working in the other fields adjacent to ours. Seeing the wild man I held with the rope behind him, my parents and people in other fields close to our field rushed to us and understood that I had captured an abductor on my own.

I told them what had happened and how I had captured the terrorist I had taken to them. People found it hard to believe the feat I had accomplished on my own. They could not dismiss as untrue what I was saying when they saw my captive with their own eyes. I was not telling a story, but showing it with a real panic-stricken person who was shaking and crying with pain, invoking his mother to help him as if she were a goddess, and begging for mercy and forgiveness. He asked us not to kill or castrate him, but I had no intention of doing so before asking me to give him some water because he was thirsty. My father poured water in a can from a gourd and put it to his mouth and helped him drink, as he could not do it himself with his wrists bound behind his back.

Many people disapproved what my father did to the evildoer, saying that the terrorist should be denied water and food so that he could die of thirst and hunger. Some people did not see the purpose of being kind to someone who would never be kind to one of us who might have fallen into his hands. And they were right about the cruelty of the terrorists because they slaughtered those who resisted being taken prisoner. But would it be right to kill someone who was bound with a rope he could not disengage? As for his fear of being castrated, his apprehension must have stemmed from the practices of his tribe where they probably castrated people accused of evil deeds. We did not inflict that kind of cruelty on other people. Some people castrated male pigs if they had no female pigs for them to mate with.

"Four other terrorists fled to the west of the former homestead of Sande Meya," I said. "I could not chase them alone leaving this bad man here behind, after he had fallen, after I struck him with my wooden-headed arrow. He would have escaped in my absence or hid in the grass to escape from me. I preferred to take him captive than chase the other four who could stop to mount an ambush to ensnare me like buffaloes do against hunters."

Before long, men gathered with their bows and arrows on their bowstrings and excited dogs gambolling or wagging their tails before they headed to Sande Meya's former residence to plunge into the bush to look for the evildoers for as long as they could. The men, most of them hunters, ran as fast as they did while chasing wild animals. They wanted to capture the fugitives and teach them lessons they would never forget for the rest of their miserable lives, if they did not kill them after spotting them and capturing them. They spent the rest of the day scouring the bush everywhere, in small groups of four with a dog in each group but to no avail. The bandits had gone away from the area and were probably heading back to Nyasaland, walking in the bush and avoiding roads and footpaths after the brush with death from my arrows.

The terrorist I captured was crying nonstop, shaking with fear about what we might do to him. We handed him over to the chief despite calls from one man who was saying that we should kill him while another man said that we should castrate him like we did with pigs before letting him return home. I told them that I would not stand for either and was not going to allow it because he was a real man and not a character in a story that is killed or who dies. He was kept tied with Gordian knots around his wrists with ropes that were tied behind his back and with other ropes around his legs, waist and neck. He was locked up in a mud-and-wattle hut in which he was tied to poles and given food so that he could recover before he could be seen off to Nyasaland or was handed over to the government who would probably exile him to the Island of Sao Tome in the Atlantic where he would live for the rest of his miserable life and die there far away from his relatives and his native Nyasaland.

Part Two: In Search of Education
Chapter 8

In my younger days there was no rule or law that compelled African parents to send their children to school. And the schools we had were mainly run by missionaries. The regime of the Portuguese ruler Antonio de Oliveira Salazar had handed over the task of giving education to African youths to missionaries, mainly of the Catholic Church. The Catholic Church established a string of primary schools in various regions of central Mozambique. Secondary schools could be found mainly in urban areas. They were few and were mainly state run and were attended by students from the colonial settlers and assimilado families which could afford to pay the fees at such schools.

There were a few state run primary schools and these again accommodated children from the settlers and assimilado families who had the money to afford to send their children to such schools. Despite their prestige as schools for the children of the elite, state run schools did poorly compared to missionary run schools which followed the same syllabuses that the government in Lisbon had established for all schools in Portugal itself, and its overseas provinces renamed after the regime in Lisbon had dropped the designation of colonies for them.

With the abolition of the designation of colonies for his overseas possessions also went the designation of empire, so that Salazar could claim that his country had no colonies and no empire but only overseas provinces which were, according to the official explanation, extensions of his European country. He thought that his ruse would make the world leave him alone and not vex him with accusations that Portugal was an imperial power like Britain or France, the two colonial powers which in the 1960s, were dismantling their empires in Africa and granting independence to their former colonies.

Salazar was wrong because nobody in the world accepted his claim and the world kept vexing him and telling his country to let its colonies become independent so that they could join the comity of newly independent states in Africa. His intransigence was such that he did not care to listen to India's call for negotiations that Portugal should peacefully surrender its colonial enclaves of Goa, Daman, and Diu in India, as India had done with France which decided to return its Indian enclaves of Pondicherry, Karaikal, Anam and Mahé in 1963 after the agreement the two countries had reached in 1956. In 1961, India decided to reclaim the enclaves by resorting to military action, putting an end to more than 450 years of Portuguese presence in those enclaves.

As for giving us education, he was in a quandary between denying us education completely and giving it to us. In his mind, giving us education was tantamount to providing us with the rope with which we would one day stifle his colonial control of us, in order to make our country independent. He was not wrong to think the way he did, for it was the educated colonial elites that had agitated for independence in the former British and French colonies, particularly the élites that had served under the imperial powers as civil servants or in their armed forces during the First and Second World Wars.

Despite his reluctance to give us education, Salazar knew that he needed Africans to serve in his colonial regime particularly as soldiers because he knew that Africans would in the end, resort to armed violence to liberate themselves from his imperial control. He decided to give some primary education to Africans and not much beyond that level. It was this category of people with such education that Salazar and his regime decided to accord the assimilado status of Portuguese citizenship in order to bamboozle them into thinking that they had no reason to revolt for independence because they were Portuguese citizens.

So far, so good for Salazar! Everything appeared to be in his favour because most Africans particularly in the rural areas were illiterate, like my parents who would not compel their children to go to school because they did not understand the importance of education. Such parents were just too happy to see their children helping them in the fields or tending their herds of goats or cows or spending time in the bush laying traps for birds and killing little animals to help feed their families.

The missionaries who had been given the task of establishing schools to educate African youths, did not go to the villages to tell our parents about the importance of sending us to school nor did they reject the children when they turned up in large numbers at their schools. They did not place a limit to the number of children classes were to have. The budget that the missionaries received from the government was not big enough to enable them to build schools everywhere. Because they wanted to establish schools everywhere and their means were limited, in some villages they sometimes made children study on the ground under trees after providing them with teachers and blackboards. The youths had to buy their own texts, exercise books, pencils, erasers as North Americans say or rubbers as the British say, to erase or rub out mistakes from their exercise books, and slates on which to work out arithmetical problems.

The slates or mini blackboards we carried in our school sacks or in our hands were the best thing we had as we could use them all the time, if they did not break. If they broke, we bought new ones because they were very cheap and were sold in the village stores.

So it was that when I began to attend school, I studied under a big and tall *nsau* tree while waiting for the missionaries to build us a school. Studying under a tree did not ensure that we had classes the year round. We had no classes when it was windy or stormy and during the rainy season. We were just too happy to wake up in the morning and see a wind whirling and whistling or rain falling outside so that we could stay at home, make popcorn by stirring maize with sticks on broken pieces of pottery placed on triads of stones with fires below them. We would sit down around fires to tell stories while eating the popcorn as thunder shook the earth and lightning made ear-splitting noises.

When the rain was heavy, we did what we liked to do best. We had rain baths called *nyantambitambi*. I and other boys would go running naked away from the huts and return back home completely drenched. Our parents and relatives did not see us naked because they were inside their huts keeping warm around the fires and sheltering themselves from the rain. We usually avoided having rain baths during stormy rains, but we sometimes went out to run even when there were storms, thunder, and lightning.

Lightning would stop us dead in our tracks as the flashes blinded us momentarily. Undaunted, we would continue to run until we decided to return to our cottages where we made fires and warmed ourselves so as to get dry.

Our cottages were like independent territories in the homesteads of our parents. Neither our fathers nor mothers nor sisters ever entered them unless they thought that something exceptional was happening when we were screaming, as if we were dying. Apart from such instances, they would not interfere with us even if they knew that we had some girls visiting us, as it was the way boys and girls socialized in the villages. Sometimes when the boys were small and the girls older, there would be situations like the one that took place with me when the half-sister of my playmate Macie and two of her girlfriends, came to play funny games with me and with my next door friends.

Chapter 9

The first school I attended in the area of Chief Marikano was under a huge and tall *nsau* tree. Every kid was registered when school began and our teacher was called Alberto Kamphiripiri. He was assiduous in doing the roll call before class every day. If we failed to attend class, he would strike our palms with a ruler the next day or on the day when we went back to school, or he made us kneel down for one hour or more until our knees began to hurt and we began to plead for mercy with tears in our eyes. I hardly failed to go to school except when I had a real reason I would present to him as a valid excuse and he usually understood in such circumstances.

Many other boys and I spent part of our early days chanting the 23 letters of the Portuguese alphabet. I learned the alphabet very fast and was able to recite it from A to Z without stopping to breathe or blink my eyelids. I remained in that group of alphabet chanters for a long time without going to the group of boys who could write or spell out words and do simple addition and subtraction arithmetic. I could not summon enough courage to tell the teacher that I had mastered the alphabet nor did anyone around me who knew that I needed to move on to the next group, ever tell the teacher that "this boy here, *senhor professor* (mister teacher), knows the alphabet and must move on to the next group."

If there was anything that made me dread going to school it was that there were some big boys who came to school after smoking hashish. They did not come to study but just to tease and bully us young boys and snatch our lunches after slapping us, so that they could intimidate us and grab our food. We were powerless to do anything against them.

The most vicious ones came with catapults and small stones hidden in the pockets of their shorts or in their sacks. Because there were so many kids in knots of varying sizes sitting, laughing, or chanting the alphabet, the bully boys had a field day with their catapults on which they placed stones and let them fly to hit the exposed bums of the little ones who wore ragged shorts after which they quickly put away their catapults.

I would suddenly hear a kid scream while rubbing his bum to lighten the stinging pain of the stone and the little ones around him would laugh because it was fun as long as it was not them who had been struck. And sometimes the teacher would come around to slap the screaming boy for interrupting the class, and no one would dare to tell him what had happened and why the boy had screamed because in most cases, boys saw the bullies catapulting the stones against their chosen victims.

Even after the teacher came to know about the crazy bully boys and what they did, he did not dare to talk to them or warn them against what they were doing or expel them from the school, if he had wanted. He could have done it, for all he needed was to tell the chief who would come running with his *cipaios* or policemen to belabour the bullies with their wooden clubs and tie them up with ropes before frog marching them out of the school and sending them to do forced labour in his fields and in the fields of his policemen. So we were stuck with the crazy boys, unable to do anything against them, to discipline them or tell them to sod off because we wanted to be left alone so that we could study undisturbed.

We would only be happy when they quarreled amongst themselves and went to the teacher to ask him to let them go outside to fight, away from our sight; to fight it out so that one of them could establish his physical supremacy over the others. The teacher would say to them, "go ahead." The dunderheads would go and later return after fighting and come to a draw. We knew that they had fought to a draw because when the two fighters came back together, they shook hands before returning to the class sometimes while laughing or while brooding.

When we only saw one of the bullies return to class, we knew that the other boy had been defeated and was ashamed to return to class or was afraid to come to school for fear of the boy who defeated him, and he never came back to school again. His defeat signaled the end of his schooling or education. Thus one by one, the bully boys disappeared from school having fought one another until only the strongest bully, we called the *xaxa* in our language or champion, kept coming to school. We little boys felt relieved and happy that those bullies who sometimes organized and incited little boys to fight after classes so that they could amuse themselves, were no longer coming to school and the teacher was also relieved as he did not have to put up with them and accept their behaviour for fear of he himself being beaten in the presence of us the kids he taught.

It happened once that a villager who stopped a fight between two boys, came to the school with the two pugilists in tow to warn the teacher against allowing boys to go out to fight. He was not amused that the teacher was letting boys fight. "What if they kill one another?" he asked the teacher who did not answer. "You will be held responsible." He left soon after he had admonished the teacher in our presence.

The event I remembered most whilst at that school was our decision to go and swim and splash in Lake Nyangangwe, which was less than half a kilometre away from the school, and which was the domain of the crocodile Man'dhangira who lazy tongues said was the familiar of the witch mother of Chief Marikano.

This particular small lake was part of a series of small lakes like it along a valley from the Zambezi in the west to the Chire, its tributary in the east, along a distance of about one and a half to two days' walk. Each one of these small lakes had the same name of Nyangangwe. Each one of them had particular characteristics. One or two of the lakes were believed to be haunted by good or by evil spirits. One or two were regarded as the domains of spirit crocodiles that were believed to be good crocodiles which did not attack people, if there was such thing as good crocodiles. There are folks out there who will say that there are good spirit crocs that will protect people from other ordinary crocs or from any other danger while they are in the water where such crocs reside. They will say that such crocs are not usually seen and people can only see them if they decide to manifest themselves in physical form when they want to be seen. One or two of the lakes were the kingdoms of dangerous crocs including those that were regarded as the familiars of witches. Probably one or two were free of any infestations, except the presence of fish which all of them had in abundance.

One afternoon before the day we splashed in the lake at Marikano, I went to another Lake Nyangangwe close to the one by our school to buy fish from the fishermen. Fishermen were still in water and pulling their long net and moving it ashore to pluck out the fish it had caught, when lo and behold, the most amazing sight came along in the net. It was a human skull. The fishermen thought nothing of it and laughed when they saw the skull. One of them removed it from the net while laughing because the rare and strange catch tickled his funny bones.

When he came out of the water with the skull in his hand, he said he was going to use it as a container for earthworms for his hooks and took it home. And no one told the man not to do so as it would result in a curse to him. The light-heartedness and humour with which they treated the grim catch was uncharacteristic of us who tended to be hysterically superstitious and should have shuddered at the very sight of a human skull coming in a net from the water.

When I saw the man holding it in his hands and showing it to us while grinning, I thought nothing of it and did not attach ominous meanings to it and nothing untoward ever happened to me after seeing it. I do not know if anything bad happened to the other people, particularly to the fishermen. Perhaps something happened to the man who decided to take it home or his relatives later asked him to get rid of it and took him to a witchdoctor to be cleansed of the evil of the skull.

What I thought at that time after seeing the unusual catch, was that someone must have drowned in the lake while swimming or, that it was the skull of one of the many people who perished in the 1958 flooding and his body ended up in that lake.

At Marikano, the behaviour of the villagers was appalling. They let the critter remain in the lake, year in, and year out while it caught and savaged people who only just escaped with their lives to tell of their ordeal in the claws and the mandibles of the critter. They never thought of tracking it down or of hunting it in order to kill it and remove the danger it posed to people, for fear of provoking the wrath of the witch mother of Chief Marikano who was supposedly its leader and who instructed it to attack people. Was that not the biggest nonsense that the villagers entertained? Does a crocodile need to be told to attack people? Isn't it in its instincts to attack humans or animals for it to eat, or because that's the only thing that a crocodile does best?

Our irrational superstition turned us into our own worst enemies. Elsewhere like in Canada, a wild animal like a cougar or mountain lion or a bear which has attacked or killed a human or which proves to be a nuisance to the general public, is tracked down right away and killed to stop it from attacking more people because once a wild animal starts attacking humans, it will attack more people, especially if it is sick or old. The same also applies to crocodiles which can survive by just eating fish, but once they attack people, they will be looking for more people to attack. And the worst of the unreasonable logic of the Marikano villagers was that the crocodile in question was in a small lake, and not in a big lake or in a river, which would have made it difficult to track down and kill. It was spotted ashore basking in the sun or moving half submerged in the water.

After a large numbers of us had bathed in the lake for three consecutive days without the dragon catching one of us, on the fourth day before we went for another splash, we saw a man bursting into the school with a contorted face rigged with frowns. He asked the teacher and us to listen to him. The din from the various voices came to a stop, as if an ancestral spirit was about to address us. We almost stopped breathing in order to hear what he had to tell us.

"You boys have been fooling for three days in Lake Nyangangwe. Stop it forthwith before Man'dhangira begins to act and catch you one by one," he said with a grave voice. "It has been seen cruising up and down in the lake as a warning to you." The man left without even saying goodbye to us as soon as he had finished delivering his warning. We heeded the warning and never went back to swim in the lake again. The croc had won before it had even taken one of us for its snack and no one came up with a plan to hunt it down in order to kill it because of our fear of an old hag who probably had nothing to do with the dragon, and to whom we attributed supernatural powers of ownership and command of the saurian.

My family did not stay long in the area of Chief Marikano because one of my young brothers fell ill with a skin disease and the healer that my parents consulted said that a witch in the village had bewitched him. He treated him and my brother got better. I cannot say whether he got better because of the treatment from the witchdoctor or his immune system got better and overpowered the infection.

The witchdoctor advised my parents that we should move away from the village before the witch could do us more harm and my parents believed in him and accepted his recommendation. We left the village without bidding farewell to any villager and moved to the village of sub-chief Ndere by the Zambezi, about two hours' walk from the village we left. We went to live in the village where uncle Lino's family lived.

But the naivety of my parents was to accept the witchdoctor's advice for us to move instead of asking him to treat us and render us immune to the witchcraft of the witch instead of us moving to another village where there were also witches who, according to my parents, began to attack us after we settled there. I believe that the best way of fighting a disease would be to seek medical treatment and boost immunity and not to run away from one place to another place because one could go to a place with more of the same disease.

At any rate, I did not regret that we moved to Ndere. I was just too happy to be closer to my cousin Zefina I liked so much and who also liked me a great deal. I was also pleased with the move because the village had a one-hall classroom of brick with corrugated iron roofing, which meant that I could attend school the year round on windy or stormy days or in the rainy season.

As soon as I began school at Ndere, the teacher acknowledged my ability to read and do simple arithmetic. An older boy assessed me and asked the teacher to move me to the next class, to Standard 2. Two years after I began classes at that school, I wrote the first government exam ever which the teacher marked. I passed after which I went to attend a bigger school at the village of Jardim about two hours walk away, which meant that I did four hours of walking every day from Monday to Friday; the walking boosted my immune system and never did I ever fall ill during the period I attended the school at Jardim.

It was at Jardim School that the indoctrination by our African teachers about us being Portuguese really started. I began to believe and take it seriously with much pride, and went about stating that I was a Portuguese by birth and that my body and the blood flowing in my veins and my soul were Portuguese, vowing to fight to the death in the defence of Portugal, if need be. Every text of Portuguese Language we used emphasized that propaganda. And Salazar himself had written some jingoistic texts we read, studied, and committed to memory. I was so mesmerized by the literary style of the dictator that I committed many of his passages to memory and would declaim them to other boys to show that I could retain what I read.

From the school at Jardim, I moved to the mission's main school at Traquino. The mission had been moved here from the region of Chief Cassano following the 1958 flooding when the mission there was completely submerged. It was moved to Traquino because this village, halfway between the Zambezi and the Chire, the river known in Malawi as the Shire, was regarded as the highest point of the Inhangoma Island that the flood had spared or that had remained dry in 1958. I became a boarder here because the place was about half a day's walk away from my village and I could not walk for classes back and forth every day.

Nothing much took place while I was there, except one nightmarish incident when I came close to doom and stared death in the eye in the most hair-raising encounter I had with a green mamba snake. It happened when government exams which I had to pass in order to attend Zobue Seminary in the land of the Zimba tribe were around the corner. I was cramming like every other student was doing. As the classrooms were noisy and the boarding house was also not a quiet place, I decided to go and study in one of the corners of the chapel so as to be able to concentrate.

I was studying when I heard a rustling sound close to me. I stood up and peered over the corner and saw a huge and long green snake the like of which I had never before seen in my life. When it sensed my presence, it turned around and decided to go back the way it had come. Instead of leaving it alone to disappear as quickly as possible, I picked up a stone and threw it at it. The brute turned around so fast that it came to me with lightning speed. When it was near me about two metres or so, it stood on its tail with its entire body in the air ready to strike. I stood stock still and faced it boldly.

If I had run, it would have lunged at me and dealt me a mortal bite because snakes are directed by vibrations and not so much by their eyesight which is said to be poor. By standing still, it was possible that I might have resembled a small stick to it or just a shade of something it could not make out. After a few seconds, it came down and turned the way it had come. I wished I had a long and strong stick to belabour the devil to death as I had done against many individuals of its evil race before. Since I had only a book in my hand and not a stick, I did the sign of the cross and turned to walk the opposite way to the evil thing after seeing it go along the wall of the chapel, enter a shrub by the wall of the chapel, and disappear out of my sight. I walked away while shivering and reciting Christian prayers without quite believing that I was still alive.

The green mamba is an arboreal snake but the black mamba, its deadlier and even more aggressive cousin, is a land snake which can also climb trees. Despite its name of black mamba, it is not at all black but grey or brown; it is the inside of its mouth that is black which accounts for its name of black mamba. The mamba is the most feared snake in Africa and with reason, for it is nervous, agile, fast, and aggressive like the devil I came face to face with on that near fatal day. The mamba is the most aggressive of all land snakes in the world. It has a neurotoxic poison and can kill very fast, usually within half hour or faster than that. In one case I read about, a mamba killed a full grown man in a minute.

As I retreated from the site of my near doom, I ran into two big boys, one of them was Gordinho who Father Jean Ribeau had slapped for laughing at his Portuguese accent. I told them what had happened to me. They quickly got hold of big long sticks and went to look for it in the direction I told them it had gone after our confrontation; I didn't dare to accompany them. They did not find it. It had gone faster than I had imagined after perhaps sensing that there was danger in the air for it, if it lingered around the chapel much longer. It was in danger of being killed as it had ventured out into the open and invaded our space.

I wish I knew how to magically immobilize a snake as I was to witness in 1983 in Mombasa, Kenya, where I saw a woman holding her left wrist with the palm of her right hand and I was told that what she was doing was rooting the snake where it was and where we could see it. The snake had dared come into the precincts of the Mutopanga Bar, which was surrounded by grass and trees including coconut trees in the eastern suburb of Bamburi of Mombasa. By immobilizing it through that simple magic, the woman enabled a man to find a stick with which to kill it. The snake remained rooted to the spot where it was with the woman holding her wrist with the palm of her hand while sweating profusely as people milled around her and talked loudly, until a man came with a long stick and beat the reptile to death. They said that the woman would continue to sweat as long as she held her wrist and that if she stopped holding her wrist, the snake would move away and disappear fast.

But I dared not ask how could holding her wrist with the palm of her other hand paralyze the reptile and root it in one spot? It makes no sense and defies the principles of logic. But African beliefs, or the popular beliefs of peoples all over the world, do not always follow scientific logic. People just believe in what they believe and things just happen the way they believe or want them to happen. The Swahili-speaking people of the coast of Kenya believed it and it worked for them.

My African mind did not have any problem accepting the belief of the Swahili-speaking people of Mombasa, although we in Senaland did not have a similar belief. I in fact believed that I had learned a new and useful trick I would use to immobilize snakes that should be killed, like the green bandit that had come out of the bush into our space so that other people could come to kill them with sticks or, I would ask someone to hold his or her wrist with the palm of his or her hand while I looked for sticks to kill them.

A few minutes after meeting the boys who had gone to look for and kill the mamba, I ran into the gardener who tended the mission's garden in which he grew vegetables and fruit for the priests. I told him about the snake which he had also seen before it ran into me. He said, "You're very lucky it did not bite you, boy. By now you would be dead and gloom would have descended on us and we would be praying for your soul to be welcomed and received in Heaven."

I had indeed been very lucky. I later prayed to God, Jesus, and the Virgin Mary to whom I recited the rosary twice that evening for having saved my life. I said no prayers to my ancestors who were probably the ones who protected me that day and not the foreign gods I prayed to. Praying to the alien gods was not a bad thing, but I should also have prayed to my ancestral spirits.

When I told uncle Lino about the incident with the mamba when I went to the village to see my family and other relatives after writing and passing the state exam that qualified me to go to the seminary, he convulsed with total shock and disbelief that I was still alive in front of him, before saying that the spirit of my late grandfather Moises he had known as a psychic man, had protected me and that other spirits of our ancestors had been very much around me on that day. "They held that evil thing still and paralyzed it when its body was still in the air and forced it to back down instead of it lunging at you, biting and killing you. They saved you from the deadly encounter."

My cousin Zefina was irreconcilable with grief, although the evil thing had not attacked and killed me. She cried and was overwhelmed with sadness and tears fell copiously from her eyes. She said that she would not know how to live on earth without me, if the evil thing had bitten and killed me. It was the sign of her undying and eternal love for me; she loved more than she did any other person. I appreciated it and vowed to love her more than I would love anyone else.

My healer aunt Albertina cleansed me that evening, although much against my will because of the strong Christian faith that I was paying attention to at that time and which made me think that ceremonies by witchdoctors were heathenish and soul-dooming and damning. I did not tell her that I did not want a heathenish ceremony because I loved her and the cultural side of my mind was still strong and telling me to accept the cleansing and protection ceremony because I was living in a very dangerous world with many ill-intentioned people, some of whom had amazing ill powers to project evil energy that doomed other people. I had no choice but to welcome the ceremony because I was a child of two worlds—of the world of Christianity with its aggressive approach against our beliefs and traditions, and of the world of my tribal beliefs which no amount of brainwashing by Christianity and the policy of Portugalization could ever erase, because it was the scene of the first impressions that entered my brain and the first ideas and beliefs it received were African and not Christian or Portuguese.

Whatever nasty things I may say about that evil snake I encountered on that near doomsday, I learned a few useful lessons about the life of all beings. I came to the conclusion that the mamba was probably sending a message to me to respect it so that it could respect me. It was asking me to respect its right to exist and telling me that there is a purpose for everything that lives on earth. I indeed know that snakes are needed to reduce rodents that destroy much of the grain in the fields. I also concluded that it is better to leave snakes alone. When I saw snakes thereafter, I left them alone and they did not bother me and they went their own way. But that particular brute deserved to be killed because it had its domain in the bush and invaded human space. At any rate, that particular devil is now dead. I read somewhere that mamba snakes did not live more than twelve years and my encounter with it took place in 1964 and fifty years have gone by since then.

Chapter 10

I found that the two weeks I spent with relatives after the exams were most refreshing. Apart from the encounter with the reptile I had decided to forget about as from the near doomsday, everything had gone well with me at the mission school before and after that near cataclysmic day. I was happy to be back in the village, where I spent most of my time not with my family, but with uncle Lino's family which rather monopolized me.

Zefina wanted me to be with her all the time. Although very feminine in appearance and beautiful beyond measure, she was a bit of a tomboy in her demeanour. She talked tough and ordered other people around. She wanted people to listen to her and not interrupt her with questions or arguments. Her job as assistant catechist in our village had made her assume a domineering attitude when she taught the basic teachings of the Catholic Church and this did not allow converts to doubt or question its beliefs.

While in the village, I had plenty of time to do what I wanted to do. I went to swim in the majestic Zambezi, which I had missed doing a great deal while away at Traquino mission school where I had to fill up a bucket with water from a tap and take it to a bathroom and use a can to scoop water and pour it over myself. Being a person from a place by a river where I went to wash and bathe every day, I never enjoyed washing from a pail. I never got used to it, would perhaps never get used to it, even if I had to do so all my life.

Despite visiting relatives at their homes or going for supper when they invited me, I also went to angle at the river with Zefina who enjoyed catching fish using a hook, bob, line and a rod, the way I had always done before to catch fish to help feed my family. Sometimes Zefina had a hard time hauling a big fish out of the water because our home-made fishing tools were not good or strong enough to do it after they had caught big fish. We learned not to try to force the fish out of the water with one pull but to tire it by going with its motion when it tried to move away, and jerk it or pull it to us when it was still or motionless until it lost its strength. We would then haul it out.

We sometimes paid some boys to take us in dug-out canoes out onto the broad river just for fun and to enjoy the breeze in the open space with no trees or tall grass to hinder its free movement. On some occasions we saw hippos some distance away. Only once did we come face to face with a pair which emerged with their jaws locked and grunting in a playful mood or in a fight at a distance of about ten meters from the canoe we were in. I had a cold shiver but it was nothing like the near death encounter I had with the green mamba at the mission. The boys and Zefina had had such encounters before and were not worried. The boys continued to chatter, roar, and steer the boat away from the monsters. The hippos disengaged their jaws and one of them sprayed us with water from its mouth before the two of them plunged into the water and we never saw them again, leaving us humiliated and nursing our impotent anger.

"A rule of thumb, Chico," said Zefina after the behemoths had left and the boys paddled the boat to land, "is never panic when you encounter hippos while you are in a canoe. If you panic and scream or wave to them, you incite them to aggression and they will ram your boat and overturn it. If you ignore them, they leave you alone and go away."

"I learned that lesson the hard way with the green mamba at the mission," I said to her.

We sometimes asked the boys to take us to an island in the river which disappeared when the river flooded. We would stay there, walking around the island, talking with people who lived there or with people from our village that went there to farm and returned home before the end of the day. We had our picnic there before going back to the village in the afternoon prior to the evenings setting in, to avoid encountering hippos which roamed in the river and sallied out to feed on land in areas away from the villages. The two of us had thus a lot of fun in order to make up for all the time we had missed being together while I was away at the mission school.

As far as I can remember, Zefina and I had never quarrelled; perhaps because we liked each other so much that we regarded ourselves as perfect and we paid no attention when we wronged each other, which I do not think we ever did. But we had a confrontation when I was with her and her family that time when I decided to go to Sofala on the other side of the river so that I could visit some relatives of ours who had been forced out of our flood-prone region during the floods of 1958. I was missing them and wanted to see them after a long time without being with them. I told her that I was going to Sofala to see our relatives.

"I'm coming with you," she said, instead of asking me whether I could take her with me.

"I don't think you can come with me," I said.

"Why not, my dear?" she asked.

"I don't think that uncle and auntie will like the idea of you travelling with me as if we were a couple and also it's a whole day's walk from the Zambezi with lions, leopards, and buffalos on the way and probably bad people."

"My parents will like the idea. I can walk and animals are rarely seen nowadays because people have been killing them with guns and bows and arrows."

My reason for not wanting her to go with me was not that she could not walk or because of wild animals. I just thought that her presence would overwhelm us with lack of privacy on the way like if she or I wanted to answer calls of nature. I could not leave her standing alone on the road while I went into the bush or let her go into the bush while I stayed on the road waiting for her, for fear of something happening to her like being scared if she saw a snake or being gored by an animal or even being kidnapped by the mapanga.

I did not wanted to see her naked nor did I want her to see me without clothes. I was then an adolescent flourishing with much sexual energy. I feared that we could fall under temptation with our libidinous urges despite the fact that we had pledged not to fall prey to temptations, which was easier said than done. Although I had vowed to treat her as my sister and she had pledged to regard me as her brother, temptation could overwhelm us. While with her, I had to control my erections; she sometimes noticed and it made her laugh at me, as if I were joking. At times, she got sexually aroused because of me. Would we always be able to control ourselves? That was why I thought that avoidance would be better than trying to control ourselves.

The sexual pressures I had to control were aroused by the fact that when we were just the two of us with no one else around, my shapely and fully grown cousin with her fully blown breasts protruding in front of her chest and shaking when she walked and laughed with sensuous smiles playing on her lips, would behave as if we were lovers, which we in fact were, without perhaps intending to do anything that was inappropriate. She did not feel

106

inhibited from holding or hugging and kissing me because it was a sport she liked to play with me. I usually shied away and did not respond to her gestures. I feared that her behaviour could excite me to a point of no return and would not mind treading on the forbidden path of sexual activity for us. I was of the age then with the strength to deflower or impregnate her. I did not tell her to stop bodily closeness with me for fear of offending her; in a way I myself liked it.

As I did not budge in the battle of wills with her and held firm in my decision not to let her travel with me, she went to complain to her parents that I was being mean and I did not want to go with her because I did not want her to see our relatives. Her parents swallowed the bait without suspecting that she was trying to use them to put pressure on me to take her with me.

"Why won't you take your sister with you?" Uncle Lino asked me.

"It's not that I don't want her to come. I don't think she can walk hard enough for us to make the journey in a single day," I said. I did not disclose to him my reasons for not wanting her to go with me. I did not want him and my aunt to wake up from their naivety of thinking that we could not be affectionate and involve ourselves in amorous adventures because we were related.

"She has already done the journey on a single day each time," he said. "Are you going to deny your sister the opportunity of seeing our relatives? If you can't cover the distance in one day, you can spend the night somewhere in a village or in a bush provided you make fires around you to prevent wild animals from approaching you."

"Okay, I'll go with her," I said. I did not want to disappoint him and my aunt and exasperate Zefina. I knew that she would like nothing better than engaging in adventures with me.

I had also wanted to go alone because I wanted to go armed with my bow and arrows. I had not yet lost the ability to use them while I was away at the mission school. Zefina had her own bow and arrow and catapults. She was the only girl in the village who used weapons that only the boys used. Some people in the village thought that her behaviour was strange, but they were not surprised. They had known her as the only girl in the village who used to fight boys with her fists and had defeated a good number of them. She had never lost any fights with boys. Lazy tongues attributed her strength or even her appearance as a very attractive girl, to her mother's magic which they said made her strong and paralyzed the boys she fought and rendered her irresistibly attractive.

When the dust had settled and I was reconciled to going with her without being annoyed with her for having misrepresented my reasons for initially refusing to go with her, I decided to be honest with her and told her why I was at first reluctant to let her go with me. I laid down rules that we would follow during our journey and subsequent stay with relatives so that she did not think that we would do as we pleased and behave like lovers, if that was what she thought we would or should do.

"We will be together when either of us have to answer calls of nature," I said. "We must never lose sight of each other. We'll survive or perish together."

"I care less if you see me naked and I see you naked, if it's for our safety," she said. "I'm not coming with you for sex."

I laughed, before complimenting her for a well expressed remark which I did not regard as entirely honest on her part. Perhaps she did not want sex, but she wanted to be her romantic self towards me which could make us lose our self control and lead us to sexual intercourse.

"Fina," I said. I used the short form of her name only I used while talking with her, "I do feel sexual impulses toward you and have a hard time to suppress them."

"Me too for you," she said. I liked to hear her admit it instead of denying the reality that was so obvious to me.

"I want us to take two days before reaching the village of our relatives. On the way we'll sleep in the same mattress but cover ourselves with different blankets."

She at first remonstrated against the idea of us using different blankets to cover ourselves at night, but she ended up accepting it for fear that I could reverse my decision to let her go with me or decide not to go altogether. I was relieved. Sleeping while covered with different blankets whilst sleeping on the same mattress was bad enough. And what of covering with the same blanket when our two bodies with bursting erotic energies would come into contact and rub, and our youthful breaths would excite arousal in us?

I had planned to camp by two shallow streams where there were sturdy huts with poles and thatched roofs which some travellers and hunters had built to spend nights in for protection against lions, leopards and hyenas at night when the critters were more abundant. I dropped my last condition which was that one of us would stand guard as the other washed in the streams to avoid both of us being in water and being taken by surprise by wild animals or robbers or mapanga, although at that time, there was no scare about the presence in our regions of the terrorists from Nyasaland because we were in the dry season. The area we would be walking through was evergreen with few habitations and was fascinatingly beautiful.

Why did I want to spend two days on the road instead of just slogging it out on a single day as I had before when I was even much younger? Zefina agreed with my idea; we wanted to sightsee the beautiful landscape we were going to travel through. Sightseeing and smelling nature and seeing animals we dreaded, was not an aspect of the Sena culture in particular or of the African cultures in general. Aesthetic appreciation of nature was not our thing; it was an aspect of western peoples or white people. Africans in general do not see beauty in things like westerners do. The elephants, lions, leopards, buffaloes and snakes are terrors to Africans. In my language, it is impossible to regard and describe those critters as beautiful as it is possible to do in Portuguese, French, English and many other European languages.

Twenty-three years later in 1987, I was in Mombasa, Kenya, going up north to Malindi and the Island of Lamu with another Mozambican exile. At Mutopanga Bar and Lodge where I had earlier seen a woman holding her left wrist with her right palm in order to immobilize a snake so that it should not escape, we found ourselves chatting with a sex worker who wanted to know who we were and what we were doing there. I told her that we were tourists. She laughed a good laugh before calling another fellow sex worker over to her.

"Hear what these guys are saying?" she asked her colleague.

"What are they saying?" her colleague asked.

"That they're *watali*," she said. Watali is the Swahili word for tourists.

"*Wajinga*," her colleague said, meaning that we were stupid. "Let's leave them alone. They're vagrants. They don't even seem to have money to pay us. They'll want to sleep with us for free."

At any rate, my colleague engaged the girl who had talked with us first and went to sleep with her despite me warning him that he ran the risk of contracting HIV and AIDS. By 1987, AIDS was killing people in Kenya. In Nairobi, AIDS had already claimed the life of one

Mozambican exile, a sex maniac in high gear who found it difficult to go a single day without sex. He was one of the very first people to die of AIDS in Nairobi. The disease was still shrouded in mystery, so much so that Kenyatta Hospital where he died, would not allow us his fellow Mozambicans to bury him as we usually did when one of us passed away.

Why was it strange for the prostitutes to hear that we Africans like them were tourists? The reason was that it was inconceivable in African minds, except in the minds of the few educated and westernized Africans, that Africans could be tourists. In East Africa, the word *watali* in Swahili, or tourists in English, only applies to westerners or white people. An African can never be a tourist. It sounds like a big joke and even madness in the ears of other Africans.

Just to illustrate the point, the authorities in Kenya have been trying to change the minds of the local people so as to encourage them to go around and see the beauty of the country and its wildlife, which is the richest in the world, by charging a third of what foreigners pay for internal flights or getting into game parks and enjoying tourist services, but the result has been dismally disappointing. Why is that so? The reason is simple. Sightseeing and tourism are not aspects of African cultures. Traditionally Africans only travel when they want to visit other people or when they are changing residence or they are going to hunt for jobs and never just for the sake of amusing themselves.

Through education, Zefina and I had become westernized and saw things differently from the locals. The two of us spoke in Portuguese, hardly in our language which we even despised, except when we found ourselves communicating with other people who could not speak Portuguese, which were most people. Because of the nature of Portuguese colonialism with its divide-and-rule policy of assimilation of those who could read and write, we did not regard ourselves as *pretos* or blacks, except when it fitted our interests, when we accepted the services of healers for fear of the unknown. The majority of the villagers who chafed under the classification of *indigenas* or natives did not consider us as blacks either. We were whites and that was why I could go around in the village with Zefina without anybody saying that we were behaving inappropriately because, for them, we were no longer Africans but whites. As long as we did not engage in sex, we were respected and admired for behaving like white people. Educated Africans regarded fellow villagers as savages.

Chapter 11

I told Zefina that I intended to travel to Tete about 300 kilometres upstream to witness the arrival of Américo Deus Rodrigues Tomas, the president of the Portuguese Republic who was coming to visit Mozambique in July of that year of 1964. Américo Tomas was a figurehead while the executive power lay in the hands of Antonio de Oliveira Salazar who was the Prime Minister. I stressed that I would like her to go with me, if the trip to Sofala turned out to be a great experience for her and me; meaning that if it would not cause us too much distress with her weakness to cope with the hardship and stress from the walk and if I was happy that she did not continue to behave in ways that suggested that she was still keen on behaving in an amorous manner towards me.

After overwhelming her with conditions and warnings, I felt I had overdone things with my gospel of moral rectitude as if she were a depraved girl of low morals, which she was not. She had maintained herself a virgin and turned down four proposals from boys who had wanted to marry her because she felt she was not yet ready to marry or, that the boys were crass or illiterates or savages. I realized that she was my cousin or older sister as per our traditions. She should in fact be advising and rebuking me for behaviours unbecoming and not me rebuking her with verbal assaults on good moral behaviour and being mean to her.

I needed her around me more than I would any other relative because we had so much in common. Also if I went alone and something terrible happened to me, there would be no eye witness to give an account of what might have happened. If I were with her, she could survive an ordeal and later tell people what happened. If something bad happened to her and I survived, I would be able to tell people what happened. And in times of challenges, we would fight together in any situation and our chances to overcome danger would be higher. And being with someone, even a woman, and an aggressive one like her, would always be better than being alone and having no one else to talk to. And I knew that loneliness could kill psychologically. Although it did not kill me during my night flight into Malawi years later, it was in fact a nightmare.

As far as I was concerned, she was a blessing in disguise for me, for, as I knew her, in difficult situations she would lay down her life to protect me and I could die fighting to save her.

When we left for Sofala, Zefina and I were prepared for the journey with our minds set and resolved to overcome any hardship, confront any dangers from wild animals or fight and defeat any bad characters we might encounter, although we did not anticipate running into fierce animals and bad people. After all, people always travelled armed along the way we were going to follow. They had killed dangerous animals whose numbers had been significantly reduced. In the past, people had captured or neutralized criminals along the path, which made would be ill intentioned adventurers think twice before undertaking perilous activities that harmed other people and which could lead them to their own doom.

For me the journey to Sofala was more of an adventure than any desire to see our relatives on the other side of the Zambezi, at a place a whole day's footslogging after crossing the river. I did not want us to footslog and make it on a single day. We were not in a hurry. I had decided that we were not going to walk as fast as to make it to our destination that same day because I had no intention of reaching the village of our relatives while completely tired and then take one or two days to recover from the hard walk. I did not want her to have sore feet on the way. I wouldn't have sore feet because I was more used to walking than her. I wanted us to reach our destination while in top form and shape and be able to smile and laugh instead of being gloomy with pain or soreness.

We left early in the morning and boarded the first canoe that took us to the other side of the river. The river is anything between five to eight kilometres wide from our village to the other side and the Zambezi broadens as it races to the Indian Ocean. The canoe we boarded was used to ferry people back and forth across the river. We paid the man more money than the usual fare most people paid and the boatman was very happy with us. He promised that if we found him on the Sofala side of the river on our return home, he would carry us back to our side for free.

Unlike most travellers who did not have much money, Zefina had a lot of money she got as pay from the missionaries who had engaged her to teach catechism and also, her healer mother made money from clients who flocked to their home every day of the week. Some of her mother's clients were well-to-do. They paid her good money. Some of them were Indians who were as superstitious as we were and they were mainly storekeepers. Sometimes, some of the rich people gave her money even after their treatment because they were very pleased with the services she had rendered to them. Although her mother did not charge the clients who flocked to her, people paid what they could afford and the flow of cash was steady and assured. Her family hardly used it. She kept it as the family's accountant, as there was no bank in our village. She ended up sitting on that money because they hardly used it on anything, apart from buying clothes. Their food came from their fields and they had farm labourers who worked to produce food for them.

I also had some money of my own which my father had given me after returning from the mission school. My father was also one of those who used his big canoe which he and uncle Lino had used to rescue people during the 1958 flooding, to ferry people across the river. Although old, our canoe was still very strong and ferried people across the river. My father employed two men as his boatmen instead of doing it himself because he liked to work in the field with my mother and produce food for the family.

The weather on the morning we crossed the river was beautiful. It was a sunny day with a cloudless sky. Zefina was her macho self, dressed with a grey khaki hat, grey trousers, and shirt and rubber shoes with a haversack with her clothes in it and about four arrows and a sharp machete attached to the haversack with her bow in her hand. Her bow was smaller than mine, but was, all the same, strong and powerful and she knew how to handle it like a man, or even better than most men. Dressed up and armed as she was, she was quite a remarkable sight.

Zefina wanted to do what men did and no one dared tell her that she was a girl who should not behave like men or do what men did. She cherished being independent and told other girls, particularly those who had received some education like herself, not to go into early marriages and to stop being slaves to men.

I had no hat on my head but was also dressed up in khaki clothes with rubber shoes too and carried a haversack with a fluffy mattress, two blankets and a few clothes and bath towels for the two of us, a sharp knife, a machete, my quiver with five metal-headed arrows and five wooden-headed arrows to kill birds we would encounter on the way for us to eat. I had a pot in my sack and two plates and two cans for us to drink water from and two bottles to keep water for us to drink during the march in the searing heat. As I could not wear two catapults around my neck as boys usually did, I gave Zefina one to wear around her neck while I wore the other one. I also gave her some stones I had prepared for the catapults so that we could shoot even small birds with them for us to eat on the way.

As we crossed the river, we saw a few hippos floating downstream. We were amused seeing them and laughed as we watched them drift downstream, floating effortlessly despite their immense weights and sizes. Whether they saw us or not, we did not know. Perhaps they did, but they did not bother us or they did not feel provoked by our presence in the river because we were not close to them.

After crossing the river, we walked for about half an hour or so before reaching the shopping centre at Magagade which was near the Trans-Zambezi Railways linking the Indian Ocean port city of Beira and Nyasaland which had just become independent from Britain with the name of Malawi. It became independent on 6th July of 1964 under the leadership of Kamuzu Banda, a highly educated and diminutive man with seven university degrees to his name obtained in South Africa, the United States, and Britain. He always wore a homburg hat, dark glasses above his extensive flat nose and was attired in English suits and carried a flywhisk like a witchdoctor. He had forced the British out of his country without resorting to violence and only after the British had imprisoned him before releasing him to lead his people to independence.

We rested at the shopping centre for a while. We had our breakfast on black tea and freshly baked bread we had bought from one of the stores before walking about the market place where we bought bananas and sugar cane for us to chew on during our march. There was fresh fish that fishermen had just brought in from the river and dried fish villagers had brought there for sale but we did not buy it because we wanted to eat wild birds we would kill on the way, as if someone had guaranteed us that we would kill any. From one Indian store, we bought a packet of tea, one kilo of sugar and bath and laundry soap.

After reaching and crossing the railway, we marched for one hour or so along a grassland area before entering woodland. After entering the wooded area, we chopped the long stems of two spindly hardwood trees and fashioned them into walking sticks for use against snakes or any baboons loitering along the path that could force us to stop and wait for them to move away at their own leisure or assumed aggressive attitudes, as the apes usually did. We were not going to stand for that and treat them like holy monkeys as they do in India where monkeys are sacred animals because *The Ramayana*, a Holy Scripture of the Hindus, had sanctified them for their services in a war between the exiled prince Rama who was the reincarnation of God Vishnu and Ravana, the demon-king of Lanka, who had abducted his wife Sita. We were going to force them out of the path with our sticks instead of using precious arrows we could lose, especially if we used them against baboons and they stuck in their bodies and then disappeared with them to die later in the bush into which we could not follow them to retrieve our arrows from their bodies.

We walked leisurely for a fairly good time without seeing wild animals at all but we could hear them in the thickets close to the way. We repeatedly stopped to try to gawk at the fascinating scenery of trees and hills unfolding before our eyes which withheld their secrets and mysteries from us as we could not peer deeper into the tall grass and the woods to see what was going on in them. We sometimes heard the distant roars of lions, which sent baboons scattering and screeching as they quickly jumped from tree to tree for safety. We laughed at the antics of nature and continued to walk as if nothing was the matter. We were unperturbed by the presence of the big cats. We knew they would not dare approach us during daytime. We were armed and would deal with them in the way in which countless of their numbers had died at the hands of men who had reduced their number with home-made guns or with powerful bows and arrows.

After walking for close to three hours, we encountered the first critter crossing the path ahead of us. We stopped and froze stock still, awed by the huge size of the python a few meters ahead of us. We were unafraid. We stood still to let it pass as its body wriggled in the grass and shook it violently on the right side of the path. When its head was in the middle of the way and it saw us or sensed our presence, it turned its head to look in our direction and it stopped. It began to open its enormous mouth and thrust its tongue towards us, as if to say that it wanted one of us for lunch. Perhaps the brute was hungry after passing many days without a meal, which they usually do after they have swallowed up a gazelle or an antelope.

I decided not to give it the pleasure of stopping us and turning against us. I asked Zefina who already had a wooden-headed arrow on her bowstring not to do anything, but stand still and watch what I was going to do to it. She obeyed. I quickly removed my catapult from my neck and placed a jagged stone in it, aimed it at its open mouth and sent the stone rattling into it. The stone went right into its mouth and struck it with tremendous force. The serpent hissed very loudly which was its own way of crying before wriggling so vigorously that the grass at the side of the path where its body was shook wildly, as if it had been shaken by a tornado.

Distressed with pain as it was, it turned its head away from us and moved it in the direction it was headed so as to escape from further punishment from me. I did not know whether I had smashed its tongue or whether it had spat out or swallowed the stone after it got into its mouth. To accelerate its flight and to prevent it from turning and waging a battle against us, I placed a wooden-headed arrow on my bow and told Zefina to do the same so that we could strike it at the same time. The arrows shoot from a few meters from the critter struck the brute at the same time and bounced back after punishing the reptile. It wriggled in pain again after which it started moving to escape into the grass to the left side of the path. We watched it speed away while shaking the grass. We remained put where we stood before challenging it. We let a few minutes pass so as to make sure that the critter had gone away and would not turn around to attack us in order to avenge its humiliation. When we were sure that the serpent had disappeared, we recovered our arrows, thanked them for a job well done before we resumed our march.

The critter was lucky, I must say, that I did not use one of my metal-headed arrows against its head, which would have doomed it to death right where we confronted it. I did not want it to die there because, if it did, it would have rotted there without anyone being able to remove it. It would produce a nauseating smell for travellers, if scavengers and vultures did not spot it and eat it up to satisfy their hunger and clean up the mess for us. I had just wanted to teach it a hard lesson by inflicting excruciating pain on it. Perhaps the inside of its mouth swelled and it lived with the pain for many days before recovering or eating, even if it found something to eat.

Zefina congratulated me on my amazing marksmanship for hitting it in the mouth. We were so excited that we hugged and kissed with our tongues, forgetting in the heat of excitement that we had decided to minimize that kind of behaviour. But our victory over the bad guy who might have been hungry and might have rushed to seize one of us for its meal, was cause for celebration and a French kiss or anything short of sex at that time was not a sin or incest.

After our victory over the serpent, we continued to walk and encountered herds of baboons, which were about the only animals that in day time did not always keep to the woods to which they retired to sleep, perched on tall trees for safety from lions but not from leopards, which were good climbers. They strayed into the path because men did not kill them as much as they did other animals as they were of no use as meat and were not as dangerous as lions or leopards or buffaloes. They were not worth wasting bullets or arrows on. The herds we encountered were usually crossing the path. They scattered, howling with fear as they saw us place arrows on our bowstrings, not intending to dispatch them against them but just to warn them against becoming arrogant and to let them know that they would be courting disaster, if they decided to make trouble for us.

With the last herd of baboons we encountered, a juvenile, perhaps not realizing that we were not baboons like it, stood arrogantly on the path in front of us, as its relatives and friends fled in panic, howling and screeching as they ran with their bare bums turned to us and disappeared into the grass and headed for the nearby woods. When I waved to it to go away, it became aggressive, grunted threats and began to bare its fearsome teeth to us. It had singled out Zefina in its aggressive behaviour, perhaps after discovering that despite her manly clothes and appearance, she had breasts and was after all a woman.

Baboons are known to fear and run away from men perhaps because it has always been men who have harmed and killed them. They do not fear women at all and will not run away from women. Zefina wanted to show it that it was mistaken if it concluded that she could not be serious against it because she was a woman. She had an arrow primed on her bow and aimed to shoot it and cause the ape an agonizing slow death. I told her not to bother about shooting it with her arrow, as it would disappear with it stuck in its body to die in the woods and we would not be able to go after it to recover her arrow. She held back and sighed with disappointment, but did not lose her temper. She had really wanted to punish the little ape rogue.

"I've to stop it doing what it has done to us, otherwise it will do the same thing to other people," I said.

I put my haversack and quiver with my arrows down and advanced to it with my long stick in one hand and a banana in the other, as if wanting to give it the precious fruit, but it was to fool it. As it extended both its arms like a human to receive the banana with much respect, I dropped the banana down and set my stick on it so fast and so hard that the blows overwhelmed it and sent it rolling on the ground howling with pain before bolting for its life. I felt sorry for it, but not guilty for what I had done to the ape, but I felt justified for the justice I had meted out to it for its arrogance and for attempting to threaten Zefina when all we had wanted it to do was to leave the path and go away and let us continue with our march.

After I had viciously punished the ape and picking up my haversack and slinging the quiver with arrows on to my shoulder to resume the march, I began to feel disappointed because we had not seen birds we could have killed for our dinner and we were approaching the first of the two streams where we had intended to spend the night. I did not want us to have bread with tea again as we had for our breakfast at the shopping centre in the morning. And that would not be much fun and my stomach was rumbling with hunger. I could not stand the idea of eating the same food as at breakfast. I thought that if we were not blessed to see and kill any francolins or guinea fowl, I was not going to eat that evening, which would not do me much good, but Zefina could eat stale bread with tea again, if she wanted. And knowing her as I did, she would also not eat, if I did not eat, as she would want to inflict on herself the same pain I would be inflicting on myself.

Luck was to smile on us after I had given up hope of seeing and killing even a turtle dove for our dinner. As we descended into the valley to the stream, a flock of guinea fowl were scurrying ahead of us. I saw them first and alerted Zefina. We drew our wooden-headed arrows to our bows and aimed at the birds without aiming at any one in particular as there were so many running together along the path ahead of us. Our arrows hit two of the birds with so much violence that they stumbled around before dying; the other birds stopped and noisily turned to check in alarm to find out what had happened, as guinea fowl usually do, thereby exposing themselves to danger. When they saw us, some of them began to run fast ahead of us before entering the grass and disappearing in it and others took to the air to be away from the place as fast as they could.

The two birds we had knocked out were more than what we needed. We could never eat and finish both of them, nor could we even finish one before its flesh went bad. So we did not regret not having killed more of them, as we did not want to kill them just for the sake of killing them.

As the sun began to descend on the horizon, we walked faster as we neared the stream where we were going to spend the night because we did not want to reach it when it would be dark and when lions and other night rogues would be on the prowl. We were tired and sweating and badly needed to bathe before preparing our dinner. After we reached the stream, Zefina did not even wait to look around to see if there were people or animals watching us and assess their intentions. As soon as she dropped her haversack, she undressed herself without even telling me to look away from her before removing a towel and taking soap from my haversack and entering the knee deep water and splashing her body into it. She had lost all sense of shame towards me. She no longer thought of the inappropriateness of me seeing her utterly naked, as if she were my girlfriend or wife.

I saw her sensuous body and her full and erect breasts that would drive any man crazy for wanting sex with her, except me to whom her body was forbidden territory under the pain of a curse that could probably lead her and me to our premature death if we engaged in sex, as my late grandfather Moises had warned me against having carnal knowledge of her. I did not think of accessing her body nor did I look at her naked with the intention of sexual intercourse with her nor did she do what she did to impel us to sin against God or transgress our sacrosanct tribal edicts and offend our ancestral spirits. We were becoming insensitive towards each other like automatons. I kept watch with an arrow on my bow, ready to let fly against any danger as she washed in the stream. After washing herself, she came out, dried herself up with her towel before putting on another set of clothes for the night and the following day.

As soon as she was ready to watch over me with her bow and arrow ready to strike terror to the heart of any human or ward off any wild animal, I also took off my clothes without asking her to look away from me. I was also not ashamed to let her see me completely naked. I did not try to conceal any part of me from her. I entered the water and washed fast before coming out to dry myself up and put on clothes for the night and the next day. We were going to sleep in the clothes we had changed into, as we had to be ready for an emergency at any time of the night as that place that was far removed from villages. We did not forget that we were undertaking a dangerous adventure that could cost us our lives.

After changing my clothes, Zefina and I arranged big logs that were already there to make two big fires for the night to keep wild animals away, although we were going to sleep in one of the huts well bolted from the inside which no animals could shake and destroy as they were of poles with no mud walls. Wild animals could see people in them but would not be able to reach them and any people were completely safe and were safer if they were armed as we were. We wanted animals completely away because we wanted to sleep without interruption and the nuisance of their sounds or noises.

When the fires became intense, we boiled water to pour on the two birds so that we could easily pluck out their feathers before cutting them open to remove their guts before washing them in the stream and roasting them on one of the fires. At the same time, we had water boiling in the only pot we had brought to make a hard boiled porridge with maize flour or *ntsima* to eat with one of the birds. I was in charge of roasting the two birds while Zefina cooked the porridge with our bows and arrows, machetes and clubs within reach for prompt action to neutralize any dangers.

Just before the sun went down on the horizon, we saw four people arriving on the opposite side of the stream. They were couples going in the opposite direction to us. After seeing us, they crossed the stream and came over to greet us and make friends with us. We were reassured that they were good people who had also reached the stream with the intention of spending the night there because continuing to walk at night would be dangerous for them. Everything seemed good, as their presence lifted some of the fear that was burdening our bodies and souls, despite our bravery and resolve to overcome our fear. No matter how brave people can be, they are sometimes bound to experience fear and panic.

One of the men, a tall and muscled fellow who looked like a warrior of yore had a spear in his hand like his male colleague while their women bore loads of whatever they were carrying on their heads, engaged us in conversation.

"I suppose you're travellers like us?" he asked us.

"Indeed, we are," I said to him.

"Who's this girl to you, a sister, or your wife?" he asked me.

"My wife," I said assertively. I wanted to protect Zefina from crude behaviour and brazen advances from the man who might have said that he would like to have her as another wife for himself, if I had said that she was my cousin or sister. The insolence, stupidity, and brazenness of men in a polygamous society like ours knew no bounds. Men tended to think that they owned women so as to behave in any manner their instincts deemed fit.

"But you are so alike that people who don't know you like us might think you are siblings," the man said. "Only that she looks older than you which is not surprising because nowadays boys go for girls who are older than them."

"She's my beloved wife. Our resemblance is just a coincidence," I said.

The man was bold and businesslike and was keen on having one of the birds I was roasting.

"You've two birds for just the two of you?" he asked. "Even one is more than you can eat unless you want to stay awake the whole night eating. If you can sell me one, how much do you want me to pay you?"

Zefina and I looked at each other before she smiled to me with an affectionate smile as if to reinforce that she was my wife. She told me that we could just give them one of the birds for free because we had enough money of our own.

"My wife says you can have one. No need to pay us." I repeated what he had already heard Zefina say.

"Your wife is a good-hearted woman, boy. May you have many children and grandchildren and great grandchildren," the man said as if to bless us.

I wish you knew that this girl with me is a no go area for me, I thought to myself without saying it. Zefina and I laughed before we thanked him for his good wishes which would never become a reality, much as we might have liked and dreamed, unless we wanted genetically warped children who would not be welcomed in our families.

As soon as we had agreed to give them one of our birds, the man shouted to his colleagues to tell them that they had a roasted guinea fowl and to order their women to make a big porridge for the four of them, where Zefina had just finished making our porridge. One of the women arrived soon after with a pot with water which she placed over the fire on the triad of stones as soon as Zefina had put our porridge on a plate.

Zefina and I waited for their porridge to be ready so that we could eat at the same time as them so as to consolidate our acquaintanceship at that place in the middle of nowhere for our common safety and security. As we waited for their food to be ready, I sprinkled salt and powdered pepper on our roasted bird after cutting it into pieces so as to make it tastier and prevent what we would eat at breakfast the following morning from going bad.

Our newly found friends and us ate under the light of the roaring fires and we kept chatting well deep into the night. They told us about themselves and where they had come from and where they were going to. I also told them about ourselves and where we were going to. The four of them decided to sleep in the open. They felt assured because they had already slept in the open at that spot before. Zefina and I went to sleep on our mattress in one of the huts. We felt uncomfortable having to sleep in the open in the middle of nowhere as there could be man-eating lions or leopards which roaring fires could not deter and also because we had never slept in the open before. To give the four people the impression that we were a married couple because of the open fire that would enable them to see us through holes in the walls of the hut, Zefina and I covered ourselves with one blanket with the other one under us on top of the mattress.

We slept with our clothes on and without engaging in behaviour that could excite our sexuality, although avoiding our bodies from touching was next to impossible. From that night on, we were assured that we could sleep together covered in the same blanket without her trying to have me do what she had done when I was a small boy in her cottage or I doing anything that could coax our libido into action. That was the test I had wanted, to help me decide whether we could go together to Tete where we would be together every day for close to a week. I was not going to deny her the pleasure of being with me nor was she going to allow me to do so. So we had to manage and control our behaviour towards each other.

We slept soundly through the night, undisturbed by the sounds of the animals prowling in the dark and what sounded like distant roars of lions which broke the stillness of the night. The two couples slept without interruption despite the fact that they slept in the open without worrying about wild animals because the two big fires kept beasts away and also because there were no known man-eating lions or leopards in this area which they knew better than we did. It also appeared that they were used to sleeping in the open with fires burning in areas where dangerous wild animals like hyenas existed or in the middle of nowhere. They seemed to have done it already.

The couples left early the following morning before the sun appeared on the horizon after bidding us farewell and thanking us again for the roasted fowl we had given them. We remained in the hut well after the sun had begun to ascend the horizon when we got up and we both washed in the stream with our bows and arrows on the sand by the water so that we could reach for them and act decisively against any threat. But there were no threats because the wild animals had retreated into the dense bush by that time for fear of armed people who would be walking along the path in the day. It seemed that people and beasts had reached a tacit agreement. People moved freely in the day along the way undisturbed by the beasts which kept to the woods because they knew that men had been decimating them during day time. Animals prowled along the path which people surrendered to them at night because darkness was their friend and they could see at night when people could not.

After washing and putting on the same clothes we had slept in, we set down on one of the burning logs and ate the hard and stale bread from the previous day with what had remained from the guinea fowl which was still a lot. There was still about a half remaining. We decided to eat the remainder at the next stream where we were going to stop over and spend another night before reaching the village of our relatives which was not very far away from the second stream.

Chapter 12

No sooner did we have our haversacks slung on our shoulders and our weapons in our hands than we waded through the stream after which we put on our shoes in order to continue with our march. We were in high spirits after the adventures of the previous day, the peaceful night's rest and sleep, and our breakfast, after which we drank a lot of water from the stream and filled two bottles with water for drinking on the way. We were different from other people who drank no water or not much water while on long marches because at school, we had been drilled on the importance of drinking water and constantly replacing the water that our bodies lost in order to keep our bodies hydrated in the tropical heat.

After leaving the stream, we once again found ourselves walking along a mainly flat countryside like the one we had seen the previous day with much tall grass and woods, a perfect home for wild animals and for human waylayers, but footpads of the highways and byways had been discouraged from pestering travellers because people went fully armed usually with bows and arrows or spears and in the past, armed travellers had captured or killed many violent outlaws. Only the mapanga from Nyasaland dared to appear in the region when the vegetation was lush but a big number of them had been neutralized like had happened at the haunted Nakasero forest ahead of us. We did not expect to encounter or hear the sounds of animals as we had the previous day, but there was no saying that it would not happen again. We would not be surprised if more dramatic events unfolded before us and greeted us with as much surprise as on the previous day and would force us to act decisively in self-defence.

We had walked for about two hours when we began to hear a stampede and hoof beats from the right side of the path which grew louder as they came closer to us. Before long, we saw one of the most spectacular, if fearsome, events right before our eyes. We saw a herd of up to twenty or more buffalos, the most fearsome beasts of the African savannah, furiously running for their lives with three determined lions in hot pursuit crossing the path ahead of us. We stopped and froze still more in amazement than fear to watch the animals cross and disappear to the left side of the way after which we resumed our march, talking and laughing, as if nothing awe-inspiring had taken place, or as if the lions would not smell us out and stalk us. We did not even think of that. It was daytime and the beasts knew that humans were then the lords along the footpath.

I liked and admired Zefina for her courage and fearlessness. She did not cringe nor did she grab hold of me for protection as women in the company of men did when scared of fear-inspiring events. We were neither afraid of the buffalos nor of the lions, which did not seem to have seen or smelled us out in the heat of the buffaloes running for their lives, and the lions resolved to chase the formidable beasts that are known to kill lions when they stop fleeing and stand their ground and charge to gore the big cats and trample them to death with their hoofs. Before long, we heard roars and a buffalo grunting. Then we heard the bovine bellowing in distress as the lions pounced on it as its friends and relatives continued on their crazed flight. We could still hear them stampeding, perhaps unaware that one of them had been seized for a meal and was desperately fighting for its doomed life.

"The cats are mauling one of them buffalos," I said gleefully.

"The unfortunate beast," Zefina said matter-of-factly. "The cats worked hard for it. It's a deserved meal for them. Everything happens for a reason."

"Without the big cats, the number of buffalos would grow unchecked and the damage to vegetation, fields, and the danger to people would be incalculable," I said as if to support her. I regarded the lions as heroes which helped check the prolific growth of herbivores so that enough vegetation existed to help humans and allow nature to revive and survive. Indeed, as Zefina said, everything happened for a reason.

Two hours after the incident with the buffalos and lions which we had put behind us no sooner than we saw them and heard their sounds, we reached the second stream between the Zambezi and our destination. This stream was as wide and with clear water as the first one behind us. Unlike the first stream much of which we could not see because of curves or meanders upstream and downstream and dense tall grass along its banks, the second stream ran in a straight line along its length and breadth as far as we could see upstream and downstream. It had less grass along its banks and had broad sandy banks. There was a village close to it on the other side of it. The sight of people we saw upstream and downstream rendered that water course more friendly and hospitable than the first stream close to which there were no people and villages and which could be said to be in the middle of nowhere.

As the layout of the second stream and the landscape around it was fascinating, Zefina and I thought that we would not amuse ourselves if we just saw it from the crossing point and continued on our journey before going through the Nakasero Forest with dangers to which our primitive but deadly weapons would be of no use. Only our courage was what mattered. And why should we fear?

People walked through it daily and nothing happened to them apart from some inexplicable phenomenon they encountered and noises from unseen individuals they heard. We ourselves had walked through it in the past when we were young and nothing happened to us nor did we hear the strange noises some people said they had heard or the strange sights they claimed to have seen which we did not see. Only that the fear of the unknown scares humans and we were no exception despite our cocky juvenile courage.

We decided to stay put at the crossing point for the rest of that day and spend the night there before resuming our walk about noon the following day so that we could arrive at the home of our relatives at around 4 p.m. or later when the sun would be going down on the horizon. We had to avoid arriving at our relatives a few hours after leaving the second stream the following day because our relatives would not believe us if we told them that we had walked the distance from the Zambezi to their village in a shorter time than it usually took people in forced marches from sunrise to sunset.

We were not going to tell them that we took two days on the day, for fear that we would set their tongues wagging and force them to think about the inadmissibility of our behaviour since we were brother and sister who should strictly respect the privacy of our bodies. If we were husband and wife, that would be a different matter, and a fine and funny story to tell them because of the romance that would characterize and be attached to it.

Arriving late the following day would convince our relatives that we had made the journey on that day and prevent them from thinking that we were engaging in a weird manner and from yapping about it while we were not doing anything unusual with our bodies. And how would we convince them that we were not doing what they would think we were doing? With those very conservative people, mere words would never be enough. They would hiss with annoyance like angry snakes, curse us and make our stay undesirable and unbearable and force us to return home prematurely.

We knew how conservative our relatives were and how much trouble they could cause us. Neither Zefina nor I doubted how they would assertively claim that we were engaging in incest. I had in fact agreed with Zefina that after our arrival, she would be with the women all the time while I would be with the men for the five days or so we had planned to stay with them. She was not to try to be with me as we did in our village where people perceived us differently. She had no difficulty understanding my point and seeing the trouble our relatives would make for us, if she was to be with me all the time the way her parents let her do in our village since our childhood without it ever occurring to them that we could be tempted into promiscuous activities because to them, we were brother and sister. Other people out in Sofala would not be as naïve and tolerant as they were, and we did not want other people to alert her parents with their suspicions and make them look foolish for letting us be together in situations that compromised the privacy of our bodies. We wanted to let sleeping dogs lie and not wake them up.

Chapter 13

How beautiful that area of the countryside was with hills to the west in the distance, grass and reeds and scattered trees along the wide sandy banks of the stream. Although it was the dry season, the vegetation was surprisingly green and lush, as if rains had just visited the area. I loved the second stream with its clear and shallow water, although a bit slower and less turbulent than the first stream. I wished that we could move from our village to live in that paradisiacal environment, to bathe in and wash our clothes and dishes with its water, and not to have to worry about crocodiles or hippos which were absent from the stream.

From where we were, the stream was full of activity upstream and downstream with boys splashing water to one another and running in the water and birds of all kinds and descriptions coming and taking off after drinking water or unable to land after seeing people at spots where they had intended to land. I could see some birds dive in the water for small fish or just splash in the water for fun as little boys did.

After deciding not to push on to the village of our relatives that day, we instead stayed around, walking downstream before going upstream. We carried our belongings with us. We could not leave them in one of the two huts that anonymous people had built as night lodges for themselves and other travellers for fear that we would find them gone as thieves could steal them if they found them unguarded.

We went downstream on the sandy bank and sometimes walked in the knee-deep water for the pleasure of it. Birds, big or small, took off at our approach. Baboons and vervet monkeys scurried away, howling with fear, after seeing us with our bows and arrows. I told Zefina not to worry about the baboons and to avoid being tempted to shoot arrows at them, even if some baboon became cocky and made threatening moves against us. We did not want to lose our precious arrows as baboons could escape with them stuck in their bodies to die elsewhere and we would never recover them. We could only use them in situations that required our defence against bad people or dangerous animals trying to attack us.

As for baboons, I told her that we would use our long sticks to bash them, as I had done to the young baboon the previous day. But no baboon challenged us and we did not want to pick unnecessary quarrels with them by provoking them, throwing stones at them or shouting at them to scare them off. We ignored them and they fled away for safety and stopped to watch us when they were at a safe distance.

We were keen on using our wooden-headed arrows, not on any little birds but on big birds we could eat like turtle doves, grouse, and guinea fowl. As we still had part of the guinea fowl we had roasted the previous evening, we did not embark on a killing spree for the fun of it, killing birds we would not eat. So we walked down the stream and back to the crossing point without killing any birds.

After eating the roasted fowl with dry bread and drinking water, we rested for a while under the shade of a big tree by the hut that was on the side of the stream we had reached before walking upstream; boys and women who had come to fetch water gawked at us without either greeting or saying anything to us. I thought that we were an uncommon sight to them. They had never seen a girl dressed like a man and armed with a bow and arrow and a stick, walking side by side with a boy instead of the girl walking behind the boy as was tradition. Everything about us was outlandish to them. I guessed they thought we were from a place with much influence of white people.

They were however not scared of us either. The boys were also armed with bows and arrows like us because it was the tradition of the people of the Sena nation. Despite our appearance as different from what they were used to seeing, we were not on a war footing nor did we look hostile to them, and they were also not unfriendly to us. We sometimes greeted them but they just looked on at us without greeting us in return.

We went as far as we wanted to go and on our way back to the spot where we wanted to spend the night, we talked to four boys. One of them sold us a francolin he had trapped in the bush close to the stream. We paid him handsomely and he was very happy. The other three boys with him became jealous of him because he had money and were not quite happy with us as we had not given them money too. Obviously, we could not just give them money for nothing. Zefina thought we should do something to make them all happy and they were ready to do what we asked them to do for us.

"Come with us to the crossing point where the hut is," I said to them and pointed to the structure. "I want you to get firewood for us to burn outside the hut in which this girl here and I will be sleeping tonight, to keep lions and leopards or hyenas away. We want no disturbance from them while sleeping."

"There are no lions or leopards in the area, only hyenas," said the boy who had sold us the bird. He corrected himself after saying what he had stated. "There are spirit lions and a spirit leopard with its spirit cubs in this region which won't attack you because they are good lions and a good leopard that protect people from the real bad big cats. They're only seen when they want to be seen because in actual fact they're spirits or ghosts."

Zefina and I had no problem understanding what the boy was saying. The people in that region were the same tribe like us. We shared the same belief that some people with very powerful juju or charms during their lifetime, turned into spirit animals after their death. Even though we were not paranoid and fearful of wild animals, not even of lions, because we were going to sleep in a hut that was strong and heavily fortified with logs and poles and the door bolted inside, the thought of lions, ordinary or spirit lions, around us at night was not a comfortable idea. We wanted to sleep undisturbed with no lions roaring, leopards coughing or hyenas howling or laughing.

As soon as we reached the spot, the boys wasted no time. They walked to the nearby bush and in no time they were back with logs that would keep burning for a whole night and even more nights. I paid the four boys equally well before they went away smiling and pleased, leaving us also satisfied that we had paid them for what they did for us. With the money I gave them, each one of them could buy shorts and a shirt or they could help their families with it. Before sunset, we lighted three fires, two on the sides of the hut and one behind it after which Zefina boiled water to immerse the bird before removing its feathers so that I could roast it while she cooked the hard porridge for us to eat with it.

We ate our delicious meal early, soon after the bird was roasted as we wanted to retire to the hut where we had also lighted a small fire at one corner to burn during the night, although we also had our torches or flash lights to hand to switch on in case of emergencies. With the three big fires about the hut and one inside and our weapons at the ready, we felt completely safe although no travellers joined us in the evening like had happened the previous day at the first stream. It was the second night that we slept together and covered with the same blanket and we respected each other.

We once again had a good sleep in the middle of nowhere, although there was a village close by where we could have gone to request shelter for the night at some homestead; they would never have turned us away because hospitality was a great tradition of the Sena people. When the night came, the place was gloomy, if not scary, as we imagined that there were dangerous critters on the prowl and will-o-the-wisps in the air. Surviving nights at such places is like being reborn after going through death because fear could overwhelm and kill one, but being with another person provides a relief or lightens the burden of fear. We had to overcome our fear because we had imposed it on ourselves by wanting adventures.

I woke with the sense of having been reborn whereas Zefina woke up, fresh and unperturbed and always with a smile on her lips and full of love for me. She was not worried about anything as long as she was with me because she knew that I could be a determined fighter and that I was a courageous boy who had faced a deadly green mamba without blinking an eye, and forced the deadly poisonous thing back from attacking me and to back down and retreat as if defeated.

Although I did not tell Zefina when we got the two long sticks with which we were armed before starting our journey, my intention was for us to use them against snakes if we encountered any and they were in situations to harm us. We killed snakes with long sticks and not with bows and arrows. We sometimes used lances with long handles to spear them but this was not a very efficient way of dealing with snakes as it did not kill them immediately. Bashing them with sticks did the job quickly and efficiently, after which we chopped off their heads or incinerated their bodies or buried them because we believed that dead snakes could resuscitate to avenge the harm we had done to them.

There was no evidence that dead snakes could come back to life and take revenge against those who killed them. It seems to be a fact though, that mambas tend to team up in pairs of males and females. If one kills a mamba, one should be on the lookout for a possible reaction from its mate. When I heard this as a boy from villagers, I did not take it seriously until I read an amazing story by a *bwana* white hunter in the adventure stories of white hunters in Africa while studying at Eastleigh Secondary School in Nairobi, Kenya, in the early 1970s. I do not remember the title of the book or the author of the story, but it was quite a scary story.

The hunter had shot a mamba in the Cape Province before travelling north to Natal in South Africa. As he travelled, he kept seeing a mamba snake following him over a distance of 500 miles, crossing rivers and any obstacles. He was able to shoot it before it attacked him after which he realized that it was the female mate of the male one he had shot in the Cape. He was lucky that he killed the second one too before it could avenge the death of its mate. There is no snake that Africans demonize and fear more than the mamba which gets its name from the Zulu word *imamba*, whatever the word in Zulu means. If it means anything, its meaning cannot be a good one or mean a good thing.

After waking up, Zefina bolted from the hut while naked, towel and soap in hand, to wash in the stream before coming out to dress and begin to boil water for tea with our stale bread while I washed in the stream. After our breakfast, we hung around until well past noon before resuming our journey so that we could reach our relatives before the sun dipped low or disappeared on the horizon. We had to be there before darkness, as it would not be much fun for them and for us to meet at night and be off to bed soon after that. And also the place was also heavily infested with hyenas.

Many people traveling in opposite directions passed us there. They greeted us or we greeted them. Some people stopped to exchange a few words and laughter with us and asked us where we were from and where we were heading to.

"From the village of Chief Nderi on the other side of the Zambezi and we're going to the village of Chief Jimo to see our relatives there," I said. Zefina left me to do all the talking. She preferred to keep quiet and not to say a single word because she thought I could handle strangers better than she could. Some of them men wanted to know how I was related to her.

"She's my wife," I said. Each time Zefina turned to look at me with a smile, as if wanting to tell me not to lie or to say: "I wish we were. Wouldn't that be the most wonderful thing in the world for us! Unfortunately we can never be."

"She's a bit older than you," said a short and stocky man with a spear in his right hand and who had thought that she was my older sister. "She sure is beautiful. Perhaps she has some *n'nchena* for you to love her."

"Young men like me nowadays like slightly older girls who know how to love and be wise with good behaviour in contrast to men of your age who prefer younger girls that you can dominate and enslave," I teased him. "She has no n'nchena or love magic. She just loves me and I also just love her. That's all."

The man took my joke in good humour and laughed a good laugh while thrusting his spear into the sandy ground. Other people with him joined him in his hearty laughter. Then the man yanked his spear from the ground and claimed he had killed a lion with it as the beast tried to raid his goats' kraal and snatch a goat from it. He and his group left while laughing, leaving Zefina and me also laughing behind them. I took his claim of killing a lion with a spear single-handed with a pitch of salt because we Sena people were not as brave as the Maasai of East Africa who fear no lions which fear them instead. In the days of yore, their boys had to kill lions single-handedly with spears as a rite of passage to qualify to marry, or at least that was what the Maasai tradition of the past required, but they were being discouraged from such a custom now in order to save wildlife as the natural heritage of Tanzania and Kenya where the Maasai live.

The Maasai do not always comply. Sometimes they have to deal with the nuisance of lions and they have to kill lions in self-defence or to protect their livestock. That is the challenge facing the Maasai that the bureaucrats making rules and laws in the Tanzanian and Kenyan capitals don't quite grasp and understand.

Years later I was quite amused when I read in a Kenyan daily that a Maasai man with a spear in hand, something Maasai are not allowed to do in Nairobi, walked by a Zimmermann store that dealt with hides of wild animals and saw the cured head of a real lion on the wall of the store. He burst into the store with his spear drawn and attacked the head with his spear because a lion had killed a brother of his. The attacker was not arrested or charged following the incident.

More people walked by, traveling in opposite directions with women carrying all kinds of produce and fruit to sell at some small village markets in the bush country. A few men passed with tethered goats or sheep to go to sell at the market. From one woman, we bought a pineapple which we ate while we boiled cassava that we had bought from another woman and we ate this with some of the roasted francolin we could not finish the previous day.

It was well past noon when we decided to resume our journey after wading through the stream and putting on our walking shoes. The path went through a less dense bush country and there were scattered clusters of huts we could see here and there with villagers going about their normal routine of tending their homesteads, going out, or returning home to the comfort of their huts. That part of the countryside was peaceful and reassuring with no or less wild animals. We continued to walk while conversing which we did not do in the denser and more menacing places between the Zambezi and the second stream when we walked with arrows on our bow strings and silently with stilled nerves, so as to hear sounds and smells and be ready to counter threats and dangers.

As we approached the Nakasero Forest, I alerted Zefina that we were about to enter the haunted place. Zefina was not intimidated. She was not the daughter of a powerful witchdoctor woman for nothing. Her mom had brought her up to be unaffected by the supernatural, she had told me. She just laughed my warning off before saying that she did not fear Nakasero and its god-damned ghosts.

I felt very creepy as we entered the forest with big trees packed together on either side of the track, preventing us from seeing much beyond the first row of trees bordering the path. I began to hear sounds and deathly screams very close to us but could not see who was making them. Perhaps I was imagining them since I had been told about them several times by different people in the past. Perhaps the noises were just in my head. Then we began to see piles of human bones of mapanga from Nyasaland that armed villagers had killed with bows and arrows, or spears or machetes and who were not buried as no one cared to bury evildoers after killing them in the middle of a forest. The bandits had also killed people they had waylaid there and who had resisted being taken away.

The killing of evildoers and the murder of their victims went on for a number of years before the forest started to be a haunted spot so much so, that the mapanga who were sent over to that region were told to avoid it. The mapanga who went to waylay villagers in the forest without knowing it was haunted, left it running because of all the screams from voices of invisible people or also because of the ghosts of their fellow evildoers and of their victims that they saw.

We walked through the haunted place for about fifteen minutes before emerging into an open space on the other side of the forest where there was a sprawling field of sorghum with banana trees scattered in it. Close by the forest in that field there were huts in which people arriving late slept to avoid crossing the forest at night, because the ghosts were reported to be very vicious at night, screaming and swearing at travellers and attacking them, which was something they rarely did during day time.

Soon after emerging into the open and free space, I took my handkerchief from the pocket of my trousers to wipe away sweat from my face after which I let out a big sigh before beginning to breathe normally as I had stifled my breath and stilled my nerves whilst going through the haunted place. I felt like I had come from the dead or had suddenly awakened from a nightmarish dream, but that it was not a dream rather a physical reality my body felt and soul experienced. I did not feel like I felt that time as a very young boy passing there in the company of adults who were talking and laughing, as if nothing was the matter.

"Did you see the strange man who walked right in front of us from the right side to the left side of the path while we were in the middle of the forest?" Zefina asked me in a very cool manner.

"I saw no strange man," I said. "What are you talking about?"

"I saw a dirty, tall, gaunt, and haggard man in rags with wiry, unkempt hair, deeply sunken eyes with long curved nails on his fingers like the devil's and, with a machete in his right hand. He walked haltingly. In the middle of the path he stopped and turned to look at us in a most unfriendly manner and waved his machete angrily at us," she said. "I knew he couldn't attack us with his machete because he's a phantom and his theatrics were a thought form of what he used to do in his lifetime."

"Were you scared seeing the former mapanga who doesn't seem to realize that he no longer belongs to the world of the living?"

"I wasn't. I even waved to him to go away and he moved away. Didn't you see me waving my hands and uttering some words?"

"Was that when I saw you agitating your arms and uttering some words I did not understand? I could not ask you what you were doing because I was so numb."

"I was chasing the god-damned thing to get lost and go to hell where it belongs. It's not a living thing. It's a zombie. It looked absolutely evil."

After Zefina told me about what she had seen, I felt that she and I complemented each other in a way that was unique. She was my spiritual safeguard while I was her physical protector, or so I thought and believed, rightly or wrongly. I became even more determined to travel to Tete with her. I wished I could go to the seminary with her, but the seminary was no place for girls. The very sight of girls was regarded as a source of temptation for the students preparing to be priests. When the time for me to go to the seminary came, I would have to part company with her and that was going to be difficult because she was the person I loved the most in the world. Without her, my life would be a nightmarish cross, too heavy to bear. If I were not related to her, I would have given up the idea of going to train to be a priest so as to be with her and marry her. But the crossed stars of our common genetics forbade me from doing so. So I had to accept the truth as a reality of our lives because I could neither shake off nor change things to please my fantasy about her or her dreams about me.

I, all the same, began to be possessive of her and I even repeatedly told her not to get married for my sake, although I could never marry her myself. She told me she was not interested in getting married, at least not then or in the near future. Each time after asking her not to get married, I pondered about the unfairness of what I was telling her and I rescinded my words, and told her to get married if she got a responsible man. I told her that I would pray for her to get a good and reasonable husband.

From the forest, we walked at a steady pace as the sun had begun to go down. For half an hour or so, we walked along the path with fields of sorghum and millet on both sides of the way before walking through villages interspersed by areas of grassland and acacia trees as we approached our destination.

We knew the place we were going to; Zefina and I had been there in the past but on different occasions. The sun was about to disappear as we entered the compound of our great uncle Josias who was related to us on our mothers' side. His young sons who were playing about in the compound watched us enter their homestead and hesitated to welcome us as they had thought that we were a couple that had got lost and wanted to get some direction from them so that we could get where we wanted to go. It had been a long time since we had been together. We, they and us, had changed a great deal as we grew up. They gawked at us before one of them recognized us and shouted our names to us to signal that he knew who we were. He and his brothers rushed to welcome us and take our belongings from us as was the custom when welcoming guests.

The excitement with hugs, handshakes, and uncontrolled laughter, joy and talking, became a cacophony that made their two dogs bark at Zefina and I, as if to tell us to go away because we were a nuisance. Chickens which were still in the compound before retreating to their pen at sunset, cackled and ducks quacked and began to run helter skelter in the compound before adults came out from the huts and the verandas to add more excitement to the euphoria, with the women ululating with joy after seeing and recognizing us. One older son of my uncle's even let out a piercing whistle that could be heard over a long distance, in a way only African villagers could do to communicate while in the bush or to let their relatives or friends looking for them know where they are.

"Unbelievable. It's you Chico and you Zefina. It's like a dream," said great uncle Josias as he came to greet us and lead us to the veranda of the hut of one of his two wives. He was a good natured man whose advancing age had begun to tell on him, with most of his hair having turned white and he had stooped a bit as if with a hunchback.

"We've come to check on you all to make sure you're alright," I said.

"We're all fine here," said the wizened Josias. "We think about you too and wonder whether everything is okay with you on the other side of the Zambezi."

"Everyone is fine at home. Thanks go to the ancestors," said Zefina before adding, "and thank God, Jesus, and Mary." It was typical of her as a traditionalist to invoke the ancestors and also God as the good Christian that she was. She never missed saying the rosary in the evening before going to sleep. She even did so in the two huts where we spent the nights by the two streams. There was no incongruity in her approach because, like me, she was a child of the world of our traditional culture and also the world of Christianity and western education. We never gave up one to embrace the other completely and we would not be able to do so, as we wanted the best of both worlds. We were not opportunists but realists.

In no time at all a chicken was seized and slaughtered to give us a good dinner. When the meal was ready, our hosts had wanted me and Zefina to eat together, as guests are always made to eat the first meal separately from the hosts. I protested that Zefina and I did not wish to be treated in that manner because we were not a couple but a brother and a sister. I told them that I would eat with the men and Zefina said that she would be with the women.

Our hosts acquiesced, although reluctantly because for them, tradition should not be violated at the whim of kids like us. Some of them guessed that Zefina and I were disrespectful of our traditions because we had gone to school and were Christians. The truth was that we liked our traditions but not everything about them. We also liked western ways but not everything about them, despite the fact that the missionaries and the colonialists told us that our traditional ways were bad and evil and that western and Christian ways were good because they were a path to salvation.

Chapter 14

During our five day stay with our relatives at Chief Jimo's village, Zefina stayed in the company of the women. She went with them to the fields, to find firewood in the bush and to wash in and fetch water from a nearby stream. She was well integrated with them and behaved toward me as if she did not care much about me or as if we had not gone there together. I admired her behaviour aimed at making our relatives, particularly the women, not to think that we had gone there together because we were in an amorous relationship with the implication of incest. And why should we be the ones to make them think so when nothing of the sort was taking place between the two of us?

I kept myself with my great uncle's boys who were very affable and joyous and who teased me a great deal. I also teased them. One of them by the name of Nkhondo, the word meaning war in our language, said that people who lived in the Zambezi Valley like me who thought they were superior and civilized and regarded the hinterland people like them as uncultured, they were the ones who were really uncouth and stupid. I did not argue with him over that. I left him alone with his belief if it made him happy and his remark did not hurt or harm me. In a way I in fact agreed with him, because our tribe was its own worst enemy with some regions always despising and underrating our own people of other regions.

"You've come to a place with strange things," he warned me. "We will go with you into the bush. If you see something strange, don't get scared or don't ask 'what's that? If you do, the front of your head will turn to the back of your head and the back of your head will be the front of your head. Do you understand you silly guy from the Zambezi Valley?"

"I do." I acquiesced without arguing, as it was never good to argue about things one did not know about or understand. That was my conviction at least. I felt it was better to keep myself in check with my mouth shut and not to attempt to wear shoes that would be too big for me, as many things that would make a western person grin were never a laughing matter with us. I knew better than just dismissing some of our beliefs out of hand.

I was told of a case of a teacher from the Angonia area in the north-west of Tete region, whose Ngoni ancestors under the leadership of Zwengendaba had fled Natal to escape the wrath of Shaka Zulu's wars of domination, and had fled to Mozambique where they were forced to leave after being defeated in a fight with the Shangaan led by Sotshangana who had also fled from Shaka Zulu. After defeating the Ngonis, the Shangaan later established the empire of Gaza in southern Mozambique and in a region of the south-eastern region of what is now Zimbabwe. The defeated hordes of Ngoni marauders continued their aimless march north, using the war tactics copied from the Zulus and causing much terror to the natives of the lands they went through. They created Ngoni colonies in Mozambique, Malawi, and Zambia with a northernmost group reaching and settling in Songea in the south of what is today mainland Tanzania. The teacher had been sent to the Catholic mission of Charre to the north of Mutarara.

The incident I am now recounting concerning the man might have been embellished to make it more amusing than what actually happened. After arriving at Charre, he was told about witchcraft. As an educated man and a Christian convert, he derided the idea, pooh-poohed the concept, and laughed it off like a man who was very drunk, saying it was hogwash only gullible and foolish people believed in. He did not know the rule of thumb in the land of the Sena people that enjoins people not to dismiss what one hears out of hand. People talked about his arrogant attitude and some women were not amused. They decided to teach him a lesson.

No one knew what his mind might have imagined or what happened to him or what he might have seen one evening after sunset, as he strolled around his school. He became scatterbrained, confused, and talked incoherently while shivering as if from blasts of a severe cold wind. He claimed to have seen a knot of hideous looking women dressed up in white gowns, performing what seemed to be some kind of a weird dance. When he attempted to approach them, his hair stood on end and the spot where they were was suddenly blotted with what looked like a very dark cloud, making it impossible for him to see them. He saw them again in the same spot where he had seen them before with the cloud having cleared as if magically when he began to back up from them. He said they stopped doing their dance. They all pointed their fingers at him, as if to accuse him of some bad behaviour, and one of them shouted in a croaky voice to tell him to get out of their village as soon as possible before they would teach him a hard lesson he would never forget for the rest of his life.

He became so scared that he packed his kit and left the village without saying good-bye to anyone a few days later, to return to his home area where members of his tribe also believed in witchcraft and whose witches did not perhaps have the ability to challenge his attitude with a stranger than fiction demonstration like the one he saw in the village where was going to teach and reside. There is no tribe no matter where in Mozambique in particular, and in black

Africa in general, which does not believe in witchcraft and in its perceived or alleged pernicious powers and consequences. Why does the belief in witchcraft persist even after western-style education with its empirical approach has taken root and spread through many regions of Africa? Is it a mere superstition that is deeply or genetically ingrained in us Africans or is there something more real to it than we can so far grasp and understand? Or will it just remain forever a mystery as mysteries tend to be?

During our stay I had much fun with my male cousins who told me that there was a ghost leopard with its ghost cubs in the area that were constantly seen and which harmed no one. Did they really expect me to buy their story about the harmlessness of a leopard? Regardless of whether the leopard in question was real or a ghost, their words did not reassure me in the least that the beast, if it existed, was not dangerous. As far as I was concerned, leopards, solitary and stealthy, are the most dangerous of the big cats wherever they may be found on earth whether in tropical Africa or in steaming areas of the southern regions or cold areas of northern Asia or in snowy and icy Siberia.

At any rate, I was not cowed because I had decided to make adventures the bread of my everyday life. Courage was the very stuff that had propelled me to go to their village, and I would have done it alone, if Zefina had not tagged along. I did not refuse to take to the bush or the stream with my cousins for fear of a leopard whether a ghost leopard or a real one.

We went to wash in the stream a stone's throw from my great uncle's residence and play on its sandy bank where we also shot birds with our bows and arrows or scooped sand with our hands in the wet areas of the stream where water that was just near the surface, filled the holes as we removed the sand. We laid traps around them and caught birds, mainly turtle doves that were part of the diet of the local people in that region.

One of the things that we did may not sound a praiseworthy activity at all, but we did it anyway and greatly amused ourselves while doing it. We isolated vervet monkeys, one at a time, on trees from their groups, and harassed them with our wooden-headed arrows or with stones from our catapults until we sometimes killed them or they escaped. Since we shot at them directly from under the trees, our arrows fell back around the trees. We did not lose them. We were often able to kill the isolated monkeys, if the trees were not close to other trees to which they could jump to disappear into the undergrowth or into the bush where we could not go to pursue the little burglars.

Sometimes the little monkeys would take chances and jump down and run away as fast as their legs could take them whilst squealing with fear, to disappear as we shot arrows or hurled stones at them. They would later find and team up with their colleagues they had been separated from. The escapees always seemed to know where their groups were after escaping from us.

It was never easy to hit monkeys on the tops of trees while they watched us aim our wooden-headed arrows at them. The little fellows were agile. They saw the arrows streaking to them and dodged the missiles and kept jumping from branch to branch. They dodged our missiles just in time, before they went past them, after which they would look at us down below so as to know what our next move would be, but we knew that they were panicky. We would sometimes take half an hour or even an hour before hitting and killing them, if they did not escape.

We never gave up as long as the monkeys did not jump down and flee. We never thought that what we were doing was a bad sport against animals that did not provoke or steal from us. And our sport was no more cruel than fox-hunting that some Europeans indulged in during which they chased foxes and their hounds caught and tore them apart. What was their reason for destroying foxes? I have a feeling that they did it for fun more than to control the number of foxes and stamp out rabies that the little canines could have caused or spread.

We left the monkeys we killed where they fell and hyenas disposed of them at night. When we went to the spots the following day and did not find the carcasses, we knew that hyenas had done their job as efficient general cleaners.

If killing birds and harassing monkeys was much fun for me, the place where my cousins took me to next was no place for fooling around. We did not take our weapons. Nkhondo said that we were not taking our weapons without explaining why. After walking in the bush for half an hour or so, struggling to find space to squeeze our bodies in a tightly packed forest with big and small trees and tall grass, we reached an ancient baobab tree that might have been where it stood since the dawn of history. In most parts of Africa it is believed that baobab trees have the predilection to become the abodes of spirits, usually good ancestral spirits, or that because of their majesty, they tend to attract spirits.

The gigantic trees are also a source of food, as it were. Their leaves can be cooked with whatever spices one likes and eaten with hard porridge or any other food, I have eaten them myself in my young days. I do not remember what their taste was like, but it was not bad at all and had no particular smell or had no smell at all. A few years ago, the BBC World Service reported on a scientific study which found out that the baobab fruit, which has a shell that is very hard to crack or break (and which in my young days I used to break with stones), contains seeds that are surrounded by an edible powder-like substance that is a powerhouse of nutrients or a super food loaded with vitamins, minerals and trace minerals. The report added that a Western company, probably a British one, I cannot quite remember, was considering the possibility of harnessing the contents of the fruit of baobab trees in order to commercialize it.

I did not need to be told that the place was haunted or that it was the abode of some invisible entities which were not hostile to us as long as we stayed reverent to them while we were there. According to my cousin, he and the other boys did at times play on the opposite side to the one where we stood in awe, while looking at the fantastic display before our eyes, as the sun ascended in the sky.

We were about five in number, three of my cousins and another boy. We watched the spotlessly clean ground, as if someone swept it several times a day, around a big hollow into the base of the baobab. Right outside the hole, we saw two spiritual earthen pots or gourds, one big and one slightly smaller, like the kinds of container in which witchdoctors keep their magic stuff. They shone as if they had been varnished with special oil. The pots were covered with black cloths below which were stringed beads of various colours. There was no question of us attempting to approach and open the gourds to see what was in them. The very idea of doing so did not cross our minds and no villager of that area had ever been reported as having tried to do so.

As Nkhondo had previously told me not to ask questions about anything strange we saw, I did not ask questions about what we were looking at. I knew that it was the stuff of invisible entities. We stood there silently with our eyes riveted on the mysterious objects and in a total state of wonderment, as if entranced.

It was only after we had left the tree and were some distance away from the baobab that my cousin began to speak to enlighten me on what we had seen. He said that in the past, a powerful witchdoctor had lived close to the baobab tree and that after his death his spirit had turned the tree into its abode, which was the reason why the place was haunted.

"When we go to that tree, we sometimes see the objects we saw today and sometimes we don't, but the place feels mysterious and haunted all the same."

When I think of it to this day, I surely find it difficult to imagine that some human kept placing and removing those objects without people venturing to that spot ever surprising him doing so. What would be the purpose for doing such a tiresome and unpaid job in the middle of a little virgin forest with so many hazards like snakes and wild animals? What was really happening there?

Chapter 15

As my cousins had told me of a man who sold bicycles he smuggled or brought from Southern Rhodesia, now Zimbabwe, I told Zefina that the boys should take us to him for us to have a look at the bicycles and buy one or two, if we liked them. The boys took us to the man in the afternoon. The man showed us his bicycles which were probably stolen as I did not believe that he had the money to buy them in the neighbouring British-ruled territory. But to our surprise, the Raleigh bicycles he had looked brand new. He had four of them and he was selling them at 300 escudos each, which was a lot of money for villagers in those days most of whom never had any money and could never even dream of owning a bicycle. Very few people had bicycles and the hoi polloi had to slog it on foot even on trips lasting a whole day, two days or even more.

I haggled with him to lower the price as we wanted to buy two of them, one for Zefina and one for me. He was reluctant to lower the price and said that he had taken a lot of pain bringing those bicycles to his village. As I was becoming impatient with him over his refusal to lower the prices, Zefina dropped a bombshell as she was the one who had the money to buy the bikes and not me, a pauper without money but who never begged her to give me money.

"We'll pay you 300 escudos a piece alright," she said.

"Give me the money and take the bikes," the man commanded without much ado. He needed the money urgently to pay the bride price for one more wife to add to his rather insignificant harem of three, so that he could have four wives after which he could hold his head high. He would no longer feel inferior to those who had five or more wives. There was a cute girl in a neighbouring village whose parents wanted to give her to him for the price of 350 escudos.

Zefina drew 600 escudos from her purse and gave it to him. The man was very happy. He spat at the money as a way of blessing his good luck and also to express his joy, before he brought us the two bikes from the veranda of the hut of his senior wife. He also gave us glue, a spanner, and pieces of inner tube rubber with which to patch up the tyres if they went flat. I thanked and hugged Zefina for buying me a bike, the first bike I was going to own. For me, it was a dream I had never thought would ever come true. Zefina already had one on which I had learned to ride. She was the only girl who could ride a bicycle in our village where like anywhere else in our tribal homeland, girls were not supposed, or were forbidden, to ride bicycles.

Zefina had learnt to ride a bike on her own initiative and against the wish of people around her including the fiery Kabulunge, our maternal grandmother, who took her parents to task for allowing her to learn to ride a bike. The old woman had feared that she would become a lousy girl after knowing how to ride a bicycle. Her fear had no logic, nor rhyme nor reason, but, incidentally, most people thought like her. For them it was okay for white, Indian, mixed race and assimilado girls, who had different personalities, to ride bikes because they were members of an elite class and in their minds, such girls were lousy anyway because they did not live by our mores and were seen mixing and laughing with boys and sometimes hugging them. For them, girls who behaved in that manner were lousy and could easily surrender their bodies to boys.

Zefina had learnt to ride a bike before she became *assimilada* or a Portuguese citizen. She proved those silly people wrong for equating girls' ability to ride bicycles with laxity of sexual morals. She chided them for being backward and snarled to them like an angry lioness to warn them to keep their mouths shut or she would assault them physically. Even our martinet grandmother backed down and kept her mouth shut like an intimidated dog folding its tail and placing it between its legs before sitting down or retreating in fear.

As she had given our great uncle Josias some money as a gift from both of us after our arrival, I felt that our relatives would not complain that she had spent so much money buying two bikes while one would have been enough without giving them any money at all. In fact, they were pleased to see our bikes that would help us travel faster and carry things in future.

As soon as we returned to our great uncle's home, I thanked his family for the good reception they had accorded us and told them that we would be leaving to return home the following day. They begged us to stay longer but we told them that we had to leave as we would be departing for Tete to welcome the president of the republic who had already arrived from Lisbon and was in southern Mozambique. At that time, we fanatically believed that we were Portuguese and should not miss the occasion to welcome the president.

They understood that we had to leave without quite understanding our reason. They wanted to give us things to carry home. As what they wanted to give us was farm produce we already had at home, we saw no need to take it as we did not want to burden our bikes and ourselves with unnecessary loads on top of our haversacks and our weapons. We had fallen in love with our bikes which we wanted to treat like babies and not punish with unnecessary weights. Our bikes were to carry us only and the few things we needed wherever we went.

Zefina and I discussed our plan for the return journey and what we were to do if we saw wild animals in front of us. We decided to use the bells on our bikes to scare them off. She was going to ride about ten meters in front of me and ring the bell if she decided to stop so that I could cue in to her move and stop to avoid rear-ending her. I was also going to ring the bell when I wanted to stop so that she did not keep going leaving me far behind and to prevent her from panicking if she did not see me behind her. Our safety was going to depend on our staying and fighting together against wild animals or hostile humans, if we had to. We did not anticipate such scenarios, but there was no telling if untoward would happen. There were enraged animals and crazy humans out there.

As we knew that we would take about three hours or even less along the well-trodden and smooth path over a mostly flat countryside, we were not in a hurry to leave early the following day. Zefina went with the girls to wash in the stream first early the following morning. After their return, I also went with the boys to wash in the stream.

At around 10:00 that morning, we took off after bidding farewell to our relatives, some of whom had tears in their eyes. Zefina also cried. I did not because boys were not supposed to cry over emotions, only if in acute physical pain. Our relatives were sad to see us leave. We were also sad to leave them behind while uncertain as to when we would be together again if at all.

We rode at a steady pace without speeding, ringing the bell when we saw people ahead of us so that they could step aside to let us pass and prevent us from running into them. Before long, we entered the haunted forest and began to ring the bells in relay so as to scare off the ghosts, and send them scurrying away panic-stricken. While at the mission school, I had read a little book on the occult that said that demons and evil spirits do not like or can stand the sounds of bells because bells irritate them and send them packing. The booklet went on to state that was one of the reasons why churches had bells. Whether that was true or not, I did not dwell on that question. I just believed it. Zefina believed it when I told her before we entered the forest which we crossed while ringing our bells not in relay but together, and no ghosts appeared to challenge us for being a nuisance to them in their own territory. Perhaps the sounds of our bells had indeed scared them off from us. I felt sorry for the poor fellows for losing a war without fighting a single battle against us.

We rode on to the first and second streams without encountering wild animals apart from hearing baboons howling in the adjacent woods. We reached Magagade Shopping Centre by 1:00 p.m. It was amazing how a simple machine like a bike had shrunk the distance that took a whole day of hard walking to cover and which had taken us three days of walking at our own pace and pitching camps in two places. We were tired after biking for three hours. We needed to rest. We decided to be at the shopping centre for the rest of the day and spend the night there. We slept in an old house of bricks with a tiled roof that had been a store before one of the Indian shopkeepers turned it into a lodge for a minimal fee for anyone stranded at the centre without somewhere to sleep. It was safe and comfortable. We crossed the river the following morning.

Chapter 16

My journey to Sofala with Zefina had been a baptism of fire for my future life not only in Mozambique but also in foreign lands where I would encounter hostile people and find myself in some blood-curdling situations. We felt invincible and on top of the world. We had every reason to pat ourselves in the back. Because the travel to Sofala had been successful, it gave us the incentive to undertake another adventurous trip without blinking an eye or pondering the pros and cons of going to a place where people spoke another language, the Nyungwe language, which, although close to ours, was different all the same, with a people with different attitudes and customs. In the land of the Anyungwe people, women smoked with the lit ends of their home-made cigars made with their own home-grown tobacco inside their mouths whereas among the Sena people, men smoked and women snuffed. I do not ever remember having seen a woman who smoked.

We were going to Tete at a time when people from other tribes amongst them Ngonis, Nsengas, Nyungwes, Zimbas, Senas, and others from all regions of Tete District with distinct mores, would be converging on the city as well. Instead of the thought of running into different members of other tribes intimidating us, it spurred us on as we wanted to see people who were different from our own people, although we would not go about asking them who they were and what areas they were from. Seeing such people would be enough to satisfy our curiosity and make us realize that they were not our fellow Senas as they would be speaking their own languages.

Zefina and I were gung-ho about it because the inducements for us to undertake yet another adventure were enticing. We wanted to fulfil our patriotic sentiments as Portuguese citizens who had pledged to spare no efforts in the defence of Portugal. We were not only Portuguese, but *muito português* for me and *muito portuguesa* for Zefina meaning *very Portuguese*. As if saying that we were Portuguese or very Portuguese was not enough, we at times emphasized it by saying in the superlative *portuguesissimo* for a male and *portuguesissima* for a female meaning that we were *most Portuguese*. The government was going to provide trains to carry those wanting to go to Tete and free food for the people who would be in the city for the presidential visit. As for water, there was going to be no problem, as people would be camping in the open on the sandy banks of the Zambezi. The city of Tete is situated on the right side of the river about 600 kilometres or so from the Indian Ocean.

Zefina's parents were glad that I was once again going to undertake a long journey with their daughter after the trip to Sofala took place without problems. And I was eager to take my cousin with an extrasensory perception who had been able to see the ghost at Nakasero Forest I did not see when he manifested himself right before our eyes. I would probably not have gone to Tete, if she had decided not to tag along with me. She also said that she would not go, if I did not go. After our companionship on the journey to Sofala, I was convinced that I once again needed her camaraderie as she needed mine.

We biked to the township of Mutarara to the north of our village with no more than our clothes, blankets, two cooking pots, two spoons, and two drinking cans and some money. The government had said that people needed to have pots and pans so that they could prepare meals with food that would be provided free of charge. If the government had failed to live up to its promise, we had the money to buy food or eat at restaurants. So we were not concerned over the government failing to give us food or not. And the government was not going to fail thousands of people who wanted to glorify it.

When we boarded a train to Tete after two days at Mutarara, we left our bikes at the home of a teacher, a man from our village, called *senhor* Jonas. He taught at the Santa Barbara Primary School which stood side by side with the Santa Barbara chapel which had the image of Saint Barbara, the patron saint of soldiers, at the top front of the chapel. She was in armour and in a semi-genuflection with her left knee on the ground and her right leg bent at a right angle and the tip of her sword on the ground. It was really a military chapel but civilians went there for Sunday services too. Soldiers of the sprawling local barracks, one of the biggest in colonial Mozambique, went there for Sunday services. There was no resident priest as the chapel was a military establishment. A priest from Charre Mission to the north arrived there on Saturdays and stayed on before returning to Charre Mission on Sunday afternoons after hearing confessions and saying masses for soldiers and civilians.

We knew the teacher and he knew us too. He was an acquaintance of our parents. He was overjoyed to see us. He welcomed us to his house with much warmth. We did not know his wife who was from the area of Mutarara. We also did not know their daughter and son who were born in the township, but the family welcomed us with much cordiality.

As we did not want to become a burden to the family apart from the space they provided us, Zefina and I went to buy groceries for us all shortly after arriving at their house. We bought enough groceries for the family to last them for a while. They were grateful for our gesture and prayed for us so that God could bless us. I thought that Zefina and I needed prayers from Christians like Jonas' family and also protection from our spiritual ancestors. We wanted every good entity with or without supernatural powers to help us and ward off evil or danger. I was in no doubt that there were dangers below the surface of the water, although the water on the surface looked calm, promising, and reassuring, a saying of the people of the Okavango Delta in Botswana as a warning to people against the danger from crocodiles.

With our bikes, Zefina and I felt that there was nothing we could not do or conquer. We were not just going to sit down the following day and wait for a whole day before taking the train to Tete. We decided to cross to Sena Town in Sofala on the other side of the river, a place from which our tribal nation draws its name by riding our bikes on the four kilometre-long bridge spanning the Zambezi. The all metal bridge was a marvel of the ingenuity, skills, and technological expertise of the white men who built it. It was built in the 1930s by the British who owned it, with the help of the Portuguese and the participation of local labourers. It was painted with the green and red colours of the Portuguese flag because it was on Portuguese territory. It has a railroad in the middle and two sidewalks for bicycles and pedestrians travelling back and forth between Mutarara and Sena.

At Dona Ana where the bridge begins on the Mutarara side, there was a white soldier who epitomized the very essence of a soldier in a green uniform with splashes of lighter green on it of the Portuguese Army, wearing gloves with his G-3 rifle in his hand. He was of medium height and steely, standing stock still. We waved to him before we walked over to have a chat with him. He was very friendly and his attention was drawn to Zefina and her enchanting beauty.

"*Que és bela, donzela!*" he said to her meaning "you're so beautiful, damsel!"

"*Obrigada,*" she thanked him for his remark. I thought she liked him but she took what he said lightly.

"*Gostaria mesmo de te casar e te tomar para a metropole e que crianças mestiçadas tao bonitas teriamos!*" he said rather unceremoniously to mean "I would really like to marry you and take you to Portugal and what beautiful mixed race kids we would have!" What the soldier said reflected the infatuation and passion Portuguese men tended to have for black women while their women did not show the same fervor for black men, although they did marry and have children with them.

"*Isto podemos sempre combinar,*" Zefina said, meaning "we can always discuss the matter." What she said was perhaps to stop him from continuing to say things she did not like or because she realized that it would be difficult to be in touch with a soldier while she lived far away from him and who could be transferred to another part of the territory anytime or, to another Portuguese colony or return to Portugal at any time. Zefina was not unnecessarily flattered by the soldier's flirting as she thought he probably said the same thing to other local girls he saw and who fascinated him with their enchanting beauty.

The soldier then showed us his weapon and explained us how he operated it without his hands moving its parts as it had a fully loaded magazine and the rifle could go off, which could cause a lot of alarm in the township. He even gave us a feel of it by letting each one of us hold it in our hands after telling us not to push or pull any parts of it. The all metal rifle was heavy in my hands. I thought that Zefina found it even heavier, although she was a tough girl. If I had stayed in Mozambique after 1967, when I would have been of military age, I would have been inducted into the army and would have been armed with the same kind of weapon or with a similar one. We thanked the soldier for showing us his weapon before we got on the sidewalk where we rode slowly at a distance of ten meters between the two of us while looking ahead all the time to avoid getting distracted and running into pedestrians or other bikers going the opposite way. Riding as we did, we could not look at the gigantic metallic structure straddling the river we had been seeing from our village.

On the other side of the bridge, we saw a black soldier with his rifle in hand and he was attired in the same kind of uniform as the white one we had talked to on the other side. We waved to him for no other reason other than that he was just a fellow black person like us. He waved back to us with a smile and excitement. We did not stop to chat with him as we were keener on getting ashore to drive into the township we had never been to before and whose history, legend, and mystery we had heard so much about for so long. Our visit was the experience of a lifetime and was liberation from a world of darkness to a world of light and enlightenment. And we had to pay due attention to every circumstance and detail.

We rode into the town with people walking about on street sidewalks going in opposite directions, before we got off our bikes and started to push them so that we could talk to someone who could help us. I stopped a man. I asked whether he knew the location of the legendary Sena Stone, the myth of which we had heard so much about, because we were eager to go and ogle it and say prayers to our ancestors there. He said he knew the place and led us to it. I paid him 20 escudos which could buy him khaki shorts or a shirt. He smiled and thanked me for my little gesture of goodwill.

For us, the visit to the Sena Stone was a pilgrimage as the mysterious landmark embodied the essence of our tribe whose beginnings are lost in the mist of times and only recounted in legends that are told with much passion. If the Christians have their Holy Land, the Jews their Jerusalem which is also holy to Christians and Moslems, the Moslems their Mecca and the Hindus their Varanasi, we the Sena people have our mysterious Stone at Sena which is as holy to us as the holy places of the aforementioned peoples are to them. On arrival we met two elderly women keeping watch on the stone. Elders, male and female, kept watch over the stone round the clock and in relay teams of two no matter what kind of weather, rain or shine; because the stone is regarded as the work of spirits who brought it to us to make Sena a sacred spot and to give us a name as the stone is called Sena.

And no one in Senaland really knows what the word Sena means apart from thinking that we are the best people in the world and that no one else is as good and human as we are. Senas have the concept of themselves as being unique from any other human beings. It is a concept that is similar to that of a chosen people such as the Biblical Jews and yet not quite like it because we do not attribute our concept of uniqueness to either Mulungu or God; we don't even worship or care about but fear God as the Lord of Thunder, Lightning, Rain or Drought, or to the ancestral spirits we at times, make offerings to, then reprimand for being naughty, fussy and unnecessarily demanding and wanting them to be happy with what we are giving them.

The Europeans laughed at us and at what they regarded as our superstition, dark belief, and sheer stupidity for revering the stone at Sena. That was the reason why they had wanted to remove the stone and take it to a museum in Portugal. Imperial powers took artefacts they looted from other lands to their countries and museums in cities like Washington DC or New York, Lisbon, Rome, Paris, London, Berlin, Moscow and Beijing; these cities are full of stolen objects from other lands. It is the Europeans who did not understand us until the power of the stone revealed itself to them and mystified them and made them to be afraid of it after conceding that it was "divine."

Sena Township, unlike Mutarara across the river, which was a European creation, was timeless and perhaps older than Lisbon, Paris, or London. According to legend, it had been inhabited by a race of dwarfs or pygmies and the last two pygmies, who could speak all the languages of the world left in 1950 and no-one knew where they went to. Phoenicians are said to have visited Sena followed by Arabs who traded with the local people with beads, ivory, precious metals, and slaves well before the Portuguese, who later built a fort there to glorify their king and country, showed up in the 16th century. It just remained a township and never grew into anything bigger, although it has more people now than ever before.

One of the elderly women led us to the stone, which stood big to our eyes and mysterious to our senses, radiating a spiritual power and timelessness. She walked us around it before leaving us standing by it to say our prayers to the spirits. The spot and the stone were not at all spooky or haunting. They exuded an aura of goodness and sacredness, if not of holiness. I crouched as men do and Zefina knelt as women do before praying to the spirits, with each one of us silently composing our own words, as we have no common prayers and no prayer books, before quietly saying them as prayers to honour the spirits and request them to be forever the guardians of the Sena people and our protectors. Zefina was the first to get up after her prayer and went to sit down with the two women on a reed mat. I joined them after my prayer and also sat down on the mat as there were no chairs there, perhaps because chairs would not be permitted as they were things that the Europeans had introduced to us and the spirits could find offence with them or would not want them.

We told the women our names after they had introduced themselves as Chasasa and Mifino. Chasasa who was tall and the older of the two spoke first, and the other woman listened to her while looking at us with her hypnotizing eyes.

"My children," Chasasa drew our attention, "the spirits brought the stone here. The imperial government had wanted to take it to Portugal. The first time they tried for 21 days but to no avail. And the second time for around 22 days and they failed again. Men would dig the whole day at the end of which they would leave to resume the work the following day."

Chasasa sighed to make sure that we were following what she was saying. I grunted to let her know that we were indeed keenly listening to what she was saying.

"Their workers would return the following day to find the work they had done the previous day gone without a trace, as if they had done nothing the previous day." She laughed sarcastically, as if to mock the naivety of the Europeans. "In the end they realized that a force beyond their power had brought the stone here to stay. The stone is indestructible. They referred to that force as divine or the stone as the work of their god and as mysterious but we say that the spirits brought it here for us and no god did so. And the spirits would not allow it to be taken away from us and it will never be taken away from us no matter by whom."

Chasasa laughed again, as if to poke fun at the men who had dug to remove the stone for 21 days and later for 22 days to no avail. "By 1906, they gave up all efforts to remove the stone and take it away from us. The spirits won the battle for us over them in their sacrilegious attempt to steal our sacred landmark."

When Chasasa stopped talking, Mifino, who was shorter than Chasasa, also talked and praised us for having made the pilgrimage to the shrine. "My children," Mifino said, "Our ancestors brought you here. You did well to pray to them. Both of you will survive any machinations bad or evil people will try to orchestrate against you, particularly you Chico who will go far away into the lands of strangers."

I was somehow wonderstruck to hear the old woman making what appeared to be a prophecy, which I believed; she was making an attempt to guess what my future was going to be and not because she had actually peered into my future. I did not think that she was a clairvoyant or a seer or a witchdoctor. I did not see how my going to the seminary at Zobue would become dangerous to me. Zobue was in Mozambique. There I would not jostle with the local people as no natives of the region lived within a radius of four kilometres of the school and the place was safe and well-protected from intruders. And in case of need, the Portuguese Army would come to our rescue in no time.

Then she looked at Zefina and smiled to her, showing the gaps that her lost teeth had created along her gum line, "you're fine, my daughter. You're as beautiful as Chasasa and I were at your age. You're like a magnet. Wealth will come to you and also a deceptive man."

Zefina had listened carefully to the granny before she pulled out her purse from her handbag and gave the woman 150 escudos to help her and her colleague to buy clothes and other things they needed. The women thanked her in unison after which we bade them farewell. From there we went to eat at a restaurant where we had hard porridge with well-prepared tilapia fish from the Zambezi before riding on the bridge back to Mutarara. Before we went onto the bridge, I told Zefina that we should not tell the teacher and his family that we visited the Sena Stone and prayed to the spirits there.

"He'll chide us for praying to what he will call false gods or evil spirits. We're versatile and he's not. We're flexible and he's not. We understand his Christian way of thinking and also the way the hoi polloi think traditionally. We want to be in tune and in peace with both worlds," I said. Zefina concurred with my thinking and we kept quiet about it after our return to the teacher's house.

In the evening, Zefina was her busy self and full of initiative and enthusiasm to help in the house. She told the teacher's wife to sit down and rest while she and her daughter called Catarina prepared dinner. The teacher and his wife and I sat down around the table and quietly chatted while their son did his school home work at one corner of the table.

When dinner was ready, the two girls brought it to the table before which they brought a bowl and a jug with water and soap and towels for us to wash and dry our hands with. Zefina held the bowl and Catarina poured water on our hands while we washed them before drying them with the towels.

The teacher said grace in Sena before we ate. The conviviality at the table was great as we slowly ate rice with fish. At some point, Zefina tried to joke about me and Catarina who had told her as they made dinner, that she was falling in love with me.

"Your daughter, Mr. Jonas, is a crushing beauty. How blessed I would be, if she could become the wife of my brother Chico here who wants to be a priest instead of looking for a girl to marry," she said. At that time I was still too young to marry and be a husband to any girl. But my cousin was simply expressing her wish for the future.

Although Jonas appeared to have sensed that what Zefina had said was a joke, he commented to her in his deeply Christian way in order to avoid offending her.

"I'd myself be happy to see Chico marry my daughter, but we leave to God what he thinks is best for Chico. If he wants to be a priest, that's God's will and His desire must prevail over our human wishes and whims."

Zefina realized that the teacher was rebuking her for what she had said by saying "over our human wishes and whims." She stopped dead in her tracks from pursuing the matter in order to avoid clashing with him because the teacher's sense of humour was so different, and so narrow, from hers, that their minds would not rhyme on the matter.

Chapter 17

We went to bed early after dinner that evening because we were tired from our trip to Sena and also because Zefina and I needed much rest as we would be leaving for Tete the following day. I slept in the same room as the teacher's son while Zefina slept in another room with Catarina. I slept uninterruptedly and woke up the following morning with a lot of verve for the journey.

There is a railway at Mutarara that branches off the main Beira to Malawi railway and goes to the coal-mining town of Moatize to the north. We boarded the train to Moatize at around 10:00 a.m. with many people, some just hitching a free ride to villages along the way and most going to Tete. How ironic that all those people were going to welcome and cheer a man who embodied our colonial subjugation!

The train we took was a combination of passenger and goods wagons more than a quarter a kilometre long. After huffing and puffing, it chugged and began to move first at low speed before gathering momentum and going fast. Trees and grass appeared to race in the opposite direction as the train speeded past them.

It went through scrubland with grass, through low-lying thorny shrubs and small trees, through dense forests, stopping only at stations where some passengers dropped and to pick up more people. At a place, the train went through a hill where the railway was built. I wondered at the immense work with machines and dynamite that was used to remove the stones and debris to enable construction to be made through the hill.

It was around 7 or 8 p.m. when the train reached Moatize. It was dark but the station was illuminated with electricity. From the train, we were led by white officers to big buses to take us to Tete about 20 kilometres to the west of Moatize. There must have been more than twenty such buses, standing in a straight line. As soon as the one in front was full, it left. And they filled up rapidly, so that there was a stream of buses with lights illuminating the bush country as they drove to Tete. It was amazing to see how efficient the colonial officers were because they were as incorruptible as Salazar, the dictator in Lisbon.

After the bus arrived at Matundo on the left side of the Zambezi, we were taken to the city across the Zambezi. The river was very narrow here and with a width that was dwarfed many times by that of the river by our village. We crossed it on a barge. A few years later the Portuguese built a bridge there to link the two sides of the river. After independence in 1975, the bridge was renamed after Samora Machel in honour of the man who in 1966 became the commander of the guerrilla army which fought against colonial rule before becoming its overall leader in 1969 when Eduardo Mondlane, the first leader, was killed in a bomb blast in Dar-Es-Salaam, Tanzania, where the rebel movement was headquartered.

Samora Machel was a staunch admirer of Mao Ze Dong and his ideology which I do not think he with his little education understood much. At independence he proclaimed Mozambique as the People's Republic of Mozambique after Mao's People's Republic of China and imposed Marxism-Leninism as the ideology of his regime. He also established *re-education camps* like Mao had done in China for those who were regarded as reactionaries and enemies of the people.

As for his personal style and demeanour, he copied Fidel Castro and wore Castro-like military uniforms and spotted a beard like Castro's. Like Castro, he would make speeches lasting many hours; sometimes as long as eight hours on a single day. People had to listen to him on pain of being imprisoned or sent to his re-education camps or even shot, if they were seen not listening to or not being enthusiastic about his speeches. The difference between the two was that Castro is tall and plump and Samora Machel was of medium height and slender and bony. He died on 19th October, 1986 when his Soviet-built presidential plane he was traveling in from Zambia to Maputo, strayed into and crashed at Mbuzini in South Africa.

Once in the city, we were led and walked to the north of the city to a sprawling sandy beach by the river teeming with people who had come from all over the District of Tete. We were out in the open and listening to people speaking in different languages or dialects and also laughing with different tones. Members of different tribal groups stayed together and never once were there scuffles between the different tribesmen or tribeswomen, except when men struggled to get hold of barrels of wine after they were delivered by trucks. The authorities had not organized people to supervise how the wine was to be distributed. It was a battle of muscles with big and full barrels being pushed and pulled this and that way with individuals shouting in different languages. They never sprang at one another for the possession of the wine and sometimes the wine ended up being lost when the barrels opened as men struggled to claim them and their contents.

Thanks God, I was not one of them because I did not drink nor did Zefina even ever think of doing so. For us seeing men struggling to own the barrels and claim a lion's share of the wine was free entertainment and we laughed a great deal.

It was quite an experience of sorts with men and women lying and sleeping on the sandy ground and never once did crocodiles crawl from the water to come ashore to snatch or drag anybody sleeping a few meters away from the fast moving water of the Zambezi. The huge crowd at the beach intimidated them. Zefina and I spread one of our blankets on the sand far away from the water and covered with another blanket, we slept with our clothes on and sharp knives by our hands for protection or defence and counter attack, if someone attempted to disturb us. Zefina needed to be fully and tightly dressed to prevent being raped. There was no cacophony caused by attempted rapes at night and men slept with their wives quietly without making love. I cannot remember whether armed policemen watched over us or patrolled as we slept to prevent disorderly behaviour or attempts at rape. No rape or unruly behaviour took place during the three nights we slept there. I do not think that the forces of law and order were very far away from us.

The following morning, we washed our faces with our hands at the water's edge of the river. We felt like plunging into the river for a swim but could not do so as we did not know whether it was safe from crocodiles in the way we knew which sections of the same river by our village were safe from the beasts.

There were several posts at the camp site at which people received food all the time. As there were a number of such posts, people did not stand long to get food which was given freely and generously. People were given maize meal flour, beans, canned sardines, or dried cod for lunch and dinner. In the day the army brought plenty of meat. We assumed it was buffalo meat mainly. Zefina and I did not want to get the meat because we did not want to eat the meat of animals we would not eat under normal circumstances.

No one went hungry. It was amazing how much the colonial government could do for us when it needed our attention to glorify colonial rulers and how little it did to build schools, clinics and hospitals and roads for us. Not surprising; it was the way totalitarian regimes did business or behaved.

After breakfast on bread and sardines we received at the camp the morning of the day after our arrival, Zefina and I decided to go into the city and walk about and do some sight-seeing. The city itself was rather small but extremely well-maintained and clean as cities and towns in Mozambique under colonial rule usually were. And not anymore now after independence, when everything has gone to the dogs with decay and neglect having become the order of the day due to the incapacity of the new rulers to administer and govern the country efficiently, and the civil war that they and their opponents like to fight to the detriment of their country and of their people. We did not need guides. The tallest buildings were three-storeys high. There might have been some that were taller. We guided ourselves with the Catholic Cathedral by the river to the north as our lighthouse because it was big and its gothic appearance unmistakable. We started from the northern end to the southern end. There were no people around and about in the streets because it was still early in the morning but the place was already steaming hot and it became like a brazier as the day wore on.

When we reached the southern end, we entered the garden of an exceptionally big stone house with a large garden with flowers of different colours and the grass was well manicured. Gardeners tended it every day, no doubt. But we saw no gardeners that we could ask about the place. However, we knew that it was where the district governor Antonio Higino de Craveiro Lopes lived. He was the brother of Francisco Higino de Craveiro Lopes who had been a past president of the Portuguese Republic. The governor had been the regional administrator at Mutarara before being appointed district governor. Like all colonial officials, he was a no nonsense man but he had loved the Sena people and their traditional dances; he used to dance with people in villages he visited as our administrator. The people gave him the name of *mbala maluku*, meaning *the mad gazelle* for no other reason than his habit of appearing at places without warning, and leaving soon after without bidding farewell to the people.

I cannot remember how we recognized it as the residence of the district governor. Either it was a plaque announcing it as the governor's residence or we just recognized it as such. There were no fidgety or fierce faced armed policemen or soldiers guarding it. That was the great thing about the residences of the colonial governors in Mozambique up to the residence of the governor-general in the capital of Lourenço Marques; they were open places that were not fenced off and guarded by armed men or trigger happy goons who could fire without asking questions. So anyone could be in the environs of such residences because there were no laws or rules barring anybody from being anywhere in Mozambique because of the colour of their skin unlike in apartheid in South Africa where there were big boards saying BLACKS NOT ALLOWED and sometimes BLACKS AND DOGS NOT ALLOWED or in rare cases DOGS AND BLACKS NOT ALLOWED, thereby giving dogs the pride of place over Blacks. The messages were in Afrikaans and English, the two official languages, and not in the languages of the people to whom the warnings were directed like in Zulu, Xhosa, Tswana, Sotho, Swazi, Shangaan and other native languages.

In Mozambique, in theory, we were all Portuguese citizens but the white settlers and the assimilado blacks like

Zefina and me that had the status of Portuguese citizens, were more equal than the natives with the status of *indigenas* we could push around and treat in a less than kind manner. But even the *indigenas* were not forbidden from being anywhere they wanted to be. The only thing that barred them was lack of means. Anyone with money could go to restaurants provided they wore shoes and they could be treated and served in similar manner. Anyone without shoes including even whites, were barred entry. In the army soldiers, of all races lived, trained, and ate together. In the past, it had not always been like that. Blacks with less or no education ate separately from the others. That was later abolished.

A short distance away to the south-west of the palace was a big mosque, beautiful and new. Perhaps it was the newest building in the city. It was the first time I had seen a mosque and I knew it was one either instinctively or perhaps I had seen pictures of mosques in our history textbooks. The building was like a child of yesterday compared to the Catholic cathedral that must have been built at the beginning of the 20th century or even at the end of the 19th century. The Portuguese had been at Tete and Sena since the 16th century. From the palace of the governor, we walked due north-east and ended up chancing on the residence of the then late Catholic bishop Feliz Niza Ribeiro, with a plaque announcing it as the bishopric. We hung around but saw nobody there. We knew the bishop, having seen him several times at our regional mission when he came on pastoral visits. I was to see him more frequently when he made pastoral visits to Zobue Seminary.

After the end of our tour, we went back to the camp site after I resisted Zefina's suggestion that we go to stay in some lodge in the city. I told her that our adventure would lose its meaning because we would see very little of what was going to happen, if we went for comfort and sequestered ourselves in the room of some hotel or lodge.

For the same reason, I told her that we should not eat at restaurants and that it would be much more fun if we made our own food at the camp site like everyone else did. She agreed with me and we returned to the camp.

I advised her to spare her money for what she had intended to do. She had decided to move to Mutarara and do business and live in the town. I knew that with her resourcefulness and determination, she would be successful in business in which she wanted to buy food from the growers, have it ground into flour, and package it for sale. And with time, she would extend her activities to other commercial sectors.

Back at the camp, we made our meal with faggots on a triad of stones that people used to prepare meals. Anybody could use any triad as long as other people were not using it. No one claimed ownership of the cooking triads as they were temporary and the municipal workers would collect them and throw them away after people returned to their villages.

Chapter 18

President Américo Tomas was going to arrive in the afternoon of the second day after our arrival. There was much expectation in the air and much excitement on the part of the residents of the city and of those like us, who had come from the various areas to see and welcome him, or at least to catch sight of his fleeting figure, if we could at all. Everyone received paper flags and I had two, one in each hand, and Zefina also had two.

As we were about to eat our breakfast of bread, canned sardines and plain tea that morning, there was a commotion at the southern end of the camping site. *Senhor* Antonio Higino de Craveiro Lopes, the district governor, had arrived and was speaking. He was speaking to people after stepping out of his car where it had stopped and was telling them that the campers should begin to move to the airport around noon to welcome the president who was going to arrive at 3p.m. His message was relayed from mouth to mouth until everyone knew the message he had conveyed.

People did not wait until noon before starting to go to the airport. Their enthusiasm was reaching fever pitch with traditional dancers moving to the airport whilst beating on drums and dancing: colourfully dressed women and their choirs left for the airport while singing and ululating. Representatives of each area of Tete District carried posters on wooden stakes welcoming the president and declaring undying loyalty to Portugal, with some posters stating that we would be forever Portuguese. Young boys and girls like me and Zefina carried and waved paper flags. Zefina and I were able to take up position right at the edge of the airport close to the area where the planes were going to land because we wanted to witness the event from close quarters.

As we stood with much patriotism bubbling in us and perspiring in that pitiless heat of the city, we saw a big military guard of honour approaching us in four files with mostly white soldiers and some black with their rifles in their hands. Four black soldiers with drums led the parade. We cheered them on as they marched to mount the guard of honour and waited for the planes to arrive. After they stopped, they relaxed and stood at ease.

Excitement from a sea of people intensified as we waited for the president. Our region of Mutarara which had more people in the city because of the carrying capacity of trains was the most prominent amongst thousands of people at the airport. Whites and blacks were together with no places reserved for whites or blacks. If Portuguese colonial rule was reprehensible in many ways, at least the Portuguese knew not to segregate people unnecessarily. That was their greatness that should not be denied or ignored. In a book in English the title and the author of which I do not remember, I read many years ago in Canada, the author described the Portuguese as having been the "least race-conscious of the European colonizers in Africa." Perhaps the writer was right.

As we waited and people talked at the top of their voices so that their colleagues could hear them because of all the drumming and dancing and roaring in that sea of humanity, we began to hear the roaring thunder of planes approaching. I saw the soldiers snap to attention, open their mouths to bare their teeth before clenching them and closing their mouths again, as if biting something in anger.

I did not understand why they had to open their mouths and clench their teeth. What was that about and for? Was it some kind of collective madness? Or was it to reaffirm their loyalty to the state?

Before long, we saw six planes, including one with the words *Air Rhodesia* inscribed on it, land one after the other. I did not know who came in the Air Rhodesia plane; perhaps the British colonial governor of Southern Rhodesia, for that year of 1964, Southern Rhodesia was still a crown colony until in 1965, a band of white rebels led by Ian Smith unilaterally declared it as the independent state of Rhodesia. I am in no doubt that the plane had come from Southern Rhodesia and not from the other crown colony of Northern Rhodesia which became independent in October of that same year of 1964 as Zambia, with Kenneth Kaunda as the prime minister before he later became the president of his new country.

Yes, the Portuguese and the British were historical allies since the 1370s. If I remember my lessons of history I learned at school in Mozambique, there were Portuguese kings like King John I who married a princess from the House of Lancaster and English royals who married into the Portuguese Royal House. The two countries had, or still have, the longest alliance between any two countries. During the scramble for colonies at the closing of the nineteenth century, however, the two allies were at loggerheads and Britain even threatened war against Portugal because the Portuguese had claimed that the territories from Angola to Mozambique were Portuguese. Portugal backed down because it would have been no match to British military power, particularly against its navy which then ruled the waves.

Out of one of the planes stepped the president with the governor general and the commander-in-chief of the Portuguese forces in Mozambique and they were received by the district governor as the people acclaimed with cheers and shouts of excitement. The president, the governor-general, and the commander-in-chief inspected the guard of hour before being led by the district governor to receive a bouquet of flowers from a little black girl who was with another little white girl and a little mixed race girl. That combination of the three races was Portugal's idealization of itself, at least in theory, as a multi-racial nation which also included Indians and Chinese both in Portugal and its overseas territories.

The colonial bigwigs made no speeches and I do not even recall whether they even acknowledged the thunderous welcome from the people. After getting the bouquet of flowers and kissing the child who presented it to him, the president and his entourage got into cars and went to the palace of the district governor where they stayed in the city. After the VIPS had left, Zefina and I stayed to watch the soldiers march back to their barracks. Their march was the most splendid and spectacular military march I have ever watched or will ever watch from close quarters.

As for us, guests in the city and for its residents, the ceremony had come to an end and the fun was over as we began to disperse to return to the campsite where we spent the evening and the night until the dawn of the following day when we began to head for the barges to take us across the Zambezi. As the first wave of people heading for the barges, we heard shrill cries from some people in the distance and word quickly spread that a chief from our area of Mutarara had collapsed and died at the dinner party the president had hosted in honour of the native chiefs of the District of Tete at the governor's residence last night. We felt sad but continued walking to the barges, as Zefina and I were intent on getting into a barge and crossing the river, so that we could board a bus of the many that had lined up on the other side of the river. This was to take us to Moatize where we wanted to board the first train leaving for

Mutarara so that we could return home to take care of our lives, relax and breathe fresh air and be ourselves again.

Zefina and I breathed sighs of joy as we boarded the first bus which departed as soon as it was full. On arrival at Moatize, we found three trains waiting to take us to Mutarara. We boarded the train that was going to leave first. As we took up our seats, Zefina made me lie on her lap before uttering some loving words. "Thank you darling for this unique opportunity for me to have gone to Tete with you," she said. "You're my brother and my hero."

I thanked her for her kind words. "You're my darling sister and my love. No one else will ever be dearer to my heart than you." We hugged and kissed with genuine platonic love with the old libidinous impulses of the past gone, as if wiped clean off the slate by some miraculous power; by the power of our ancestral spirits and of the Christian gods, as both they and our ancestral spirits would not permit incest between the two of us. Incest was abominable to our ancestors whom we revered and to the foreign gods we worshipped.

Before long the train started and left the station. It worked hard to return us to Mutarara. My days to go to the seminary were about less than two months away and I had begun to think of it already. I was determined to become a seminarian and part company with Zefina. It was hard for me, but life had to continue for both of us in our different ways.

Chapter 19

We arrived at Mutarara in the afternoon after taking the train at Moatize that morning. As soon as we left the train, Zefina and I went to Jonas' residence. We reached it in no time. As the teacher's wife had shown Zefina the place where she hid the key to the house so we could get in, if we returned when the family was not in, our first concern after unlocking the house, was to go and wash at the river which was about ten minutes' walk away from the house. A few days of not washing properly in Tete because of the presence of so many people at the camp site by the Zambezi which had made it impossible for us to wash without people watching us, was beginning to tell on us. We felt dirty and uncomfortable. We even thought that we were stinking. I think we were.

We took towels and soap and went down to the river where there were two places at which men and women bathed separately because members of the two sexes bathed whilst naked and traditionally men and women did not bathe together at rivers, streams or lakes. Zefina went to wash with some women at a corner where women were washing clothes, bathing, talking, and laughing loudly while I went to where there were a few men and bathed there.

We did not spend long at the river because we wanted to ride our bicycles into town and buy groceries before

187

returning to the teacher's residence. We had missed riding the bikes and we felt exhilarated when we saw them and rode them once again. Before returning to the teacher's residence, we once again went down to the river to see whether we could find any fisherman with catch to sell us, although we knew that it was unlikely that we would get fish in the afternoon as fishermen caught fish at dawn and brought it ashore for sale at the waterfront and at the town market in the morning.

There were no fishermen in sight and we were desperate, but later found two big boys who had caught some fish with hooks. They were happy to sell it to us because no one had ever bought fish from anglers who caught fish for home consumption and not for sale. They scraped the scales off the tiger and tilapia fish they sold us, cut them open to remove their guts before washing them in the water. They even carried it for us to the teacher's house, as we pushed our bikes back up the hill from the river. The family were still not back home yet. The teacher was still at school where his daughter and son studied whilst his wife was out in the field where she grew grain and vegetables for the family.

As Zefina knew everything about their kitchen, she wasted no time making herself busy with my help. I could not just sit down and watch her work because Jonas was not at home yet for me to sit and chat with and recount our adventures in Tete. She began to cook the fish with garlic, onions, tomatoes, and spices before making the porridge for dinner. When the family returned, they found dinner, warm and appetizing, on the table waiting for us all to eat. We were all hungry and wanted to eat; Zefina and I had not eaten since yesterday.

Before eating, we exchanged greetings and the family was pleased to see that we were back in one piece and also grateful that the enterprising Zefina had cooked for us. Jonas said grace for our safe return and the food God had placed on the table for us, ignoring that it was Zefina with my help who had made and placed the food on the table and not any god at all. I wished I could rebuke him for that, but I could not do so as it would not have gone well with his fundamentalist way of looking at things which made him attribute anything that was good or went well to God.

As we ate, our hosts were all ears wanting to know how our trip to Tete went, what we saw, what happened in the city, and how our return journey went. I talked at length and stressed that our trip had been worth the trouble because we had seen the city and many people from different areas of the district and their cultural displays, dances and performances. Jonas who had been to the city several times knew the place quite well but not his wife and children who had not been outside of Mutarara much.

They told us that during our absence they, as a family, had prayed for our safety and were convinced that their prayers had saved us from trouble or any disaster. Zefina and I were also happy that nothing untoward had happened to us at a place where there were so many drunken people who had been boozing their heads off with the wine the government had provided freely and in large quantities.

The teacher begged us to stay at his house for a whole week before saying that he, his wife and children had decided to regard us as members of their family. We agreed to stay, but not for a week, although we ended up staying for about a week or so with some days spent on an adventure to southern Malawi which had just become independent about two weeks earlier. Zefina also wanted to explore the town and find a house where she could live in so that she could do business at Mutarara. She felt that she had enough money to try her hand at some business. She also wanted to change and become a town girl because she was tired of living in a village with people she snobbishly described as uncouth, particularly the boys who thought they could entice her to fall in love with them and marry her.

"It's a good idea," Jonas said. "If you've money, invest it here to make more money. Don't just waste it, doing nothing with it, or doing a lot of useless things with it. Jonas told us of a house that a departing Portuguese settler returning to Portugal after making a fortune in town, had given him that he was not using; he took care of it all the same to ensure that it remained in good condition until he could find someone to rent it to or until he could sell it. "You can live there and use it for your business for free, provided you take good care of it," Jonas said. She exploded into a joyous laughter, perhaps not quite believing that the teacher was so kind as to let her use the house free of charge or that such a windfall had actually happened to her. Not having to pay rent would enable her to put more money into her business and employ someone to not only help her in her business but also help her take proper care of the house.

"God bless you, *senhor* Jonas," Zefina said.

I also thanked Jonas to reinforce Zefina's sense of gratitude.

I had an exciting idea that I had not discussed with Zefina because I had not regarded it as really important until that moment, I interrupted to announce it whilst we ate.

"Zefina and I will to go to Nsanje to see how things are going on there after the British granted independence to former Nyasaland. I've an uncle called Twobob who is the son of my late great uncle Joseph who was the younger brother of my grandfather Moises."

"That's a good idea," Zefina said. She was fired up. "We must go. I want to see uncle Twobob you've told me so much about him."

"I hope the authorities won't deny us permission to go to Malawi because the neighbouring country is a bad example to us," I said.

"A bad example in what way?" asked Jonas.

"Because Malawi is independent while the Portuguese won't quit Mozambique. If they turn us down at the border, we'll not go. We will come back," I said.

"You can use one of the bush tracks people use instead of using the border post," Jonas advised us.

"The people using bush tracks are regarded as natives or are Malawians coming to grow food in Mozambique and not like Zefina and I who are Portuguese citizens. If we do so and the authorities ever find out, we'll be in real trouble," I said.

Jonas, who had resisted taking Portuguese citizenship for reasons best known to him, concurred with what I said because he knew how the Portuguese would react, if we, as Portuguese citizens, used unorthodox ways to enter a foreign country. Zefina wanted the two of us to be in the good books of the authorities. She did not want us to become fugitives living on the run and in hiding whilst being sought out and hunted down like animals. I also did not want us to flee to Malawi and live there as refugees, if we did something that could go wrong. We loved our land whether under colonialism or not. It was the best place we had and knew better than any other place in the whole world.

There was no need for us to become vain or useless heroes instead of living our lives as good citizens under the law, albeit a colonial law, as some people would decry. I thought we had to make the best of a bad situation because the two of us could not change Mozambique's colonial situation on our own and trying to do so would be courting disaster. Although I then thought that independence was a good idea, I was not convinced that things would be hunky dory with independence in Mozambique. I had reservations about it because I was fully aware of the mess that Congo, having become independent in 1960, had become, with politicians there at one another's throats with the backing of militias and mercenaries and the involvement of the United States and France on one side and the Soviet Union on the other, supporting rival parties or sides to the detriment of the Congolese people.

Independence would be a good thing with wise leaders but a nightmare with power hungry dictators with no interest in the people and their freedom at heart. I hoped that Malawi would turn out to be different from Congo. And if we became independent, I wished that our country would become a shining example to the rest of Africa; some countries had already gone to the dogs soon after becoming independent.

The following day being a Saturday and a free day for Jonas as he did not teach on weekends, he took us to have a look at the house he had decided to let Zefina use when she moved to town. It was near his house. It was a brick and zinc-roofed building that had been built as a store. It was large with stalls and section for keeping goods and a self-contained back room with a bed, a table and three chairs, and running water. There was no better deal Zefina could have bargained for than that and for free as well. It was like a dream come true. As it were, what she needed was bedding, kitchen utensils, and cutlery. We bought pots and kitchen utensils in the afternoon of that day from an open market in town and took them to the house.

Jonas actually told us to try to live in the house while we were in town so as to have a feel of it before Zefina moved in, if we did not mind. Zefina and I thought it was a good idea because it lifted the pressure on space our presence was having in his house. We decided to buy food, cook, and eat in their house with them instead of us making our own food at the other house. Jonas also agreed to this proposal because he did not want us to buy food for them and also for ourselves, as, *la noblesse oblige*, we would do. In fact, we had bought fairly large quantities of food before our trip to and on returning from Tete. There was still some of that food left.

I once again thanked Jonas for his kindness and congratulated my cousin for her good luck that had come her way in the twinkling of an eye. Unfortunately, at that time though, I could not invoke our ancestral spirits to thank them for their blessing for fear of upsetting the religious Jonas. I was always mindful of his sensibilities and careful not to affront them and offend him. We did not mind him speaking in ways that belittled our weak belief in the Catholic Church.

"My sister will share with you the gains she will make from using your house, *senhor* Jonas," I said. "She's a kind-hearted soul." In order to talk in a fundamentalist way that pleased him, I added, "Fina will not fail in her efforts because Almighty God will help her."

"I attach no strings to my decision to let her use my house. What's the point of it sitting there with no one making use of it or living in it to take better care of it?" Jonas said. "I demand no money from her. I regard her as my own daughter and you as my own son. If God will bless her with success, I'll also feel blessed and will be happy."

"Let's leave everything in the hands of God. If I succeed, my success will be a blessing to you *senhor* Jonas and your family as well," Zefina said.

We inspected the building and its attached back flat before returning to Jonas' house. We were pleased with everything. We had an early dinner so that Zefina and I could be back at the other house while it was still light and bright. We were going to use an oil lamp when darkness fell as electricity to the house had been disconnected after the former owner had left, and there was no need to have it reconnected before Zefina moved in because something might happen that may prevent her from going to live in it.

Before we left, Jonas gave Zefina the key to the house. I had told him and his family that we would be attempting to go to Malawi the following day, which was a Sunday, when there would be minimal traffic between the two territories. We did not want them to be alarmed and start looking for us, if they did not see us. We left Jonas' residence while pushing our bikes with our belongings on the saddles. The family escorted us there and left soon after arrival as they wanted us to go to bed early because of our trip the following day.

We did not go to bed as soon as we had planned because we thought that we needed some kind of adventure in town. We rode to the shopping centre where stores were open up to 8p.m. We bought some sugar, tea, and canned sardines and bread and returned to the house where we made tea and drank it slowly before retiring to bed.

As there was only one bed, we slept in that bed and covered ourselves with the same blanket. We slept soundly without interruption of any kind and no fear of wild animals as had happened at the two streams where we spent nights on our way to Sofala. We had gone to bed and decided to sleep as much as possible in anticipation of the adventure on the following day. When the day broke, we continued to sleep until 9 when we woke up. I washed while Zefina prepared breakfast after which she went to wash as I spruced myself up. When she was dressed and ready, we sat down and ate breakfast while chatting about what might happen to us in a foreign land where we were going without being sure that we would be able to find my uncle. What if he had left Nsanje and had gone to Blantyre or Limbe I asked myself. Blantyre and Limbe are twin cities of Malawi.

Chapter 20

We left the town by 10 o'clock riding our bikes with the Portuguese paper flags; we got into Tete with them flying on our handlebars. We cycled on a road running along the rail track to Malawi. After two hours of steady cycling, we were able to cover the twenty-seven kilometres between Mutarara and the Malawi border. We went into the immigration house where there was a white soldier who we told we wanted to go to Malawi after showing him our citizenship certificates. He was actually pleased to see us displaying the Portuguese flags on our bikes. He made us sign declarations in which we wrote our names and declared that we would be back in Mozambique in three days.

"Hope you'll not go to Tanzania to join a terrorist organization there and later come to fight against your country," he said.

"What terrorists are you talking about?" I asked him. I had not understood what he was talking about.

We had heard nothing about a terrorist organization that had been formed in Tanzania to fight Portuguese rule in Mozambique, but the soldier knew better as he was well-informed by the Portuguese intelligence service or he himself was part of the Portuguese military intelligence service."

"We can't fight our own country. We're Portuguese to the core of our bodies and souls," I said. "If there are terrorists against us, we will fight them tooth and nail or to the last drop of our blood to wipe them out."

The officer stamped our declarations after signing them and making photocopies of them so that we could show them here on our way back to Mozambique. He kept the originals in a drawer behind the counter which he locked with a key. He gave us the copies before wishing us good luck and opening the door for us and the gate to enter Malawi where we removed the Portuguese flags from our handlebars as soon as we were out his of sight; we could not ride our bikes in Malawi displaying the Portuguese paper flags, that would be an insult to the Malawians who could harass us for insolence that according to them was typical of us the Portuguese. Malawians referred to anybody from Mozambique as *mapwitikizi* meaning the Portuguese and regarded us all, blacks and whites, as an arrogant lot. They said that we were all Portuguese regardless of whether we were black or white. "*Onse ndi mapwitizi*," they said in their predominantly Chewa language, to mean that "these guys are all Portuguese people."

We did not go through any immigration process in Malawi as the Malawians did not have a border control post at the border. Their immigration was about five miles inside their territory from the border. We bypassed it using a side track around it which the Malawian villagers used. We saw a policeman in uniform at their control post as we rode by from a distance. He might have thought that we were Malawian villagers. Their control post was mainly for people driving cars or using vehicles transporting goods between Mozambique and Malawi and not for pedestrians.

After biking for two hours on a dirty road in a territory covered in grass and short trees that was heavily infested with hyenas at night between Mozambique and Malawi, we reached Nsanje. I could no longer remember where uncle Twobob's residence was in the area, as I had visited him when I was a young boy. As the people of southern Malawi are Senas, we had no trouble communicating with them. We went about asking people who did not know the man until we found one man who said he knew the house and the man we were looking for. I was relieved because the possibility of being stranded in a hyena-infested area and of me and my cousin having to spend a night in the open without huts and water as we had been blessed with on our trip to Sofala, scared me and was forbidding.

We entered Twobob's compound while pushing our bikes, their wheels making light noises on the ground. When he saw us, Twobob gawked at us, not knowing what to make of our approach to his residence. He no longer recognized me as he had last seen me when I was a small boy and I had changed a lot physically since then. I explained to him who I was after which he exploded with joy.

"Blood of my blood," Twobob said. His wife and children came to us and congregated around us before welcoming and asking us in. Before long we were shaking hands, patting on shoulders, smiling and laughing with Twobob's boys and daughters who were born after I had last seen their father who was then not yet married. His sons chased a hen to be slaughtered for a welcoming meal for us.

"And who's the beautiful girl with you? Is she your wife?" asked Twobob fixating his eyes on Zefina.

"I'm too young to have a wife, uncle," I said. "She's my cousin. Her mother is my mother's older sister."

When Twobob's sons realized that we had come from Mozambique, they began shouting the word *mapwitikizi*. I felt uncomfortable being called Portuguese in Malawi for fear of Zefina and I being harassed as arrogant persons. But their shouts of mapwitikizi did not cross the boundary of their compound and did not spread beyond my uncle's residence and no neighbours of theirs came to gawk at us and object that we were in their village, as if we were objectionable aliens from another planet. And to make sure that they did not continue calling us Portuguese, I told them that I did not like them calling us Portuguese, and that if they did not stop, Zefina and I would leave right away. Their father also weighed in because he did not want to be known as having played host to arrogant Portuguese guests from Mozambique.

Knowing that we could not be in Malawi without identification papers, the following day Twobob took us to the local chief, who was a great friend of his, who without hesitation, issued us with ID cards without asking questions or demanding bribes. Those cards made us Malawian citizens who could live and settle in Malawi. They carried our names and stated our village as Nsanje and our false dates of births and bore our photos. At that time, getting Malawian citizenship was that simple for Africans from neighbouring countries and we could have stayed in Malawi right away without returning to Mozambique, if we had wanted. But we wanted to be in Mozambique and leave only if the situation became politically unbearable, which we did not expect to happen and we hoped that it would not be difficult in the near future or in the future.

As we had not gone to Malawi as fugitives and we did not want to live in that country, although we felt blessed for having its citizenship IDs, we also wanted to return to our beloved region of Mutarara. We did not want to lose the citizenship cards of Malawi either because we felt that we might need them one day, if the political situation in Mozambique became violent and we had to seek refuge in Malawi or enter Malawi. Upon our return to Mozambique, we had to keep the matter of the cards to ourselves and not talk about them to anyone, otherwise the Portuguese authorities would arrest us and throw us in prison, which would not be much fun, if it happened. We wanted to be free like birds and enjoy life with all the good things it had to offer us.

There was not much that happened while we were in Malawi. I helped Twobob with repairs he was making to his compound while Zefina accompanied his wife to their field and helped her cook meals after returning from the field. And after two days, we left Nsanje to return to Mutarara. At the immigration, we handed back the copies of the exit declarations that the soldier who allowed us into Malawi had issued to us, with no questions asked to declare what we were bringing back from Malawi because we had brought nothing with us. We were not even searched and we passed the border post without our Malawian IDs being discovered.

Back at Mutarara, we once again fraternized with Jonas and had meals with his family while staying and sleeping in his other house he had placed at Zefina's disposal. Zefina felt that she had no time to waste as she had wanted us to go to the village and collect the money she needed to start her business with. She wanted me to return to Mutarara with her because she wanted my help. I was eager to help her, as there was nothing else I could do at home in our village while waiting to go to Zobue.

As sleeping on the same bed with Zefina was making me increasingly uneasy, I told her that we should not go on sleeping in the same bed indefinitely. So we went shopping for a bed and got a simple metallic bed with a mattress for a very cheap price and we bought some bedding and pillows. As there was only one bedroom in the back flat, we slept in the same room but in different beds. She was as comfortable with the arrangement as I was.

Chapter 21

Back home I went to my parents and told them that I was going to help Zefina start a business at Mutarara and that I would go from there to go to the seminary. My parents were happy to know that I was going to help her because they liked her and she liked them greatly as, when I was at the mission school, she had always gone to see them once a week to check on them and make sure that they were fine. And Zefina's parents also appreciated that I was going to help their daughter and thanked me for having taken care of her during our trip to Sofala and to the far flung Tete.

"We took care of each other," I told them. I wanted them to know that our companionship was not a one way street in which I helped their daughter but a two-way road in which we took care of each other to ensure our mutual safety. "I like Zefina. She's very beautiful. I wish I could marry her if we did not have some common blood."

Uncle Lino and aunt Albertina laughed after hearing my frank and daring words, which, coming from a close relative, some parents might have regarded as provocative or as insolent. Zefina was also amused. She was pleased that I let her parents know what I thought of her while bewailing our star-crossed situation.

"Marry her if you want. We'll look the other way," aunt Albertina said. I knew that she, as a spiritual medium who enforced the laws higher forces had decreed, would be daggers drawn if we took her joke seriously and thought we could marry, and went ahead to try to do so.

"The problem is not with me," her father said as if to enforce the ban preventing us from coming together as a couple. "You and I have no common blood, but you and Zefina are star-crossed because your mothers are blood sisters. I know that some other tribes allow marriages between close relatives like the two of you, but not us the Sena people."

What my aunt and my uncle said proved that I had been wrong to believe that they were so naïve as not to think that there was a strong amorous attraction between the two of us. Our mutual obsession with each other had told them a story and they only trusted that we would not cross boundaries which we did not. My aunt with her amazingly uncanny intuitiveness would have known it without being told, if we had made love. She probably knew what Zefina had done to me when I was a very young boy who could not perform, but regarded it as nothing, or certainly not as incest, as I had not messed up her virginity because I was just a small boy.

From the home of my parents I collected all I had wanted to take away, my clothes and books. I did not have much to take away. My father gave me some money so that I could buy more clothes at Mutarara before heading for the seminary. Zefina also collected more clothes and books to read during her spare time but left most of her clothes behind. She would need them when she went back home to breathe the purer air of our village, as she put it. She regarded Mutarara with its incessant road and rail traffic and military planes taking off and landing all the time, as a polluted and smelly place because of the gases that land and air traffic emitted, although she liked it better than the village for being an urban area.

We did not stay in the village long. With Zefina smelling business success in the air, she was eager to start straight away. July had gone by and we were in early August. The clock was ticking on fast for me to leave for the seminary in early September and Zefina was becoming uneasy with my decision to go so far away from her and be about 400 kilometres away from Mutarara. She wanted me to give up the idea so that I could stay and live with her at Mutarara.

I remonstrated with her and told her that I stood to gain by going to the seminary where I would acquire more education which could help me to understand the world better and perhaps help me get a lot of money in the future. I told her that I was not so sure whether in the end I wanted to become a priest. Being the adolescent that I was, I did not think that I wanted to have a wife yet. At that time, I had two girls in mind, Gwedje's sister Maria or Catarina, Jonas' daughter at Mutarara, if it came for me to have a wife which would be six to seven years from then, 1964, when I would be about twenty years old or so. She finally agreed with my ideas, saying that they were sounder and made more sense than me staying with her doing business. She once again stressed that she was not keen on having a husband at that time, and that one of the reasons why she had moved from the village was to avoid being harassed by uncouth boys who were asking for her hand in marriage.

We rode back to Mutarara on our bikes and went straight to the house that Jonas had made available for her before going to greet him and his family on the afternoon of the following day. We had been going about town to take stock of the existing business so that Zefina could do something different and not have to compete with them. She did not want to be a merchant of clothes like most other businessmen. As she had already planned, she decided to buy and stockpile maize and sorghum from producers and set up a flour mill to grind and package flour for sale. There was no such business in the town and most

African families were still using pestle and mortar in their backyards to make flour.

Her decision to acquire such a machine was a big costly gamble which could pay big dividends after acquisition in Tete and operation at Mutarara. We ordered it through a businessman who ran a business between the two urban areas. The man was honest. Zefina had given him a lot of money to pay for the machine and he could have taken off with it or he could have denied that she had ever given him money and nothing would have happened to him as she had not involved a lawyer in the transfer. He brought the machine himself and helped us to set it up as he had experience operating industrial machines. The machine ran on gasoline.

After word had gone around that there was a milling machine in town and Zefina had advertised in the small community newspaper of the town, people were relieved and began to queue at her store, some coming to buy flour that she packaged and others bringing their grain to be ground for them for a fee depending on the size of the loads they took to her. Before long Zefina thought that as the machine was working five days a week,　if she was going to force it to work that way, it would break down in no time. She did not want to buy another one straight away. She decided to run it four days a week from Monday to Thursday when it ground and packaged flour to sell in her store and also ground the grain that people brought to the mill.

As she had engaged an experienced employee to operate the machine, she stayed mostly in the store where I helped her sell the packaged flour. As we sold the packaged flour at higher but affordable prices for most people, she soon began to make a profit. On Saturdays we went to buy grain from producers which a man with a truck delivered to the mill for a fee.

I was much pleased with the success of her enterprise. Before I left for the seminary, she employed an enterprising young girl called Isabela who was going to live with her and be her companion after my departure. She dreaded having to live alone, although it would be quite safe for her. But she wanted someone she could talk to and keep her company so that she did not get bored and become depressed.

Chapter 22

The time I was at Zobue Seminary from 1964 to 1967 is a story with details that are long enough to constitute a memoir of their own. My intention in revisiting this episode in my life is to have a brief remembrance of things past, delight my memory with them and give an overview of the feel and smell of the place and of what I did there; of what I gained or learnt from having decided to be there against the wishes of some of my friends like Gwedje, who had thought that I wanted to be a priest because I knew that I was an impotent man.

Despite my enthusiasm to go to the seminary, I was depressed to have to part ways with Zefina and head in another direction. I went to the railway station at Mutarara to team up with the old students returning to the seminary and new ones like myself joining the school for the first time. As I had known the date of the departure and the time we had to take the train bound from Moatize, I bade her farewell. She was crying as we hugged and kissed and said goodbye to each other. I also said goodbye to Isabela, her helper, after eating breakfast with them that morning of 12th September 1964. Zefina had decided not to see me off at the station because, as she said, she would not like to be seen crying in public in the presence of other people. She did not want to make a public scene in the presence of my colleagues. I agreed with her and I walked to the station alone carrying some money, a suitcase with my clothes in and two blankets, although I knew that I would be given more of those things at the seminary.

When I reached the station at seven-thirty that morning, I found the other boys from my mission already there. They had arrived on the afternoon of the previous day and spent the night in the open wrapped up in their blankets to wait for the passenger train that was going to leave for Moatize at eight o'clock that morning. I was excited to meet and reunite with the other students I knew. I shook hands with them and we hugged with smiles and laughter before I told some of them how I had spent my holidays. Some of them in turn also told me how they had spent their vacation days in their villages or travelling to other places to see relatives and acquaintances. Everyone had had a good time with their loved ones. We were sad that the vacation was over but excited to go to school for another year of hard academic work.

As eight o'clock sounded, we heard and saw a train chugging and emerging from the long bridge over the Zambezi down below and announcing its arrival with steam blowing before pulling up at the station, where it stayed for half an hour before continuing to Moatize. As soon as it stopped, passengers alighting there came out rather slowly as they were tired after an overnight ride from Beira or other places on the way before we scrambled into it, as if we were afraid that it would take off without us and leave us stranded there with no means to get to our destination.

As soon as we were on board, the old seminarians of my mission exploded with joy as they ran into their old colleagues from Manica and Sofala, who, like them, were also going back to school. For them, it was an exciting reunion of old boys. Knowing none of the older folks from the other regions, I stayed away from their excitement and was sure that with time, I would know them all and become friends with them. I remained quiet during the entire trip watching villages or grass or forests retreating behind us as the train sped along after stopping at different stations before reaching the station at Vila Caldas Xavier, a township well before Moatize that was named after a Portuguese conqueror who had quelled an anti-Portuguese revolt by a tribe called the Makololo, who appear to be a section of our tribe. After independence, the place was renamed to Kambulatsisi, which was perhaps the former name of the place after the name of a local chieftain before the Portuguese renamed it Caldas Xavier. The post-independence revolutionary government changed the names of many places that bore the names the Portuguese had given them such as Lourenço Marques which became Maputo and continues to be the capital city of Mozambique.

We left the train at Caldas Xavier and boarded a number of trucks that the priests had sent to whisk us away to the cool mountainous region of Zobue in the land of the descendants of the once feared Zimba cannibals, about 130 kilometres to the north-east of that station. The descendants of the Zimbas were now a peaceful and gentle people who spoke with hands clasped in front of them as respect to whomever they were talking to or even when talking amongst themselves. Most of them had become Christians or predominantly Catholics which was the only religion carrying out missionary work in their regions in Mozambique and also across the border in Malawi, where Scottish missionaries had also done much missionary work.

We arrived at the seminary after a rough drive lasting three to four hours over a rather broad, bumpy and dusty road. Although the Portuguese had built a vast network of railways in most of Mozambique to connect the territory with the neighbouring countries and to serve and connect various regions of the territory to seaports, larger than other European colonial powers had done in their colonies, they did very little to build roads. This they did hurriedly later when facing an insurgency, fighting to rid the territory of

207

colonial rule. Outnumbered and outgunned on land and with no means effectively to counter Portuguese air activity against them, the rebels relied mainly on landmines to destroy vehicles and demoralize Portuguese troops on land. And the unpaved roads were ideal for placing landmines and the rebels used them effectively. When they realized the importance of paved roads, it was too late and what they did was too little too late.

Despite the bad state of the roads, we reached our destination with no accidents and all in good shape, except one boy who kept throwing up because of motion sickness which only happened during the bumpy ride and not in a smooth-travelling train. The seminary was four kilometres to the north of Zobue town on the border with Malawi at the foot of the Mountain of the Cross, which was so known to us at the school because the first students to attend the school when it was founded in 1948 had planted a cross at the top of that mountain. The cross was there during the time I lived at the school. It is possible that the natives there had a different name for their mountain. I did not have the means to know whether they called that mountain a different name from us because we were barred from having contact with them, for fear of us seeing their girls and sinning in our thoughts. And Zimba girls were very pretty.

The first students had also worked very hard. They planted mango, lemon, orange, banana, guava, peach, and papaya trees, and an avocado tree, around the school. So the school was more than self-sufficient in fruit. We could never eat it all. And there were no monkeys who raided the orchards either. The school had a garden of its own growing cabbage and a full time local employee who tended it. Cabbage was one of our basic foods with beans and pork and beef from pigs and cows from a kraal belonging to the seminary. A pig was slaughtered or a cow was shot with a rifle every Saturday for us to eat with ntsima, the hard mill porridge, and sometimes with rice on festive religious days. We had a local man who cooked the food for us.

The Seminary was an immense U-shaped building of concrete with zinc roofing. Its right wing contained the chapel, class rooms, and the quarters where the priests lived and the left wing contained dormitories for us students and our dining hall. There were three detached buildings, one was our latrine, one was the kitchen with a bathing hall and another one was the granary containing maize which was ground into flour in a mill belonging to a German resident called Ludovic who lived on the opposite side of the Mountain of the Cross.

A bit higher up the incline by the base of the Mountain of the Cross to the north of the main building, there were volleyball and basketball fields. And further up still there were three soccer fields, one for young boys like myself then, another for middle older boys and yet another one for senior boys. The three fields stood side by side. The two smaller fields stood on the same level while the biggest one stood on much more elevated ground. We used the big field for physical exercise from Monday to Saturday, but not on Sundays when we had a break from most daily activities and students had more time to read and study or play outdoor sports or indoor games. The big field was also where our students played football matches against the Army usually. Sometimes the Malawian team from Mwanza opposite Zobue in Malawi came to play us, and we once went to play a return match in Mwanza.

And on that one day, we played a return match at Mwanza, our team trounced the Malawians on their own territory despite the aggressiveness of one of their players called Banda, as the president of Malawi was called. On our way back to Zobue, the displeased Malawians rained stones on us along the road but they did not hurt any one of us because the two trucks returning us to Mozambique were moving fast on their equally bad section of road, as bad as it was on our side in Mozambique. It seemed that the Malawians could not understand that our team from a colonized country could have defeated their team from an independent country. The defeat humiliated them and their youths decided to make us run a gauntlet of stones over twenty kilometres from Mwanza town to the Mozambique border.

I did not like to play soccer. It was not my favourite sport because I did not do well at it. I played it because students were organized in teams and, willy-nilly, everyone had to play, except when someone was ill. My favourite activities were physical exercises, running and above all reading. I would claim to be ill when my team was playing so that I could stay away and read novels, newspapers from Beira and copies of *La Libre Belgique* father Robert Roesems, our Belgian teacher of French, received from home and placed at our disposal after reading them himself so that those of us keen on reading in French, could read them as well. I also liked scouring the area on picnics and going on excursions into the forests or climbing mountains and seeing streams of pristine water spouting from their sources up the mountains, before cascading down mountain sides before becoming brown and muddy brooks when they reached flat areas down below. There were no big streams or lakes and fish was unknown in Zobue.

We spoke and studied in Portuguese and students could face consequences, if they were heard speaking their mother tongues which were only allowed on the first and third Sundays of every month. Portuguese united us all and made us friends. I became friends with boys from tribes the Senas despised as if they were untouchables or even, without evidence, described as cannibal tribes because people in our area said that they ate humans. I lived, ate, and played with them. No swear words or fighting was permitted. Above all, no one was to prefer some boys more than others. All those rules were good and mostly observed. As for friendship of all towards all, that was a dream.

The big problem facing the Catholic Church that imposes celibacy on its clergy was manifesting itself at the seminary. When people are deprived of intimate feelings with members of the opposite sex like Catholic priests are, there is greater tendency that, under sexual stress, some priests end up abusing boys or women. It was visible that some boys had struck up intimate friendships or were falling in love with other boys, although it was doubtful whether some of them ever engaged in gay activities which the Catholic Church then described as a cardinal sin with no reprieve from hell. Such activities, if discovered, would have led to the dismissal of those involved in them from the school.

I pretty much liked everybody, although there were some boys I just liked more than others. Also some boys liked me more than they liked other boys but it was nothing like being in love. At different times, three boys asked me to become their particular friends because, as they put it, they had fallen in love with me. I refused and told them I was in love with two girls named Maria and Catarina back home and I could return to them if I decided to quit the seminary anytime I wanted to do so. I did not want to be regarded as a boyfriend or a girlfriend by another boy and that was that with me. I now recognize the freedom of people to decide on their sexual orientation, including the freedom of same sex relationships.

If there is a field in which I excelled, it was in the academic field. In all the classes I attended each year, I earned great marks in all the subjects except drawing or art which has never been my forte or my cup of tea to put it in a very English way. I gained higher grades than anyone else in Latin and French, except in Portuguese where there was always someone with 17 out of 20 whilst I scored 16 out of 20. All the courses were marked out of 20 which was the equivalent of 100 per cent. A total of 8, 9, 10, or 11 out of 20 were weak marks. Totals of 12 to 15 were good grades and 16 to 20, great marks or distinction.

By the time I left Mozambique, I could speak French fluently but had no English at all as the school only started teaching English in the class that I was to attend in the following year of 1968, if I had not left the seminary. French, though important to me, proved to be of little use in the neighbouring countries that had been British colonies. Initially, the lack of English came to prove the chink in my armour when I resumed school in Nairobi in 1970 after interrupting my studies at Zobue in 1967.

My years at Zobue seminary proved to be a political revelation. Although politics was not part of our education, it came to us as a result of the evolving situation in Africa where the British and the French were granting independence to their colonies while the Portuguese dictator Antonio de Oliveira Salazar, vowed to stay put and never to relinquish his grip on his African colonies. Our Spanish, German, Belgian and Swiss teachers did not promote the assimilation policies of the Portuguese government nor did they discourage it. The 250 students, mostly Africans with a few mulatto boys and a Chinese boy called Adolfo Vieira who was a great friend of mine, had the status of Portuguese citizens. There had been a white Portuguese boy from Tete who had been a student there before my time. He had to quit after developing serious stomach problems, perhaps because his softer system did not agree with the food and the water which was tapped into pipes from the mountain side when it was still pristine and not from down below after becoming murky.

I ran into the boy while with Zefina in Tete where he told me about having been at Zobue as I was about to join and explained to me why he had to leave. The boy was infatuated with Zefina. I walked away and left the two of them to talk things over. But they did not agree. The boy wanted her to go live in Tete. Zefina liked the city for a visit but thought she could never live in it. And that was the end of their little chat. I did not feel sorry for the boy or for my cousin because they had attempted to establish a relationship, not breaking up an already existing one, which would have been tough had it been the case.

Although we stood up firmly and sang the Portuguese anthem when colonial administrators visited us and we made speeches welcoming the officers, expressing our undying sense of patriotism towards Portugal, the spirit of rebellion began to creep up in us slowly but surely, like cancer spreading in and eating up a body. Our sense of patriotism towards Mozambique waxed as that for colonial Portugal began to wane and a feeling of rebellion exploded in us when the leaders of the Portuguese Church in Mozambique, probably under orders from the Salazar regime, decided to kick out our European White Father teachers and replaced them with Portuguese Jesuit priests.

For me, the move to replace our teachers was the straw that broke the camel's back. The students were flabbergasted because of the political implications of the move and not that we were against the white Portuguese Jesuit teachers. How could we who took so much pride in the Portuguese Language we spoke better than most proud owners of the language, and cherished Portuguese manners and culture, be against them as individuals? Were we ourselves not Portuguese citizens? No one accused us of xenophobia because the Portuguese Jesuits were whites like our former European teachers.

I felt I had to leave Mozambique on any adventurous trip without knowing what would be waiting for me. Would I have left, if I had known that there would be monsters studding my path ahead waiting to wage war against me? And was the adventure worth the trouble? We shall see whether it was worth the trouble or not. I suppose it was worth the pain because I survived the pitfalls, overcame

213

difficulties, and triumphed over enemies. I gained much more in terms of experience and education than if I had stayed in Mozambique, where I might have ended up fighting with Portuguese forces against those who were struggling for independence, whose tyrannical ways I came to detest with as much intensity as I disliked colonial rule.

As for Zobue Seminary, it died a tragic death in the end, vandalized by men who fought their wars for political power and supremacy. The Zobue region became a battle zone in the war between Portuguese forces and pro-independence fighters which lasted ten years. It survived that bitter episode, pretty much unscathed, but it was totally destroyed in the sixteen year civil war that ensued in 1977 after independence in 1975, between the party that had fought for independence and another movement which opposed the totalitarian ways of the liberation movement with the support of the rebel regime of Ian Smith in Rhodesia and of apartheid in South Africa. Only one small section of a wall of the main building is still said to be standing, according to an old boy that made a trip to the site to check the situation on the spot and pay his tribute to our alma mater. What happened to what had once been one of the best schools in Mozambique is a crime, a shame and an insult to the youths of Mozambique who could now be there receiving a good and sound education.

Chapter 23

I can never say enough about my years at Zobue Seminary. Attempting to give a detailed account of those years would be a monumental task, if not an impossible one. I will, however, recount some exceptional events that remain indelibly stamped on my mind before the narration leaves Mozambique to give an account of my life in three, if not four, African countries.

To start with, I must say that Zobue Seminary was a place of intense prayer; so intense that the earth and the heaven reverberated with them and their power. As for myself, I just prayed as a matter of routine without ever being overly devout as a few boys we mockingly called *their Holinesses* were. I do not think that I was meant to be a fervent worshipper or a man of prayers, but I had to be in the chapel with everyone else for the morning mass after reveille and bathing at six o'clock. At noon, the chapel's bell rang for the *Angelus*, a prayer that reminded us that the Lord's own good angel let Mary know that she was about to become pregnant by the power of the Holy Spirit. When all the important prayers were said in Latin, we said, "*Angelus Domini nunciavit Mariae. Et concepit de Spiritu Sancto,*" followed by the Hail Mary prayer also in Latin. That prayer reasserts the Catholic doctrine of the divinity of Jesus Christ when it says that the "*The Angel of the Lord declared to Mary. And she conceived of the Holy Spirit.*" According to those words, Jesus is the son of God and in his gospel John goes further to state that Jesus he refers to as the Word, was with God and was God before descending to earth and being incarnated as a human.

When the Vatican thought that Catholic prayers should be said in all languages rather than just in Latin, a dead language, although it was the Catholic Church's language, millions of its followers could not understand it, we began to say it in Portuguese: "*O Anjo do Senhor anunciou a Maria. E Ela concebeu pelo poder do Espirito Santo.*"

The Benediction prayer was held in the chapel at six in the evening before dinner at seven and the nightly prayer before bedtime was also held in the chapel to say goodbye to God and implore him to keep us safe from mischief makers when we were asleep. We also said grace before and after every meal at the three meals we had daily. And on top of all those prayers, we also had to say individual prayers such as reciting the rosary and prayers the priests at confessionals prescribed to us to say so as to have our sins forgiven and regain God's forgiveness, favour, and grace. Prayers swamped us and they kept evil at bay and evil only visited the place after the place was abandoned as war loomed larger on the horizon, by which time I was already safely tucked away in Kenya, living a different kind of life and facing other challenges.

After describing the location of Zobue Seminary and noting its academic importance and the religious activities there, I must talk about some events that I lived through or witnessed because they actually happened and are different from fictitious events. The events may not all appear in this narration exactly in the order they happened.

The first event I want to revisit is an earthquake that struck the area one night. Being a mountainous region, it is not a surprise that it took place, although earthquakes can happen anywhere in the world and at any time. I cannot say whether I was dreaming or not at the time when it struck. That earthquake might have scored highly on the Richter scale but it caused no damage or loss of human life in the area as there were no storey-high buildings or a city. It did not hurt the villagers in their huts, although it terrified them as much as it did us at the seminary. We suddenly woke up from our sound sleep as the earth shook and our beds creaked and swayed violently and the high-ceilinged roof of the immense building rattled as if it were being torn away. If it had collapsed, it would have been disastrous as it would have trapped and entombed us with no hope of us ever being rescued.

In my dormitory as in all other dormitories, we jumped out of our beds and rushed to the doors in total darkness with one young boy in my dormitory repeatedly shouting the word war. No one tried to reach for a power switch after jumping out of our beds to light up the place. No one thought of doing so because there was no time to do so and we were only instinctively concerned with survival. It was as if we had been trained to avoid switching on power during an earthquake as it could cause fires. In a split second, more than fifty of us we already out of our dormitory and in total darkness found ourselves between the two wings of the building having arrived there at the same time as the boys from the other dormitories.

We were terrified to the core of our hearts and trembling with fear without knowing whether the ground under our feet could open up anytime and swallow us. We knew that a major earthquake had struck the area and we were all talking loudly about it when father José Latorre, the Spanish Basque who was the seminary's rector or father superior, came to us with a lantern in his hand to tell us that a big earthquake had hit the area and asked us not to return to our dormitories as a secondary bolt could strike again. And it did not take long before another bolt which was as powerful as the first one came, and we felt the earth under our feet shake and sway again. And the building held firmly and survived once again. People who have never had such experience with earthquakes as I did can never quite conceive of the terror that earthquakes can sow in the hearts of the people who experience them.

We remained in our night clothes with no one daring to sneak into a dormitory to pluck a blanket, any blanket, and rush out with it so as to wrap up with it. The dormitories, our places of sure comfort and safety, looked dark, menacing, and spooky from the outside. Fortunately it was during the warm season. If it had been during the cold season, we would have suffered a great deal as Zobue can be freezing cold.

We remained terror-stricken in the compound waiting for the day to break and see the sun, as if the sun was going to bring us salvation. It was only after the sun had started to appear that we fearfully dared to go into our dormitories to pick up towels and soaps, brushes and toothpaste and walk to the bath hall, instead of running as we did every day, to bathe in the large bath hall where there were two pools that were filled with water in the evenings and also about twenty taps. As a boy who had always enjoyed immersing my entire body in water, I never used the taps. I always plunged into the pools regardless of whether it was during the warm or cold season.

We were profoundly shaken and felt like mental and physical wrecks. Our minds could not let the earthquake go and our legs wobbled as we walked like zombies, as if our bones could not stick together. After washing and dressing, we went into the chapel and a special mass was said that morning to thank God for having looked after us and for having prevented any physical harm from affecting any of us. We pleaded with him to prevent any further earthquakes from occurring in the area again and God appeared to have listened as no more earthquakes hit us. It was after several days that we began to recover from the trauma, regain our composure, feel reassured that the experience was past us and started to forget the event.

About a week later, we heard that the earthquake had caused a casualty at Zobue town itself. A soldier broke his arm as he jumped from his bed and fell to the ground. We did not know how severe his injury was. We did not want to know more about it simply because it would have kept us thinking about the earthquake and made us live with perpetual fear. We wanted to be liberated from the terror that nature had unleashed against us and free our minds from it.

Another event which remains as fresh in my mind as if it had happened yesterday was what happened after Father Latorre, who was well-informed as he listened to the radio broadcasts from the capital of Lourenço Marques, had spoken to us at mass in the chapel. He had said that a severe drought had gripped Mozambique and that the situation was reported to be hopeless with the spectre of famine rearing its ugly head if it did not rain to permit the peasants to grow food. Even the mountainous region of Zobue was dry and badly needed showers or heavy rain in order to revive the vegetation. We were all moved before the priest decided that we would dedicate the following day as a day of prayers for rain.

We devoted the mass the following day to ask God to help his people in Mozambique and from the chapel we sallied out in a procession while praying and singing for about a distance of a mile before return to the seminary. Lo and behold! After four days, heavy rain began to fall in Zobue and all over Mozambique. The thirsty land needed water and was heavily soaked and some areas experienced light flooding which did not adversely affect their residents, as the water percolated into the ground or disappeared quickly after irrigating and fertilizing the land. And more rain came and irrigated the land.

Even if I did not wish to attribute the instant rain that followed to our prayers as many of us were convinced that our prayers had brought rain to the Mozambique, I also seemed to find it difficult to believe that it was a mere coincidence. I think that God heard our prayers and commiserated with the people of Mozambique. But God has not always commiserated with the poor people of Mozambique. He has sometimes abandoned them to their own devices when merciless men unleashed wars for the sake of political power.

He is not always pleased with us because of our transgressions and crimes against one another. Those in power violate human rights on a massive scale. Their actions lead to criminal wars which claim hundreds of thousands of lives and regress the beautiful country that is ours to the Stone Age and all that, in order for them to maintain power or for the others who oppose them to achieve power.

I sometimes heard father Latorre tell us about what was happening in the second half of 1960s. He seemed to be very keen on events taking place in what was then referred to as Red China. I heard him say that it was heating up there. The Cultural Revolution was the time from 1966 to 1969 or thereabouts, when Mao Ze Dong stopped all activities in China and forced the closure of schools and universities so that everyone could go to the countryside and engage in revolution and struggle against the enemies of the people. In particular, people who were dubbed as reactionaries and agents of imperialism who were paraded with cardboard placards hanging with strings from their necks sometimes with words like "I'm an agent of US imperialism. I deserve to die" on them. Obviously people who were forced to wear such cardboard did not write those words themselves.

In 2008, while doing a university course on the History of Modern China in Canada that was taught by a Chinese professor who was sent for re-education during Mao's rule, I was appalled to learn that over two million people perished as a result of the Cultural Revolution and about two hundred million people were negatively affected by it. Mao, the genius of manipulation, later turned against the Red Guards he had created to unleash the terror of his Great Proletarian Cultural Revolution when he realized that they were getting out of hand and they were becoming a threat to his own power.

On another day father Latorre said, "Red China has just tested a hydrogen bomb, which is a more powerful bomb that an atomic bomb."

The Zobue area was not known as a flight route for planes. When we occasionally saw planes, we knew that they were military planes from the airbase near Tete, about one hundred and twenty-five kilometres to the south-west of Zobue. The planes we had seen before that day when we got a big surprise were rather slow. They would drone and circle over us as if to survey the land or carry out air reconnaissance before returning to base.

It was at break time at around ten o'clock that morning when we were surprised by screaming sounds of two jets flying so fast almost near supersonic speed and so low that our hearts were struck with terror again, like the fear that the two earthquakes had sown in our hearts. The ground shook and the zinc roof of the giant building rattled with much noise when they passed over us. They were over Zobue town when I saw them first, as if heading straight into Malawi. I thought they were going to crash into a border mountain. They turned towards our direction before crossing into Malawi and in a split second they were over us and we watched them fly and disappear between two mountains to the north of us before returning and overflying us again. Then they went back to base. They were back in the afternoon of the same day flying in the same pattern as they had done in the morning.

At that time, the Portuguese Air Force in Mozambique had American-made F-84 jets. The F-84 aircraft had seen much action during the Korean War in the early 1950s where they had been in dog fights against Soviet-built MiG-15 fighters that the Soviet Union had supplied to North Korea and were flown by Soviet-trained Chinese pilots. America had given those F-84 planes to Portugal to help it bolster the western military alliance but Portugal sent them to Mozambique without American permission. The decision by Portugal to boost its military power in Mozambique with those planes caused much friction between the two allies. Portugal did not retain them in Mozambique for long. It send them to Angola where they were needed to counter Angolan nationalists who had started to take up arms to oust Portuguese rule from their country about four years before Mozambicans launched their armed insurrection.

After I saw the planes, I asked myself what had impelled the military to send their planes and make a show of force over us. Had they been tipped off that anti-colonial rebels were in Zobue? No, the rebels had not come there yet and it would be years before they would reach the area. Were they just training or saying goodbye to Mozambique before heading for Angola for real action? I did not know.

There was another surprise in the offing. Despite being ideal terrain for wild animals, Zobue did not really seem to have wild animals, perhaps because of its dense forests which were not ideal for herbivores which prefer grasslands with fewer trees because they eat mostly grass and their presence attracts carnivores. Apart from the hyenas we sometimes heard growling at night from a distance while we were safely tucked away from them within the confines of our dormitories, I do not remember having seen other animals like baboons raiding the seminary's orchards. I never heard lions roar or any other critters grunt or screech or squeal. Hyenas came to the seminary for the bones of the cows and pigs we discarded by the kitchen. They came at the dead of the night while we were in our dormitories and no one ever encountered them. As we had no dogs, they did not worry about barking or any other noises. The Zimbas did not appear to have dogs. They did not seem to like them like the Senas liked to have hunting dogs.

I do not even think that the Zimbas hunted wild animals like we did in Senaland. The most I saw around the seminary was a hare. Even snakes were rare. We killed a snake one day though. A group of us were walking in the bush to the north of the seminary when we saw a snake, a spitting cobra, with its body in the air gawking at a hare we had not yet seen and preparing to lunge at it and inject it with its deadly poison. As there were so many stones about us, we all picked up stones and rained them on the demon. It tried to run away from us but the torrent of stones landing on it was such that we killed it in no time. The hare that was startled when we began to lapidate the snake was also targeted with stones and killed. I do not know what the boys who took the hare did with it but the snake was burned to ashes. The incident with the snake was amusing, though not much of an event. It was a distraction.

There was a surprise for me one sunny morning when I saw the Spanish father Moreno with a band of Zimba locals. I modified his name and it is the only name I modify in my entire story because of some not so catholic aspects of the man I include without distortion. I prefer to alter his name in case he is still alive rather than fiddle with the aspects of the events concerning him because my story is about telling the truth regarding events as I witnessed or lived them. I believe that father Moreno was essentially a good man, although many of my former fellow seminarians would not agree with me on that account. He taught Portuguese and Bible studies mainly.

I saw him return to the seminary with a rifle that was used to shoot the cows with it in his hand with a bevy of locals carrying a leopard he had shot at a place to the north-west of the seminary. They had tied its legs and inserted a long pole through its legs from its head to its rear. The priest walked ahead as two men bore the dead cat with the pole on their shoulders and other locals walked silently behind them, as if in fear of the terror-inspiring cat, although it was dead.

I had never seen a leopard before, although I had heard many scary stories about the terrifying spotted cat. The critter, although dead, looked fearsome. Its eyes still radiated terror. Its teeth sent cold shivers down my spine and its claws were terrifying. Father Moreno only wanted its skin after the men skinned it. I did not linger around with them for long, as the bell had rung and I had to rush to a class. Before I left, father Moreno said something about the leopard to me and some other boys who might have been there with me, but I do not remember whether there were other boys with me there or not. I think there were one or two boys with me.

"The leopard had got into the chicken coop of a settler called Ludovic," he said. Ludovic was a German who lived quietly behind the Mountain of the Cross on the other side of the seminary. He was a technician who serviced our power generator and made sure that we had electricity at all times. He also installed any machines that were brought to the school and repaired them when they broke down. Something was said about his military exploits with the Wehrmacht or the German armed forces during the Second World War. He was also reported to have downed many allied planes, either as a Luftwaffe pilot or while operating anti-aircraft guns against allied planes.

He might have been a war criminal or a criminal against humanity hiding and living comfortably in a good house he had built for himself of bricks with a tiled roof, in the bush area of Zobue where he had a mill that also ground our maize for us at the seminary. I would not have been surprised if he were a former Nazi criminal. If he were a Nazi criminal, I do not even think that Ludovic was his true name. I did not think that he is alive now as he was already old in the 1960s. Salazar, Portugal's ruler was a master manipulator who cooperated with both Britain his country's historical ally, and Nazi Germany who he admired politically. He had SS officers train his army and the Gestapo train his PIDE secret agency. Even his youth organization was styled after the Hitler youth organization. This same man sheltered a million Jewish refugees during the war in Portugal.

I listened to father Moreno before beginning to trot to class, as I had to be there to pray with the other students before the class began.

"After gorging on hens, its stomach bulged and it was unable to get out through the hole it had used to get into the coop. When it heard Ludovic approach the pen this morning, it snarled and sent the German running back to his house before dispatching one of his labourers to come tell me to go shoot the cat. When I reached the place, I found men shaking with fear and with axes in their hands. I tracked the animal which had got out of the coop with the fearful men behind me, but they panicked when they heard it snarl. They made for the nearest tree where they were shivering with their axes still in their hands."

"It is a bad idea to run away from a leopard and climb a tree because the leopard is a good climber and that's how at night it gets baboons which suffer from night blindness as I have been told, while the cat sees as clear in the day as at night," I said before I ran to my class without waiting to hear the priest comment on what I had said. Perhaps he did not know as much about the behaviour of leopards as I did, although I had not killed one as he did that morning. I had spent my young days listening to stories about the characteristics of various African animals, particularly those which strike fear into the hearts of people such as leopards, lions, buffalos, elephants, rhinos, hippos, and crocodiles and mambas. The most demonized of the lot are leopards, buffalos, hippos, and mambas with mambas and buffalos being the kings of them all.

I came to know in Canada while reading books by Jim Corbett on the man-eating tigers of Kumaon in India, that despite its smaller size than the tiger or the lion, the leopard is the most fierce and dangerous of all the big cats. The Sena fear him more than they do lions who tend to be gregarious and move in prides in territories in which they will not allow other lions to trespass, whilst the leopard is a loner and stealthy. According to Corbett, one leopard in India was reported to have killed 500 people so much so that the matter raised alarm and was discussed in the British Parliament in London. In 1926, Corbett killed the leopard of Rudraprayag after it had killed 125 people.

The following day, I was with father Moreno who had come to know me more than other boys of my class because I had scored the highest mark, 18 out of 20, which is 90 percent, in an end of term exam in the Bible studies he taught my class. He made me stand up before telling the class that I had scored the highest mark and congratulating me on my unparalleled achievement. The exam had been mostly about the Books of Genesis and Exodus of the Old Testament.

"Father," I said. "Are you happy you got your leopard's skin?"

"It's now drying. I'll take it to my family when I go to Spain."

"They'll be happy with you, won't they?"

"Of course, they will. Neighbours will envy them."

He smiled to me, which he rarely did to people, before saying, "the men who came with me almost came to blows yesterday."

"Why?" I asked him.

"Each one of them wanted to eat heart of the leopard, not the leopard itself. They believe that eating a leopard's heart can make them very brave and courageous."

I was not surprised because my own tribesmen think that eating crocodiles is very good as it can make a person acquire crocodilian qualities and become a survivor like the saurian which has been on earth since prehistoric times. We also discourage pregnant women from eating weird-looking animals like salamanders, tortoises, hippos and others to prevent their babies from resembling those animals after they are born. Most pregnant women will eat vegetarian food or pretty fish, avoiding ugly looking ones.

On another day, father Moreno was asked to go and shoot a python which had eaten an animal and was unable to move as happens with pythons after swallowing a big meal. After he shot it, several Zimba locals brought it to the seminary. The priest wanted its skin only. I never asked him later what the men did with the fresh meat after skinning the serpent. It is possible that they divided it among themselves and took it home to eat or the priest had them bury it.

Despite my amicable chats with him, father Moreno was not much liked at the seminary. He was dour and mean when talking to the students and used degrading language. Some boys even thought he was a racist. I did not think he was a racist as there was evidence that he liked black women, but he definitely did not relate well to most students. He seemed to be on good terms with the locals who went to him to have their pictures taken for official documents particularly those required for Portuguese citizenship certificates. He appeared to exploit his profession as a good photographer when women, particular young girls, went to him for pictures. After taking their photographs for official documents, he would ask those pretty and westernized female descendants of the Zimba cannibals to crouch so that he could take more pictures of them. The unsuspected girls would crouch and their skirts kind of opened up and exposed their inner thighs and underwear. He photographed them in such positions and later developed and kept the pictures for himself.

One day he made the mistake of showing the pictures to boys in the presence of father Jean Ribeau who baptized me at Traquino mission and who had slapped the boy Gordinho there for laughing at his accent. The puritanical Ribeau was not amused when he saw some of the pictures. He told him directly in his dragging French Swiss accent in Portuguese: "*Moreno, amigo. Tu nao devias ser um padre. És sujo. És um porco, amigo,*" meaning "Moreno, my friend. You should not be a priest. You've a dirty mind. You're a swine, my friend."

Moreno kept quiet and stopped showing us the photos and we were silent. We were unable openly to support either Moreno or Ribeau, but we supported Ribeau because we felt that Moreno should not have taken advantage of the naïve girls to take scandalous snapshots. I was embarrassed with the whole incident, although it was not my shame but Moreno's. No one was amused or laughed. I did not know what Moreno did with the pictures later, whether he destroyed or kept them for his wicked satisfaction. Did he masturbate while looking at them?

We knew that the two priests would not fight. If it had ever come to blows, I would have no doubt as to the outcome. Ribeau, a sturdy former soldier of the Swiss Army, would have made a mess of Moreno, a soft and slightly plump civilian survivor of the Spanish civil war which saw Francisco Franco emerge as the indisputable ruler of Spain and who ruled his country with an iron fist as *the Caudillo de Espana pela gratia de Dios* or the leader of Spain by the grace of God.

Father Ribeau was a very good man but he was too serious for my comfort. His only slight show of humour I can still remember was while at Traquino Mission and he was talking about the evolution of the human race when he said to me and the other boys that "I believe it's the white men who have descended from apes because we whites have more hair on our bodies than you blacks." He made his joke without smiling and with a serious tone that failed to bring up his intended humour. As a joke what Ribeau said can pass but may not even be distantly supported by scientific evidence.

The work of the anthropologist Rd. Leaky in East Africa indicates that the human race began its evolution as individuals of one kind at Olduvai Gorge in Serengeti in what is today mainland Tanzania. An ape-like human skull from Olduvai Gorge I had seen in the Nairobi Museum in Kenya was carbon dated to two million years old. Recently a human-like foot print was discovered at Olduvai and was found to be two million years old. Evidence strongly supports the theory that humans originated there and from there they spread to the rest of the world.

As to why the same people subsequently acquired different and distinct physical features, no reasons have been offered to explain this phenomenon. I am no scientist, but I tend to think that some factors such as food and climate came into play to effect genetic mutations. But all humans regardless of race retain the same universal traits such as the same distinct blood groups, the same emotions of courage and fear and cowardice, love and hate, hunger and fullness, and all other aspects.

Kabulunge, my autocratic maternal grandmother who brooked no contradictions to whatever she said, once explained to me and some of her other grandchildren about how the humans acquired different skin colours after having been created by God as blacks. It is one of our myths but I could not dare tell her that it was just a story like any other as she would have jumped on me and trashed me so thoroughly that she would have turned me into a sorry sight. For her the story was true. It happened. And that was that and she would have no nonsense from anybody contradicting her on that account.

"There were no humans as the Spirit of Mulungu hovered over the earth," she said. "Then God made three humans and they were all black. One day the Almighty ordered them to go in a certain direction to a place where there was a pool where they were to wash. Upon reaching the spot, the men found a pool with boiling water and the men were afraid to enter it and wash. They hesitated but feared that they would anger God if they went back to him without washing. One of them entered the pool and screamed as the water boiled his skin. He stayed there for a fairly long time despite the heat. When he came out, he was pale and became the ancestor of the white people. The second man plunged into the pool, screamed because of the heat before coming out after a short time. He was half-cooked and became the ancestor of the Arabs and Indians. The last man was so afraid of the boiling water that he did not enter the pool at all. He only touched the surface of the water with the palms of his hands and felt it with the soles of his feet. His palms and soles became white while the rest of his body retained the original colour God had given the three of them. This man became the ancestor of us black people." We looked at the palms of our hands and at the soles of our feet which were indeed white while the rest of our bodies were black. I was convinced that the old girl was right, wise, and knowledgeable.

Father Jean Ribeau was a cocky man and could be unnecessarily bold. One day he saw some Portuguese soldiers in full battle dress with their rifles around the seminary. He went to tell them that they should go away, stressing that "we don't want to side with you or with the terrorists." The word terrorists was the official term the Portuguese government used to refer to Mozambican rebels fighting against the colonial rule in the northern region of

Mozambique near the border with Tanzania where they trained and were armed with Soviet and Chinese weapons.

That was a bit foolish of him to do and say to the soldiers. If he had said the same thing to a group of rebel soldiers, they would have beaten him up or killed him, as they did in 1964 to a Dutch priest in the northern region of Cabo Delgado who did not even provoke or swear at them. The soldiers were a common sight at the seminary. They came there and frequently played football matches with us and more often than not, we thrashed them. We were on very good terms with them, particularly with the black ones we found easier to talk to some of whom were relatives of some of our students. They were more approachable and eager to talk to us than the white ones.

Some of the soldiers had returned from the north where they had seen action against the rebels and they told us much about their clashes with the terrorists. They came to fetch water from our taps with big tanker trucks after a battalion of them set up a base at Zobue town following either the abduction or the surrender from Malawi of *senhor* Baltasar Chagonga, one of the leaders of the rebels of the so-called terrorist organization in Tanzania. I will deal with his case when talking about the VIPS who honoured us with visits to the seminary, although he was no VIP to us. He did not come to us nor would he have been allowed or we would have wanted him to come to us because for us, as Portuguese citizens then, he was our enemy and a terrorist leader.

But before I talk about the VIPS, I must give the names of the other priests who taught us at Zobue and who were among the finest men I have ever met and, from whom I learnt many values, particularly the imperative need of adventure and of being bold, no matter what the consequences. They were adventurous as missionaries like the missionaries of all other Christian religions such as the Baptists from America, the Lutherans, the Anglicans, the

Scottish Missionaries to name but a few. They brought us the Gospel, education, and medical services. They lived with us in our rough lands away from their families and the comfort of sophisticated Europe.

I have so far mentioned father Jose Latorre who had replaced father Prein as our rector. Father Prein with a goatee beard was at the seminary in the first year I was there. I think he fell ill and went to Germany for medical care and to recover before subsequently returning to Mozambique where he became the father superior of my mission at Traquino in 1967, the year I left the country.

He had done missionary work in Tanganyika and counted amongst his students' Cardinal Rugambwa of Tabora who was one of the first Africans the Vatican made a cardinal and Julius Nyerere who became the first president of Tanganyika, which had been a former German colony later mandated to Britain after Germany's defeat in the First World War. British troops from Kenya chased the Germans from there after when they entered Mozambique where they clashed with the Portuguese who fought with the anti-German coalition during the First World War.

I have also named fathers Jean Ribeau, Robert Roesems, and Moreno. There was also a priest by the name of Fernando Aytorre. He was a short, round and happy-go-lucky Spanish Basque who taught us mathematics and music. He taught my group of young boys which was known as Angelic Voices, to sing in Latin and Portuguese. He also taught us a few songs in Spanish and in his Basque tongue which is a unique language that is not related to any other language in the world. There are two such languages in the world: the Basque of Spain and France and the Hunza of the Himalayas.

A Belgian father André de Bels, a man of style who combined French elegance with Portuguese vanity which he must have acquired when he lived and studied in Portugal, taught my class Portuguese which he took much pride in speaking and he taught it with much style. Unfortunately father de Bels did not remain at the seminary for long after I had joined it. His departure was quick because the Portuguese government hounded him out of Mozambique after discovering that he had masterminded the flight of a number of former students to Malawi even before it became independent from the British; from there the students went for further studies in the United States. It was a pity that the seminary lost one of its best teachers.

There was the German father Anton Diener. He was short and bald-headed. He was intensely pious and sometimes rushed in his behaviour, but was otherwise an overtly good man with a fine sense of humour. He disliked Hitler with a passion. He always swore when he talked about Hitler and stressed that he would never have liked to see the monster. At the end of the Second World War, he was a POW of the British whose behaviour towards him he deplored. "British soldiers kicked me and spat on my face." I heard him say once. I suppose that such things would happen even with the most disciplined soldiers like the British whose behaviour compared to the German soldiers because war is a state of insanity.

Even the sanest person like Field Marshal Montgomery had a hard time on deciding what was to be the right way for his troops of occupation to behave towards German civilians; he wanted to treat them well but he did not seem to think that the Germans were innocent of what the Nazis had done. He even called the war the German War rather than the Second World War. When he thought that his soldiers were becoming too friendly to the German civilians, he would issue orders for soldiers to avoid being friendly and stop smiling to the Germans. It is Montgomery himself who says it in his memoirs.

Father Diener had done much missionary work in the land of the Sena people who language he knew and spoke without accent. He taught mainly religious studies, Latin and English. He also spoke French and at times he taught French.

The most imposing figure of them all was father Franz Schupp, a tall man with a pot belly and a long beard. He was a heavy smoker who used a pipe and the smoke stained his teeth and tainted his beard which had a golden-blackish colour as a result. He called himself Francisco rather than Franz, his German name, perhaps he thought that Francisco was better and sounded more romantic than the harsh-sounding Germanic Franz. He was a POW of the Russians at end of the Second World War. The Russians did not feed him apart from giving him salt and he ended up losing one of his kidneys.

His missionary work in the land of the Sena people had made him a Sena man with a limitless sense of humour that is typical of the Sena people. He taught mathematics mainly and sometimes he gave examples in class while speaking in Sena despite the presence of boys from other tribes who did not know the Sena language. They somehow were able to follow what he was saying and cherished the beauty of seeing a European speaking an African language he regarded as his own language and, taking pride in it. He could say in Sena things that could not be said in any European language because the concepts of what he was saying had no equivalent in European languages.

His sense of humour was such that he laughed himself sick when two senior boys parodied him in a theatrical show which they presented in Latin, showing him at a geometry class about triangles. One boy stuffed blankets on his stomach to give him the resemblance of a pot belly like his, put on a cassock and wore a fake beard to look like him. The other boy was demonstrating with a blackboard and a chalk his understanding of the lesson he had taught as the priest's double or lookalike shook his head and stroked his beard in agreement with the student.

After giving a lesson, father Schupp would always send someone to the blackboard the following day to demonstrate to other students that he had understood what had been taught the previous day. He would shake his head and stroke his beard as a student explained to the others what he had taught. That was the behaviour the two boys were ridiculing in Latin. It was the most hilarious theatrical show that sent everyone laughing without control after the boys had staged their show in the spiritual hall which also served as our theatre hall. It was also in the spiritual hall where the father rector gave us moral causeries for half an hour or so in the evenings every evening.

In 1966, a tall and slender German priest by the name of Hinkelmann joined the teaching staff at the seminary as a science teacher. He was perhaps the blondest man with the bluest eyes I had ever seen both before and since. He never taught my class but I just knew that he was a wonderful man.

Besides those European teachers, there were also two African teachers who taught the last primary class that was being phased out before Zobue just became a secondary school. After seven years at Zobue Seminary, students who made it to the end there went on to the major seminary in southern Mozambique for another seven years to study philosophy and theology before being ordained as priests.

Chapter 24

If talking about earthquakes, warplanes, leopards, pythons, and hyenas seemed to be a bit off the beat, let me now turn to outsiders who came calling at the seminary to see the majestic bush institution which in its heyday, was one of the finest learning institutions in Mozambique. I still remember the events as if they have just taken place. For me, all that is important because I witnessed it and lived it as history and not as mere tales from the pages of fiction.

One of the most distinguished visits we got was from *senhor* Antonio Higino de Craveiro Lopes, the district governor for Tete. Zefina and I had seen him in Tete but it was from a distance. When father Latorre, the rector, informed us that the district governor and the commander of the Portuguese forces in Tete and their wives were going to pay us a visit, there was expectation in the air, for, as long as I remember, no high-ranking government officials had bothered to come to the seminary during my stay there. There were reasons expounded to explain the indifference. Some people said that the government did not like the school because it was run by a non-Portuguese staff or, that it was the focus of rebellion. For sure, the government knew from their infiltrators in the rebel movement in Tanzania, that a couple of former students had gone to join the nascent rebel movement in Tanzania. Unfortunately, one was using his real name of Faustino Kambeu on rebel broadcasts of the Sena Language from Dar-Es-Salaam. The

Portuguese Intelligence was able to discover that he was a former student at Zobue Seminary.

We, however, prepared ourselves as thoroughly as we could to accord him the most dignified reception possible. We cleaned and spruced up the place. For once, we rehearsed *A Portuguesa* as the Portuguese national anthem is patriotically called. Most of us had been singing it every morning before classes at our mission schools but the seminary never bothered about patriotism and we never sang it there except when the governor came to visit. But none of us had forgotten it. We rehearsed it just to refresh our memories and make sure that we sang it in the best manner possible when the time came in the presence of government officials.

The governor arrived in the afternoon. We were in the spiritual hall silently awaiting him and his cortege with no one coughing or burping. On arrival, they were received by the rector and other priests who brought them to the hall. We began to clap our hands as soon as we saw the rector lead the way to the dais where there were five chairs for the governor and the military commander and their wives and the rector, while the other priests sat with us. The governor wore a suit and the military commander wore a light green military uniform and their wives were spruced up in the most fashionable aristocratic way possible with hats with feathers and all.

As soon as the guests and the rector had reached the dais, we started singing the lyrical and martial anthem faultlessly, with our voices floating in the air. The guests were highly impressed, particularly the ladies who smiled as we sang, probably because they had never heard it sung elsewhere as beautifully as we did at the seminary.

After the anthem was sung, the guests and the rector sat down followed by us. Antonio Jenquene, a boy from my mission who had the best diction in Portuguese, delivered the welcome speech during which he waxed lyrical about

237

our pride as Portuguese citizens. I thought the boy overdid it, but what else could he have done? Criticize Portuguese colonialism which even the most rebellious boy could not have done on that day in the presence of those all-powerful officials. And let's face it: were we students or Portuguese nationals? Had we not pledged to be and remain forever Portuguese? Were we not Portuguese citizens, regardless of whether we felt colonized or not? At that time, we simply could not show the government officials our rebellious face without incurring the severest consequences. What would have been gained by insulting the officials?

Luis de Camoes, the epic poet of the *Lusiads* said, "It's no bravery to be a lion amongst sheep." The reverse which is my own thought about our position towards the government officials, is also true: "it's foolish for sheep to be brave amidst lions."

After the speech, the rector made a brief introduction of the visitors to us, although most of us already knew who was who in the gubernatorial cortege. We clapped hands at the end of the introduction after which the governor said a few words to thank us for the resounding reception we accorded him and his team. We clapped for his good words.

Let me be frank here. Those officials were civilized people, to us at least. They were so considerate; they came without a policemen or a soldier accompanying them, and yet, they had plenty of policemen and soldiers to escort them. In many African-ruled countries then, government officials were escorted with armed goons wherever they went to in order to threaten and beat up their own people. I think it is very easy to criticize colonialists and overlook the abuse of power in African countries. Lack of honesty, civility, and humbleness on the part of African rulers proved to be the undoing of many African countries.

So impressed was the governor with Antonio Jenquene, the boy who made the speech, that he later presented him with a gift of 1,000 escudos, a fairly good amount of money in those days. After the governor's brief speech, the guests and the rector led them out as we clapped our hands. The rector led them to the priests' residences where there was a reception for the distinguished guests. We left the hall, very excited that we had received our governor well and that we had played our role as good citizens. As it was a public holiday to honour the governor's visit, we went back to do what each one liked to do best. I went to read Portuguese newspapers and the editions of *La Libre Belgique.* Portuguese newspapers had introduced me to Cassius Clay the black American pugilist who later came to call himself Mohamed Ali. I could see myself as Cassius Clay, walking like him and sparring against imaginary opponents in the ring. I talked about him to other boys who cared to listen to me.

The visitors left the seminary later that day and returned to Tete perhaps the same day. For me the visit was one of the great events in the annals of the school. It was history, and at least the colonial governor had not come to rail against us or intimidate us or destroy the seminary, as Mozambican dolts did later in their war for political power.

A few weeks after the governor's visit, a foreign VIP came to the school. It was a most unusual visit. Strictly speaking it was not a visit but just a courtesy call , not even a courtesy call but a drop by from Mr. John Chakwamba, a Sena tribesman from southern Malawi who was then minister of agriculture in the government of President Kamuzu Banda of Malawi. He was brought to the seminary by the colonial administrator of Zobue. He arrived while we were busy working in and around the seminary as we did in the afternoons, to clean and maintain the school by clearing grass, tending the orchards and picking fruit. Word reached me where I was working that a minister of Malawi was around and I saw a Land Rover he had come in. I hastily went to where he was and found the minister talking with father Robert Roesems in English and with some boys who had been studying English for quite a long time at the seminary and could manage conversing in English. The words on the Land Rover which had brought the minister said "Government of Malawi" and standing and leaning on it were two Malawian police officers in khaki uniform. They did not engage anyone in conversation. No one talked to them either. Perhaps one Ngoni boy spoke to them in Chichewa. I do not remember.

After some time, the caller left without even ever going into the school or without us welcoming him as we had done with the governor. There was no reception for him because he was a foreign dignitary and was not a Portuguese like we were. So there was no reception or a speech to welcome him. That is all I can remember of that rather uneventful visit, but I came to know later while living in Canada, that John Chakwamba had more than once tried to run for the presidency of Malawi without success.

On the 10th June 1966 there was a public holiday in memory of Luis de Camoes, the one-eyed poet laureate who lost his right eye while battling Moors in Tangier in North Africa in the fifteenth century. He is the author of *The Lusiads* epic in the style of Homer, with Greek gods and all that glorifies the voyages of discovery by Vasco da Gama by sea from Portugal to India. We the seminarians went to Zobue town on foot for an open air mass. It was a sunny day and excitement was in the air for me because the seminary was like a stuffy place and I needed to get some fresh air and have the chance of seeing women and girls.

During mass there was commotion as secret agents ran here and there without us being told what was happening. Father Moreno who remained there after we left the town to return to the seminary and was in the good books of the secret agents told us the following day, that one of the leaders of the terrorists had given himself up. But the truth, as I came to know it later, was that Baltasar Chagonga who lived in Blantyre in Malawi had been kidnapped by the Portuguese secret agents, drugged, and brought to Zobue from where he was whisked away in a helicopter to Tete on the afternoon of the same day. It seemed that during interrogation, he had disclosed that the rebels who had earlier attempted to infiltrate Tete from Zambia and were soundly defeated, were again planning to launch attacks in Tete through Zobue, which might have explained why a battalion of the Portuguese Army from Tete was hastily dispatched to take up position at Zobue on that same day.

If the visit from the governor was a goodwill one, the call that we got next looked like a visitation from the angels of death, as after it, nothing was the same again or went well. The body of Zobue Seminary became ill and its illness heralded the end for that great institution. I was profoundly ill morally, unable to think of the seminary as a good place anymore. I dreamed of flying to faraway places, soaring in the air never to return again as long as freedom did not become a reality to Mozambique after the departure of the colonial regime.

Unlike many people who did not dare to think, I dared to do so and I had visions. As to what I really wanted to do, I was undecided. Go to Mutarara to be with Zefina. What would I gain from that? Being with her would never be an adventure but stagnation. As a 15-year old boy or thereabouts, I was not yet ready to marry, although all the time while at seminary, I dreamt of the three girls: Zefina, I could not marry; of Catarina, Jonas's daughter or of Maria, Gwedje's sister, who I could marry. The choice would be mine between Maria and Catarina. Much as I would like to take the two of them as my wives, Jonas, Catarina's deeply religious father, would not allow his daughter to be in a polygamous marriage. So I would have to choose between Maria and Catarina.

The explosion that set in motion the cataclysmic descent to hell came one day. It was at break time.

Someone saw a car with our late Bishop Feliz Niza Ribeiro in with two other senior prelates, the late Bishop Francisco Teixeira of Zambezia and the late Archbishop Custodio Alvim Pereira of Lourenço Marques. As was the custom, whoever spotted the Bishop's car first, even when he arrived unannounced which he did at times, had to rush to the chapel to ring the bell so as to let the students know that the bishop was around. That was the only time when the bell rang outside the regular hours it was normally rung. So, some one rang the bell that morning and before long I saw a car pull up and out came the three bishops after it had stopped. Without much ado, Bishop Niza Ribeiro introduced the Archbishop Custodio Alvim Pereira of Lourenço Marques whose name I knew from the class on Morals and Civics, and the Bishop Francisco Teixeira we already knew as he had come to visit us previously. For him Zobue Seminary was very important as it also received a big number of students from his Zambezia diocese.

"We're from Quelimane and have come through Malawi," said Archbishop Alvim Pereira, the highest Catholic Church leader in Mozambique then, after we had congregated in the spiritual hall to welcome him and his two fellow bishops. "When we were at Zobue town, Bishop Niza Ribeiro here told us that Zobue Seminary was close. I told him that we should call on you." He was silent before continuing. "In God's grace, we've the pleasure to be here with you today." We clapped to him. He and the other bishops smiled and appeared to be happy.

We applauded to him without suspecting that the Archbishop was not telling us the truth. And events later showed that he was probably lying. At any rate, we were excited to see those religious potentates who stayed at the seminary until the early afternoon of that day when they left. Father Latorre announced after our meeting with the bishops that the rest of the day would be a public holiday to honour the visit of the three bishops.

Chapter 25

When I was at Zobue Seminary from 1964 to 1967, I went on holiday three times. In 1965, I and students of classes with odd numbers stayed behind at the seminary while students of classes with even numbers were allowed to go home on holiday. After spending the month of July at the seminary, it was arranged that we spend the month of August at Boroma Mission which was established in 1895 and was about twenty kilometres to the north of Tete where we would spend the rest of our vacation before returning to the school to resume our classes in September. I was excited to go and see Boroma which was also a teacher training college for primary school teachers. It was where a number of the teachers I knew at my mission of Traquino had trained. I also wanted to go to Boroma to be near the Zambezi, a river that had become part of my soul and with which I identified because, for a long time I had bathed in it, I had drunk its water and I had eaten fish from it. I did not mind that the river sometimes punished us with flooding, as it did in 1958.

As the seminary did not have a bus, the enterprising father Moreno spoke to the army in Tete who agreed to use its trucks to take us from Zobue to Tete. Boroma Mission sent its own big truck to pick us from Tete and take us to the mission. The trip in military trucks and a big truck from the school was a rather bumpy affair over rough roads. I enjoyed every bit of it as I was not particularly keen on comfort. Comfort was the last thing I sought or wanted or was after. I had not lived a particularly comfortable life. My youth had been hard walking long distances to school. Zobue Seminary was not intended for a soft life either. In principle, according to the Church doctrine and its logic, training to be a priest is not an invitation to a cup of tea or a treat of free lunch. It was intended to be difficult and hard so as to prepare individuals for a life of sacrifices and deprivation as missionaries and church leaders and for martyrdom to God, if necessary.

All that sounded good as my life had been hard and I had decided that it should be a series of adventures demanding courage. If I had not adopted such an approach, I would never have made the decisions I took in my life and would not have survived some of the situations after I began to move on, without knowing whether I would live or die in the process. So the trip to Tete was an easy travel compared to some episodes I had gone through in the past and would face in the future.

One day at Boroma I almost had a narrow escape when a crocodile was preparing to attack a friend of mine and I when out of nowhere, a guardian angel appeared and alerted us about the imminent danger we were in. I was angling at a place where the previous evening I had caught so many tilapia fish that was enough to feed all my colleagues from Zobue. The following morning, I went back to the same place where I had caught the fish hoping that I would repeat the feat again. I was with another seminarian who had been with me the previous day. We had cast our lines and were holding our rods waiting for the fish to bite, but there were no fish around perhaps because they had seen the danger looming over them and had fled to be safe.

As I looked out at the water with the rod in my hand, I saw something coming to the surface of the water and submerging when it thought I had seen it. I saw it twice before I told my colleague who also saw it come to the surface and submerge. We dismissed it as a log without asking ourselves what log could remain still at the same spot in that fast flowing water of the mighty Zambezi. The Zambezi has to be seen to be appreciated as mighty, and it has been dubbed as mighty for a reason.

Then a boy appeared for apparently no apparent reason as he was coming neither to angle nor to bathe because it was not a bathing spot. The beach for bathing with shallow water was upstream. I greeted him in Portuguese and he answered in Portuguese after which I told him about the thing that kept coming to the surface and submerging. I told him to look where I pointed my finger at the spot where I had seen it.

"You guys are in danger," he said after seeing the thing. "That's not a log. It's a crocodile preparing to attack you. You must leave. It's calculating the distance and the time it will take to reach you."

We pulled our lines out of the water before beginning to run as fast as our legs could take us, stopping after we had thought that we were at a safe distance. Before thanking our guardian angel and parting company with him, he told us his name and said that he had completed primary school and would be joining the seminary in September of that year. I had really wanted him to come to the seminary to be my friend but I did not see him when old students returned and new ones joined us. Had he failed to turn up for other reasons or was he actually a guardian angel who did not need to come to a school for humans? Or to look at it in the African way, was he a human boy our ancestral spirits had guided to save us just in time or was he a spirit in human form?

Let me believe that he was neither a guardian angel nor a spirit in a human form. The other seminarian and I were just lucky to have escaped from being caught in the jaws of a crocodile and dragged under the water for the crocodiles' lunch. I believe that the saurian we saw was not alone in the water at that spot. Despite that incident with the crocodile, the holidays in Boroma father Jean Ribeau chaperoned, were a great event for all of us who went there. We had a good time and enjoyed every bit of it. Our hosts the Portuguese Jesuit priests and the nuns, had afforded us a good reception.

In 1966 I went back home for the holidays. I found Zefina well established in Mutarara and doing fine in her business. She had been entertaining a man in the village she later married while I was at Zobue. The man did not want to go and live with her at Mutarara. Their living apart was the reason for their constant friction and the man ended up taking another woman with whom he lived in the village. Zefina did not accept the situation nor did she want an official divorce. She did not need to divorce him officially although she regarded the situation as a *de facto* divorce because she had no intention of ever allowing him near her or, of marrying another man, as, according to her, she was not meant to sleep with more than one man in her life. I left her to her decision which I respected. I just wanted her to continue to be successful in her business and live her life the way she wanted to live it.

The year of 1967 had dawned well until that ominous visitation by the three church leaders which no one suspected would bode ill after it had happened. Our White Father teachers had been told of the decision to kick them out of the seminary but they kept it to themselves until the month of June arrived prior to our holidays, when they thought it fit to inform us that the White Fathers whose congregation had been fundamental to and had founded the seminary, were no longer going to continue teaching at the school; the Jesuits from Boroma were going to replace them.

It was father Latorre, the rector, who announced the decision to us in the spiritual hall. No one said anything. No one shouted with indignation or to express opposition or disapproval which would have done nothing to change the decision that higher powers had taken without consulting us or asking for our opinion. Continuing, the rector said, "This year we will let everyone go on holiday instead of alternating who goes on vacation between classes with even and odd numbers. We the priests will remain here packing and to help our colleagues who are replacing us to familiarize themselves with this place." The decision made sense as the White fathers had wanted to wipe the slate clean and let the Jesuits begin afresh.

The new Portuguese Jesuits were not late in coming on familiarization tours. They started coming before classes wound up and we left on holiday. I remember only one by his full name. That was father Antonio Sarreira, an old friend of the Portuguese dictator Antonio de Oliveira Salazar. Father Sarreira who received our group in Tete and took us to Boroma in 1965, was an old man. He was an extremely brilliant mathematician and engineer. I had heard about him and his genius from the teachers at my mission whom the priest had trained as teachers at Boroma.

Others were father Peixoto, the new rector, who had received part of his education in England; Father Marques who had studied in France; and fathers Pinto, Gama, and Guerra. Others such as Vieira and Custodio were not priests as yet, but had gone through the first rituals towards priesthood.

I went on vacation and had a good time with Zefina and Jonas and his family at Mutarara. I noticed that Catarina, Jonas' daughter, had become an adult from the adolescent that she was in 1964 when she told Zefina that she had begun to love me. While in the village, a male cousin who seemed to be very intuitive and was constantly going into trances prior to becoming a healer, recommended that I ask aunt Albertina, Zefina's healer mother, to cleanse me because he thought that I needed such a ceremony as he foresaw stormy episodes ahead of me. I did not refuse or argue. I readily welcomed his idea as I thought that I was about to face big challenges ahead of me. The cleansing ceremony would play the double role of eliminating evil forces of the past and the present as well as strengthening my protection for the future.

Christianity and education had done much for me but I had not stopped belonging to the world I came face to face with after my birth. And I never felt I should discard my traditional identity to embrace Christianity entirely. I simply could not and would not, apart from rejecting some barbaric aspects of our culture like subjecting widows to sexual orgies with their brothers-in-law after the death of their husbands as a way of cleansing them of evil and a few other objectionable behaviours. Apart from those objections, I believed that the two worlds complemented each other for me and that I needed both of them. And I decided to be open to other ways and accept their useful principles and reject ideas which denied people their basic freedoms such as certain aspects of African ways that are tyrannical, religious fundamentalism of any colour and stripe, fascism and communism.

After staying with and helping Zefina in August, I returned to Zobue to try the new system and give it the benefit of the doubt. A good number of students did not return after the holidays. They either stayed at home or engaged in other activities or went to other schools.

Relations between the new staff and the students were characterized by confrontation and the Jesuit military-like way of running the school disgusted many boys who were used to much more freedom under the White Fathers. And many students were abandoning the school in such numbers that I felt that if things went on that way, the seminary would have to close altogether.

One morning a boy called Marcos Bulande and another called Antonio Miguel and I sneaked into Mwanza in

Malawi where we met an agent of the rebel organization in Tanzania who said that he would receive us and make sure that we went to Tanzania. I did not think that I wanted to go to Tanzania but in the end, I decided to venture to Tanzania and from there I thought I would work my work to some other place. I had always thought of going to France because of my fluency in French; I could not contemplate England much because I knew no English then, but I would go there, if the worst came to the worst. England would definitely be better than living in Tanzania. As for English, I thought, that should not be a problem as I would have to learn it, as I had learnt Portuguese and French.

Marcos Bulande thought we should not even return to the seminary and we should just move on from Mwanza. I told him that it would be a bad thing to do as we would be reported as missing and the army and the security forces would start looking for us and would enter Malawi where they could catch up with us, drug and drag us to Mozambique as they had done with Baltasar Chagonga.

"The best thing," I said to him and the other boy, "is for us to return to the seminary and after a few days, leave to our places and meet at Moatize on 16 November and return to cross the border at Zobue."

The boys agreed. Back at the seminary that evening I was summoned to the office of Custodio, the new staff member in charge of disciplinary matters and my teacher of Portuguese Language, who had been informed that I was absent from the school that day. I lied to him saying that I had gone to the village to get some sugar cane. He swallowed the lie, and I got away with it. I was the first to leave the school and I went home. Left behind, when the other two boys requested to leave to go home, they simply went to Mwanza instead of going to their homes and later teamed up with me at Moatize on the date we had agreed.

I left Zobue at the beginning of November and went home for two weeks. Zefina and I went to our village for a week. She was the only one I confided in that I was leaving Mozambique. She did not express objection to my decision. She wished me well. During my stay in the village, I asked aunt Albertina to do another cleansing ceremony on me again so as to cleanse me further and strengthen me against the evil of humans and evil spirits. Just the gravity of what I had set out to do compelled me to seek such support. It was the fear of the unknown. I knew that courage alone would not be enough to protect me or prayers to Christian gods do the job as quickly and as efficiently as our healers were able to do. And I knew my aunt and her strange powers better than anyone else.

The cleansing would guarantee that the evils that caused ill luck were swept away. This basic belief explains why Africans in general are not concerned so much with trying to know what will happen in the future. They believed that if they are free and protected from a bad past and current malign influences then they will become strong and the door is barred to future evils; the future should take care of itself, which does not necessarily mean that there will be no problems. Problems never cease to crop up as long as there are bad individuals and evil spirits which Christians refer to as the Devil or devils.

Part 3: Diaspora
Chapter 26

There was nothing that was going to stop me. I was on the way. I had taken the decision to leave Mozambique while fully aware that things could go wrong because I was fleeing from my duties and obligations as a Portuguese citizen and was not leaving the country legally. I was doing something which I was not supposed to do. The penalty, if caught for trying to do so, would be abysmal. I could expect torture or even death by torture. That was how the Portuguese regime went about implementing the death penalty that its own laws had abolished. In theory there was no death penalty in Portugal and its colonies as the law did not allow the courts to pass capital sentences. But the death penalty existed all the same through the barbarous torture and treatment of prisoners which eventually killed them.

After a trip by train lasting the greater part of the day from Mutarara on November 16, 1967, I arrived at Moatize at around about three or four o'clock in the afternoon and headed straight to the Moatize Parish where I ran into Antonio Fortunato, a student I had left at the seminary and who had left the school after me. He had started to work for the mission. I think he was teaching there. He was pleased to see me. As an old friend, I told him what I was up to. He took me to a Spanish priest who welcomed me and told me that I could spend the night there and showed me exactly where I was going to sleep on a mat he provided for me. He regretted that it would not be comfortable, but comfort was the last thing that I would demand in that situation.

The Moatize Mission was run by the Spanish de Burgos Fathers. Their patron saint is St. Francis Xavier who took Christianity to Japan, China and India after Ignatius Loyola, he and others had founded the congregation of Jesuit priests in 1534. Francis Xavier, who is incidentally my patron saint, died in Asia in 1556 and his remains can be viewed in the Basilica of Bom Jesus in Goa, India.

The De Burgos Fathers and the White Fathers in Tete later became a thorn in the flesh of the Portuguese government. They denounced the way Portuguese forces conducted their war against the pro-independence rebels they called terrorists and the massacres they perpetrated against villagers, the biggest of which being the Wiryamu massacre of 1972. One afternoon white and black soldiers of the Sixth Commando battalion based at Tete, were dropped from helicopters close to the village of chief Wiryamu before marching on it and beginning to kill everyone on sight, as according to them, they had received orders not to spare anyone. They wiped out more than 400 villagers that afternoon. It seemed that those who had sent them to kill the civilians had also wanted them to perish after their hideous act so as to erase all the vestiges of their decision, by either forgetting or failing to send helicopters to whisk them away. As they returned to base on foot, they fell in an ambush mounted by the rebels they were able to beat back.

The De Burgos Fathers who came to know about the killings relayed the information to Father Adrian Hastings in Britain who reported the matter to The Times in London which took up the matter and stirred worldwide condemnation of Portugal. The Portuguese at first denied that a massacre had taken place but evidence mounted against them and The Times kept up the heat by publishing all the reports that the De Burgos Fathers had supplied to Adrian Hastings. In the end, relations between the Portuguese government and the De Burgos and White Fathers fell to rock bottom, forcing the two congregations to withdraw their missionaries from Mozambique whilst the Portuguese regime said it had expelled them.

Some hours after my arrival at the mission, two boys who had pulled out of the seminary arrived at the mission on their way back to their regions in Sofala. They were Antonio Quinze and Miguel Nhavicondo. I did not see Marcos Bulande and Antonio Miguel with whom I had agreed to meet at Moatize on that day for the onward journey to Zobue and Malawi. I was disappointed and realized that I had been let down and betrayed. I was alone which was a blessing in disguise because being alone would make me less conspicuous but it was also a curse because being alone meant that I had no company and the anguish and fear would not be light on me. I had realized the importance of being with someone rather than being alone when I went to Sofala and subsequently to Tete with Zefina. In the course of those trips she saw things I did not and I saw things she did not and we let each other know what the other had missed. I also discussed strategies with her to counter what would confront us.

I learnt from the two boys that the situation at the border had changed and become very dangerous to would be escapees. The secret service agents were on the alert after they had learnt that a number of boys from the seminary had crossed the border into Malawi to go and join the terrorist organization in Tanzania after leaving the seminary instead of going home. Boys from Zambezia to the east of Malawi who had until then transited back and forth through Malawi were forced to take a roundabout trip through Mozambique to return to their villages in Zambezia. Secrets agents were going to the seminary to pick up boys abandoning the school to make sure that they went to their regions instead of running to Malawi and going to join the rebels in Tanzania.

"Secret agents are patrolling the border and entering Malawi in search of escapees," Antonio Quinze said.

I shuddered after hearing that piece of news. And the two boys asked me to call off my plan so as to allow the situation to cool down, and reschedule it for a later date when the three of us would meet at Moatize and head for Zobue and Malawi. After having been betrayed by other boys, I could not trust these ones either. I refused because my adventure was a rolling storm and a roaring thunder I could not stop to please friends. It could only be stopped by the physical superiority of the enemy. They pleaded with me to reconsider but to no avail because I knew that they would not live up to their promise as Marcos Bulande and Antonio Miguel had also failed to do.

The two boys left early the following morning by train to Mutarara and on to Sofala. At around nine that morning, I boarded a bus which made two weekly runs back and forth between Salisbury in Southern Rhodesia, through Tete to Blantyre in Malawi. It is driver was a Portuguese gentleman called Pereira who was very friendly to female peasants along the road between Moatize and Zobue. He allowed them into his bus with their loads of farm produce.

The trip went without a hitch until we reached Zobue. It arrived at Zobue at around 1 p.m. or so. I got out of the bus in front of an Indian store whose owner had died of a heart attack in 1965 and was cremated in the open by his store before his ashes were sent to India to be scattered in the Ganges. I had to get out there so that I did not reach the border control about a kilometre or so from there as I would be questioned at the border as to where I was going and be arrested to face damning consequences. As soon as I got out, I saw right in front of me white government officials in uniforms with epaulettes, all because 17th November was a public holiday in Portugal dedicated to the Virgin Mary. I supposed they were from mass at Zobue Mission, which was still being run by the White Fathers after the other White Fathers had been kicked out of the seminary.

That day was one of the few occasions when I panicked and trembled uncontrollably. I walked away from there and went to one side of the store before anyone could stop me and ask for my identification papers. I took a path that cut through a maize and banana plantation so as to be away from the store as soon as possible, before entering the field and taking shelter in a little dilapidated structure of bricks with a roof still standing. I breathed hard and sweated. I was unsure whether I would extricate myself from that situation and survive to see another day dawn for me.

I was in a real fix. I also felt that anybody seeing me in there could think that I was a criminal or a thief on the run and might attack me. I could not stay there long nor could I hide in that shelter because half of it had either been destroyed or had collapsed. I walked away from there through the field onto the main road to the store of *senhor* Santos who had arrived in Mozambique from Portugal in rags and had overnight become a wealthy businessman. There were people everywhere on the road. I wobbled as my legs trembled. The younger son of senhor Santos I knew well because he and his older brother who was in the same class with me at the seminary but was not a seminarian, had a donkey called Francisco. They used to come to the seminary with their donkey to collect hay for it when we trimmed the grass around the school. They unnecessarily kept calling the donkey by its name in order to annoy and provoke the boys like myself who were called Francisco.

At first several of the boys called Francisco were not amused but we decided to ignore the situation and not warn the two brothers because there was nothing we could do against them or to force them to change the name of their donkey. We could not beat them because we were seminarians who were supposed to tolerate provocation and humiliation like Jesus had done when he carried the heavy cross on his shoulders and later died on it.

The boy noticed that I was shaking. He might have thought that I was ill and needed medical attention but he did not come to ask me whether I needed help. After walking past Santos' store, which was very close to the border, I took the road to the left which went to the seminary and beyond into the country of the Zimba people.

As I walked on, I heard a truck coming behind me. I turned and saw that it was full of seminarians who had probably gone to attend mass at Zobue Mission or for some other activity in the town. I turned away from them and hid my face with the sack containing my few possessions, mainly clothes and a blanket and my identification papers and school certificates. I had taken a sack because I did not want to take a suitcase. For a person on an extremely dangerous flight, a suitcase would be cumbersome, difficult to carry and handle. With a sack which was not heavy at all, I could run as fast as my legs could carry me, if I had to bolt for it. The seminary had taught me to run. On the day Baltasar Chagonga was brought drugged from Malawi when we seminarians had walked to Zobue on foot in the morning, I and three other boys returned to the seminary running at full speed without ever stopping anywhere and covered the four kilometres between the two places in perhaps less than forty-five minutes. I did not think that anyone could chase and catch me, perhaps if people chased me with dogs.

After the truck had zoomed past me and gone on its way without stopping, I walked to a brook that was usually dry, except when it rained heavily and water came cascading from the mountains. Past that stream, I followed a left path off the road to the seminary. There was tall grass on both sides of the path with shrubs and trees. I instinctively thought that I needed natural cover instead of continuing to walk and take stock of my situation and bearings. Thinking that people might have seen me wobbling as I walked along the main road between the Indian and Santos' stores and could decide to follow me, I decided to jump from the path into the grass and walk further away from the path. There I ducked and lay well camouflaged under tall grass so perfectly like a soldier in an ambush waiting to attack an enemy.

The only thing I did not have was a rifle and I wished I had one and knew how to operate it. I had a small sharp knife I could use to threaten and attack any person trying to harass or arrest me. My gentle heart had in a few minutes hardened from one that would like to avoid violence, if possible, to one that was determined to fight back and inflict unacceptable hurt to a would be enemy. I told myself that in a fight for survival, I would have to do away with the feelings of kindness and pity because my enemies like the mapanga terrorists from Nyasaland I had confronted when a younger boy, would not pity me or be kind to me.

Nothing happened for twenty minutes after which I returned to the path and continued to walk until I reached an intersection. There I turned to the right of the other path and began to walk towards the road to the seminary so that I could follow it and veer off it before the seminary to take another path to Malawi which was about four kilometres away. But there was a loud wedding party ahead of me which I had to avoid.

As I walked on, I ran into two men going in the opposite direction. I greeted them and they returned my greeting. Fortunately they spoke Portuguese. As they had never seen me in their village, one of them asked me whether I was lost and needed help to find my way.

"Oh, no," I said. "I'm fine. I'm from the seminary on my way home."

"Ah, you're from the seminary? There is one of you who also lives there ahead of us. Come see him, if you want."

I agreed to go and see the student and followed them. I had no idea who the student was. When we reached the cluster of huts where he lived, the man called the boy who was in his cottage. The boy came out. I recognized him and he recognized me too. He was not a seminarian. He was one of the two boys who studied at the seminary without being a seminarian. The other boy was the older son of the senhor Santos. Because he was not a seminarian, I had never talked to him, although he was in the same class as me but in a different stream as our class had two streams.

We greeted each other as if we had been friends. He welcomed me and asked me to feel at home before we went into his cottage. We talked amicably. I had initially told him that I had just left the seminary but had to wait in the neighbourhood for the Moatize-bound bus the following day to board a train from there to Mutarara, which was actually where I was coming from.

"In that case you can stay and sleep here until tomorrow."

"Thank you for your kindness."

As I was not certain whether or not he was a secret agent, I kept the original story for about an hour or so before telling him the truth.

"That's okay. You can stay here and I'll walk you to the border before dawn tomorrow."

I could not do otherwise. I stayed there, knowing that, if he were a security agent, he could dispatch someone to go and summon secret agents who would come to arrest me. I was not going to allow him do so. I would bolt into the bush I knew so well and head to the border and enter Malawi and there hide in the bush to avoid the secret agents who were patrolling the road in Malawi. I was monitoring his bodily and facial expressions before I realized that he was genuinely against the colonial regime. I trusted him so much so that in the afternoon, we took a stroll from his residence and we ran into two pretty girls whom he told I was a cousin of his visiting him. One of the girls was manifestly attracted to me and told him in Portuguese that she wanted me to be her boyfriend and lover. I had always feared that my handsomeness would be my undoing.

There was no way I could ever entertain that girl because I was in an impossible situation. I could not stay in Zobue with her or go back home to tell Zefina that I needed her support to get a Zimba girl from Zobue to Mutarara. She would never be amused. She would have breathed fire on me for deciding on another girl from the Zimba tribe that were still thought of as cannibals when Catarina, Jonas' daughter, at Mutarara, was dying for my love. She also knew that Maria, Gwedje's sister, wanted me to marry her but she preferred Catarina for me and not Maria. I could not go to Malawi and get back to Zobue for her because once out of Mozambique illegally, I would be an outlaw. And Malawi was not my destination, anyway. I thought the situation would require a genius to plot a story around it and come up with a satisfying climax and resolution.

"You're very beautiful, my sweetheart," I said to her. That Zimba girl was indeed beautiful and she was bold for having said what she said. "I don't have much time to discuss the matter with you today. I'll come back again. If I find you still hunting, I will take you with me to become my wife."

The girl and I hugged before shaking hands. She had that kind of smile and a body which exuded sex and which was enhanced by the pleasant smell of the perfume she had over applied on herself.

After the two girls went on their way, the boy told me that the girl who wanted me was a distant cousin of his and was very well behaved. I felt sorry for the girl and for

259

myself. I was really depressed at the thought that the girl went home believing that I would return for her. The boy was not disturbed by the whole episode which he regarded as a big joke, and he reassured me that he would later encourage her to go on hunting until she found a boy who could marry her.

After we returned to his place, I decided to bribe him. I was certain that I could trust him and he deserved my gratitude. I gave him 250 escudos from the money Zefina had given me. It was a good amount that he had not worked for. He was very grateful. He gave a half of it to his mother who was also very happy. We ate early and stayed up until nine before we went to sleep. Even if I had wanted to sleep, I could not do so. I did not lull myself into believing that I was completely safe and saved. I needed to be awake so as to hear the first cock crow. When I heard it, I decided it was time to be on the move before daylight could catch up with me while I was still in Mozambique. He also thought it was a good time to escort me to the border which was about a kilometre or so from his residence, so that he could return home to sleep a bit more before going for classes at the seminary in the morning. At the border, with him in Mozambique and I in Malawi, we shook hands and bade each other farewell after which I was alone to face different kinds of enemies that night.

Chapter 27

If at Zobue I ran the risk of being suspected of planning to leave the country and being arrested, I now faced a different assortment of hostile phenomena that were more menacing than the danger of humans because I could neither run away from them nor skip them. It was like everything around and at some distance was conspiring against me. The pitch darkness of the moonless night, the forms and shapes of the trees and grass, of other beings my mind imagined and the shapes of squatting mountains to the north of me, some of which I had climbed before, assumed lives of their own and threatened me in their own different ways. They all appeared ready to spring against me and make a mess of me or reduce me to pulp.

I had the sensation that I was no longer a living person. I was just a zombie moving in a place and a world that were not real but surrealistic and evil through and through. I stilled my nerves and body against dangers that I seemed to sense about me as I kept walking very fast but never ran, for fear that if I started running I could panic, fall and hurt myself or could even alert critters which might not have been aware that I was passing, and have them start chasing me.

Then the most terrifying idea came to my mind when I thought of encountering hyenas. I knew that the hyenas I had heard growling while in the safety of my dormitory at the seminary were free citizens of Mozambique and Malawi and that night and darkness were their time for loitering in search of food. I would be totally at their mercy and they would quickly devour me if I encountered them. I had no protection from or defence against them.

I also thought of the leopard that father Moreno had shot at Ludovic's residence and brought to the seminary for skinning to have its skin, and the Zimba locals wanted its heart for them to eat and become as brave as leopards. I could vividly see its terrifying eyes, teeth, and claws in that darkness. I guessed that the brute had not been the only one in the area. I was sure that it had a father or a mother, brothers and sisters, uncles, aunts, cousins and others of its kind that were still alive and could be on the loose at that time. I also knew that although loners, leopards were more terrifying than the gregarious hyenas. They preferred to attack or spring on their victims from behind, thereby leaving no chance for their prey to offer resistance, fight them off or scare them off.

As I had not expected to cross the border and walk in Malawi at night, I had not thought of having a torch or a flash light with me which I could spot on to the eyes of any wild animals I might encounter and blind them, even if momentarily. Unlike at Zobue town the previous day when I wobbled and trembled with fear, that night I was walking steadily and almost breathlessly, but overwhelmed with fear all the same.

As darkness began to fade away and give way to light, I knew that I had made it and that the danger from hyenas and leopards, or even lions if there were any in the area, was past me; the burglars were back in their dens or deeper in the woods for safety, away from the terrors that daylight with the presence of humans represented to them. They also knew fear as everything that lived on the surface of the earth experienced fear of some kind and got frightened. As more light came, my heart began to lighten up and my body to relax. I smiled to myself because I had made it and was still alive.

By six o'clock when it was bright with the sun's rays beginning to appear with much life and vigour, I began to slow down my pace and walk in a leisurely manner before I bypassed the Malawi border control along a side walk. The Malawian border control was well inside Malawi unlike the Portuguese one that was right by the border. Two Malawian police officers saw me as I walked by. I did not even think that they guessed that I was from Mozambique. They might have thought that I was just a Malawian boy hurrying to school.

I was in a region of Malawi where the tribe is also Zimbas like those in Zobue. They spoke Nyanja which is similar to Chichewa, the predominant native language in Malawi; the government of president Banda, a Chewa tribesman himself who could no longer speak his language and preferred English when addressing his nation, and someone translated his words to Chichewa, had imposed this as the national language of Malawi with English as the official language.

At eight o'clock that morning, I arrived at the residence of *senhor* Cerejeira, the contact of the rebel movement known as the Front for the Liberation of Mozambique, Frelimo in short, who lived in Mwanza. He had three wives and was a heavy drinker. There began my encounter with a different kind of enemy who were avowedly hostile to freedom.

Chapter 28

The word liberation is often used to mean freedom. In a thesaurus, the word freedom would probably be given as a synonym of liberation. So has the case been with the former rebel movement known as the Front for the Liberation of Mozambique, Frelimo, which is the acronym of the Portuguese words *Frente de Libertaçao de Moçambique*. The movement came together after originally two nationalist groups decided to unite. The movements were the Democratic Union of Mozambique or Udenamo in short which was secretly formed in southern Rhodesia when it was still under British rule, and the African National Union or Manu which was formed by Makonde tribesmen in exile in Tanganyika. Manu actually stood for Makonde National Union, the Makonde being the name of the tribe straddling the region between the northern province of Cabo Delgado of Mozambique and the southern region of Tanganyika. The group was later joined by the National Union for an Independent Mozambique or Unami which had been formed clandestinely in Tete by Baltasar Chagonga, the man the Portuguese secret agents kidnapped and drugged in Malawi before bringing him to Zobue the day we were there on 10th June 1966 for an open air mass.

In its initial document after its foundation, the leaders of Frelimo had stated that their aim was to liberate Mozambique so as later to enable the people of Mozambique to establish a democratic state of their choice.

But the founders were quickly edged out of the leadership when some aggressive individuals usurped power and either threw the original founders out or had them murdered. The aim of the new leaders was to liberate Mozambique and no longer to introduce democratic freedom afterwards. By their own actions, the new leaders made clear the distinction between liberation and freedom. This notwithstanding, the romantic supporters of the movement in the West in particular, did not understand that the leaders of Frelimo had made clear the difference between liberation and freedom. They insisted on calling Frelimo freedom fighters, which they were not.

For propaganda reasons, the Portuguese decided to refer to the nationalists as terrorists. That was the word I heard first while in Mozambique and saw in Portuguese newspapers of the time; it somehow stuck in my mind and refused to go away despite my best intentions and disagreement with the term terrorists for the people who were fighting for our independence but definitely not for our freedom.

Can Frelimo which has become a manifest embodiment of tyranny be regarded as freedom fighters in the true sense of the words as men who sought to establish a system based on democratic freedom? Not really, but perhaps in one strict and narrow sense, if we were to accept that liberating a country implies freeing it from control by another regime, but such liberation does not necessarily mean freedom with collective and individual liberties for the citizens. How many countries have been liberated from one tyranny to find themselves in a worse condition under new, more despotic tyrants?

Were such countries freed from the previous despotism free countries? Another reason why members of that despotic organization were referred to as freedom fighters was the Swahili Language semantics. The Tanzanians referred to their Mozambican protégés as *wagombania uhuru* which literally means fighters for independence. But in Swahili the word uhuru also means freedom as in *uhuru wa kwabudu* meaning freedom of worship. So the Swahili words were translated as freedom fighters because it sounded better than pro-independence fighters or fighters for independence what is what Frelimo fighters should have been called, and not freedom fighters.

I disagree with such antics on semantics of those who translated the Swahili words with a view to bamboozling people into thinking that Frelimo men in Mozambique were freedom fighters. In my view, freedom fighters should be those who actually fight to liberate a country from some kind of tyranny to replace it with democratic freedom and not people who fight to liberate a country from internal or foreign tyranny and then impose a tyrannical system such as Frelimo in Mozambique.

The term freedom fighters is a misnomer for people who liberate a country and impose a dictatorship of their own as happened in Angola, Mozambique and Zimbabwe where Robert Mugabe replaced the former white minority regime with a tyranny of his own that actually makes the regime he replaced appear a bit saintly.

If we look at the history of European countries which today constitute the comity of the most countries in the world, we can see cases like England liberated in the past by Oliver Cromwell from a dictatorial monarchy but he did not liberate England in order to establish freedom for the English people. I agree that in the confrontation with the monarchy, he had wanted Parliament to assert its rights and reduce the power of the king.

But after he had dethroned the monarch, had the king put to death and become the supreme leader of England, he imposed his own brand of tyrannical rule called Puritanism that was very harsh, with his suppression of the right of the people to enjoy their lives and entertain themselves by abolishing theatres and sports, making swearing and walking on Sundays, except for going to church, punishable with fines and imprisonment. He forced the people to fast once a day every month on a religious day instead of letting them celebrate and eat as they used to do.

He made makeup for women illegal and forced them to wear long dresses which fell to their heels so as to cover their bodies completely. He behaved in the same way as the Taliban who force women to wear *purdahs* and *burqas* to cover themselves completely with light clothes with holes over the eyes to enable them see, and to compel men to sport long beards and punish those who violate this edict on the holiness of wearing long beards, with public flogging or even execution.

Was Cromwell a freedom fighter? Perhaps for those romantic supporters of Frelimo in Britain who insisted that Frelimo were freedom fighters. So if Frelimo, in spite of its tyrannical nature, were freedom fighters for Mozambique, we can also say that Oliver Cromwell and his regime were freedom fighters for the English people. Will the English people of today agree with that? Perhaps a few Englishmen will think that he brought freedom to England. I know that the English of the time, were fed up with his rule and that was why they decided to return to a constitutional monarchy.

What of the French revolution which overthrew or liberated the French from a monarchist regime but made the French live under a terror of unprecedented ferocity during the revolution? Were Robespierre and his group who imposed the rule of terror in France, freedom fighters? Not even Napoleon who stopped the revolution and imposed his own dictatorship on France can be regarded as a freedom fighter. The Weimar Republic after the First World War in Germany was an anarchic experimentation with democracy. The Nazis liberated Germany from the anarchic republic and imposed one of the worst despotic regimes in the history of mankind. Were the Nazis freedom fighters?

The despotism of tsarist Russia paled into insignificance when compared to the totalitarianism of the Soviet regime that liberated Russia from tsarist rule. I find it difficult to think of Lenin and Stalin and the other leaders who followed them in power in the Soviet Union, as freedom fighters. What of Pol Pot and his Khmer Rouge regime in Cambodia which came to power in 1975 after militarily liberating Cambodia from a pro-American regime and imposed a rule that decimated two million of their fellow Cambodians? I would insult my own intelligence, if I were to regard the Khmer Rouge as freedom fighters.

Frelimo has known nothing but dictatorship with very ruthless leaders. Before it came to power in Mozambique, its rulers were opposed and challenged rather than acting peacefully and some people were killed for opposing them. I escaped with my skin intact after opposing them and they have always hunted me down ever since. After Frelimo came to power after independence in 1975, other people opposed its dictatorship with the force of arms in a civil war which lasted sixteen years from 1977 to 1993 and killed close to one million people. And more recently from 2013 to 2014, the Frelimo regime once again was engaged in a mini civil war of short duration with Renamo, the same group against which it fought the sixteen-year civil war. Why has it been opposed by force of arms? The reason is that Frelimo leaders are alien to concepts of freedom and they have therefore never been freedom fighters.

If they had been freedom fighters, Mozambique would have been a shining example of freedom today like Britain where no one sees the need to take up arms to fight for their liberties because people live in freedom and exercise their political and social rights. In fact, in Britain, it is the people who are the masters and not so much those in power who exercise power with the mandate of the people while in Mozambique, those in power do not have the mandate of the people and are in power after rigged elections and the same people have previously exercised power through the force of arms.

What went wrong and why did the original ideals of freedom for the people not prevail?

If we look at George Orwell's *Animal Farm* we will find some interesting parallels between what happened in countries that were liberated from one kind of tyranny and were placed under another brand of tyranny even harsher than the one it replaced. The animals had thought that their lot would improve after chasing their human owner away. That was not to be because the Pigs soon brought the farm under their own control and a new rule that made the rule of their former human owner look like child's play and very benign. Greed to control resources, thirst for power, megalomania and the absence of a system of checks and balances, propel individuals to impose themselves as unchallenged leaders and to rule their countries brutally.

What was worst with Frelimo is that the tyranny of its leaders began well before independence and became even worse when its rulers became the government of Mozambique after the Portuguese withdrew in 1975.

Why am I ruminating here?

I am doing so in order to help people understand why I did not fit into that organization after I had joined it and why it is wrong to hail people who have committed many abuses and violations of human rights not only in Mozambique but also in any other country. What I will narrate next will give an overview of the situation I found and faced in Frelimo when I joined it in Tanzania. I thought it would be better to give some explanation before describing the situation I encountered.

Despite my disagreement with the leaders of Frelimo and my abhorrence of their inhuman deeds, I did not agree with the Portuguese who claimed that Frelimo itself was a terrorist organization, although its actions against its own members and civilians have always been terroristic in nature and character. And while in Mozambique, I remember that despite our sympathy with the rebels, we always referred to Frelimo as terrorists because that was the term the Portuguese had drummed into our heads. When I use the word terrorists for Frelimo, it is not so much to disparage the organization but to revive history with humour. It was in that context of seeing history with humour that a newspaper in Nairobi in 1975 mused about Samora Machel as the terrorist of yesterday becoming the president of today in Mozambique. The newspaper knew that the Portuguese used to call Samora Machel a terrorist.

After dissecting the situation I found when I came into contact with Frelimo, I can now continue to narrate my adventures both when I was in it and after it, pleased that I have tried to explain things so that people can follow my story without asking why this or that happened or took place. My ruminations will also explain why there was instability and even a civil war after the departure of the Portuguese from Mozambique.

When I say that Malawi was one of the countries I lived in after leaving Mozambique, I am not quite telling the truth. Malawi only served as a transition path for me. I stayed there for only one week before I went to Tanzania after arriving in Blantyre which was then the capital of Malawi.

On the first day upon arrival in Blantyre, I became a victim of Frelimo's devious sabotage schemes before I even began to understand the goings-on in that organization. After arriving there, I went to the suburb of Bangwe where I found some fifteen boys from the seminary waiting to leave for Tanzania. There, I came to know the late Bonifacio Gruveta who, as the governor of the province of Zambezia after independence, ordered and oversaw the public execution of two individuals suspected of being thieves. The men were executed at the football stadium in Quelimane.

After greeting me, he wanted to know if I had documents from Mozambique.

"I've a diploma, a school leaving certificate, a birth certificate and my Portuguese citizenship certificate."

"You can give them to me for safekeeping, camarada,' he said, calling me comrade. We'll give them back to you later."

"My name is not Camarada," I said to him. "My name is Francisco Moises and don't call me Camarada again."

I did not know then that the members of Frelimo had adopted the Maoist way of calling each other comrade so much so, that few people even bothered to know the names of other people. The appellation of comrade started replacing names and began to give a faceless and communistic aspect to the organization. Being called comrade and hearing people calling each other comrade all the time began to sound normal to my ears until I began to refer to others as comrade after the shock of using that term has worn off. He said nothing after I rebuked him for calling me comrade. I knew that the wuss did not quite like it and detested me. I surrendered my documents to him, thinking, and believing that I would get them back later either before leaving Malawi or in Tanzania. No one later ever said anything about my certificates. I began to detest that gangster-like behaviour on the part of the people who wanted to be our future leaders.

I came to learn many years later that Bonifacio Gruveta was under instruction from his superiors in Tanzania to collect certificates and diplomas from Mozambicans arriving in Malawi so as to prevent the owners from ever leaving Frelimo, becoming the property and slaves of Frelimo and unable to go anywhere else to further their studies. That was their way of making sure that

Mozambicans did not get past the level they themselves had reached in education or of preventing Mozambicans from reaching the level of education a few of them like their leader Eduardo Mondlane, had reached. They knew that without school leaving certificates and diplomas, schools would find it difficult to accept and place youths in their classes and it would also prevent Mozambican youths from applying for scholarships to further their education.

After a week in Blantyre, we left the city by bus and we reached the Zambian border late in the evening of the same day and the bus just drove on through Zambia for about 70 kilometres before reaching the Zambia-Tanzania border at Tunduma late that evening. Papers were processed for us to enter Tanzania the following morning. We passed Christmas at Tunduma rather uneventfully before leaving the place like cattle packed in a huge truck for Nachingwea where Frelimo had its guerrilla training camp.

For two days we travelled along the worst road I had ever seen in my life, which made the bad roads I had travelled on in Mozambique far better. Big trucks laden with goods bound for Zambia and from Zambia, mainly with copper going to Tanzania, had broken down and some had swerved off the road and were half plunged down valleys with no hope and means of ever being pulled out because Tanzania simply did not have the resources, capacity, and ability to do so. We travelled through the most amazing land with rugged mountains and hills separated by valleys and gorges which looked as virgin as they were from the time they had come into existence. It looked like no humans had ever set foot on them.

We finally made it to the base at Nachingwea, a dismal place in a bush and in the middle of nowhere with nothing for us, we who had come from a prestigious academic institution. It was apparent that our arrival was not quite appreciated by the largely semi-illiterate men already there who felt rather inferior towards us. Instead of celebrating the arrival of our group which was made up of brilliant boys with good secondary school education, they began to hate us with a passion with some of them calling us priestlings in order to lower our dignity and humiliate us unnecessarily.

Chinese instructors trained the rebels in guerrilla warfare and also indoctrinated them with Maoist ideology. Every guerrilla was issued with the little red book by Mao Ze Dong called *Citaçoes do Presidente Mao Tse-Tung* in Portuguese or *Quotations from Chairman Mao Tse-Tung* in English. The instructors even taught the guerrillas to sing songs in Mandarin in praise of Mao. Mao's little book was full of fantastic statements that the guerrillas had to commit to memory, bashing imperialism and its lackeys. While at the camp I read the little book very quickly. I had been chosen to be a political commissar who had to know Maoist ideology inside out in order to indoctrinate the comrade guerrillas.

It even states that "the atomic bomb is a paper tiger," which in Chinese ideology means something that is *fearsome and yet powerless*. In Mao's concept, the atomic bombs of the American imperialists and of Soviet Social imperialists as he called them after he fell out with Nikita Khrushchev, would be useless against China as the Chinese people would swamp the invaders in a sea of people.

Surely, was Mao so ingenuous as to think that the Americans and the Soviets would need to enter China after firing their ballistic missiles from land-based silos or submarines thousands of miles away or dropping their nuclear bombs from bombers? Mao wrote such fantasies before China had nuclear weapons of its own. When it had them, it dubbed them as defensive weapons against the offensive weapons of the American imperialists and of the Soviet Social Imperialists. In case of a nuclear war then, China and its people would have been reduced to a radioactive waste and the Americans or the Soviets would not have needed to enter China before nuclear radioactivity dissipated.

He would be right in thinking so, if the Americans or the Soviets were to fight a war against China with conventional weapons. The sea of Chinese masses would have drowned the imperialists or the social imperialists and defeated them. Even then I thought that the Americans and the Soviets knew it and they would never dare invade China from land or from the sea.

It was while there that I first saw Samora Machel, the guerrilla commander, who would become the first president of Mozambique after independence. He was quite a comical figure moving like a peacock in his Fidel Castro-like uniform and always pulling up the sleeves of his shirt as a man about to fight another man. He did all that to demonstrate his self-importance. He was sporting an unruly beard like that of his Cuban hero.

Information about him has always been scarce and so much contradictory information was fabricated about him that has not been borne by people who knew him in Mozambique and in Tanzania. The man whose parents called Magarila at his birth, a name he disliked with passion as it was close to the word gorilla, belonged to the same Shangaan tribe of southern Mozambique as Eduardo Mondlane, the American-educated leader of Frelimo who was killed in a bomb blast in Dar-Es-Salaam two years later on 3rd February 1969. That event paved the way for Machel to become the leader of Frelimo with no elections whatsoever within the organization. He would also become the first president of Mozambique without election.

Samora Machel became the guerrilla commander after the death of Filipe Magaia, the first guerrilla commander who had attained the rank of second lieutenant in the Portuguese Army before Frelimo came into existence. Magaia was killed by one of his own officers in the northern province of Niassa on 16th October 1966 as a result of a plot that involved Machel himself according to Lourenço Magaia, the man who fired the three shots which claimed the life of the first guerrilla commander in chief. Matola revealed the plot to kill Magaia while talking with me and other Mozambican exiles in Nairobi, Kenya, in the early 1980s.

After firing on Magaia who died three days later, Matola was arrested by the men in the group who had decide to execute him on the spot before relenting and handing him over to the Tanzanians for investigation. He was handed over while tied up with ropes (for lack of chains and handcuffs, I suppose!). The Tanzanians held him for five years in a maximum security prison at Mnazi Moja in Dar-Es-Salaam after which they released him without ever explaining why, and disclosing any information they got out of him while investigating him.

Matola died tragically in Nairobi in 1989 after being struck by a hit and run truck, an accident some superstitious minds in the community of the Mozambican exiles in the Kenyan capital described as the revenge of the spirit of Magaia he had killed.

After Magaia's death, Machel not only replaced him as commander-in-chief but also took over and married Josina Mutemba who had been Magaia's fiancée. Josina died years later at a hospital in Dar-ES-Salaam, Tanzania, either from leukaemia as sources in Frelimo stated or after being poisoned after Machel discovered that she was pregnant and suspecting that her pregnancy was the work of another man. He had previously had a child with her though.

According to various reports from people who had known him in Mozambique including some of his own age mates and classmates, Samora Machel failed to pass the exams for his primary education certificate, although he later claimed to have reached Form 2 and to be a nursing graduate. It was however known that he had been at the central hospital in the then Mozambican capital of

Lourenço Marques in a capacity that no one seems to be able to identify. Some people claimed that he had studied nursing and failed, but Solomon Mondlane, in a short work on Samora Machel in English, says that he had worked in the hospital's morgue where the sight of the dead people he handled sort of desensitized him about death, and this explained his total lack of respect for human life and why he became such a cruel man as the guerrilla commander of Frelimo and subsequently as the president of Mozambique.

As some of us were regarded as still too young to receive guerrilla training, we were selected to go and join the Frelimo School in Dar-Es-Salaam by the Indian Ocean, which bore the pompous name of "The Mozambican Institute." I never quite knew whether it was a primary or a secondary school. The more grown up amongst our group remained at the base and Frelimo never quite made adequate use of them as commanders or in any other capacity. Some of them had a hard time there after Samora Machel targeted them for humiliation because they could not take the man's insolence lying down. Two or more of them went over to the Portuguese when the opportunity to do so presented itself, and others fled and ended up living in Tanzania, Congo, and Kenya. Some stayed and were sent to fight in Mozambique where they died in combat against Portuguese forces.

Chapter 29

I was in Dar-Es-Salaam at last; an African settlement the Arabs had called Dar-as-Salaam meaning the Haven of Peace. While here I deem it opportune to say something about the word Mozambique which was from the name of an Arab ruler. The Arab by the name of *Musa bin Biq* had made himself the sultan of an island off the coast of the northern region of Nampula. When the Portuguese arrived there, they called the Island Moçambique which was their translation of the name Musa bin Biq.

There was nothing special for me about Dar Es Salaam because it was not the exciting place I had thought it would be, and there was also something special for me as it was the place where I was involved in a struggle for freedom and in which I failed when I lost to the forces of tyranny. In 1968, the city itself was old and dilapidated with practically no development taking place because of the policies of Julius Nyerere who was the first president of Tanganyika after Britain pulled out in 1961, and later in 1964 when Tanganyika federated with the Island of Zanzibar to become Tanzania. There were some crumbling buildings and structures the Germans had built before the First World War before Britain took over the administration of the territory as a League of Nations-mandated territory for 43 years from 1918 until independence in 1961.

The late President Nyerere was an idealist man with the interests of his people at heart but he was so conceited that his behaviour precluded him from opening his eyes and mind to see things in their proper and right perspectives. He had genuinely believed that the path to progress in his country lay in the hands of his people who should have been confident in their own ability to work hard and develop their nation. But he introduced socialist policies which he called African Socialism and these killed the spirit of initiative. Like the socialist thinkers and idealists before him and those who attempted to implement the ideas of idealists like Karl Marx, he failed to appreciate that human beings were by nature selfish and were motivated by the promise of personal gain. He closed his eyes to the fact that his fellow citizens would work hard, if not harder, if and when they felt they stood to profit from whatever they did. But Nyerere nationalized little personal businesses like stores and barber's shops and did not allow Tanzanians to do anything for their own profit. He wasted his time on socialist ideologies and his obsessive fear of his people being exploited by capitalists. Mere ideas did not meet the needs of his people nor did they fill up their stomachs.

Nyerere was an autocratic ruler but never a brutal one like many an African country has known. He was a great scholar who got a Master's Degree in Economics and History from the University of Edinburgh. He had been a teacher before entering politics, the reason why his official title for his personal pride, gratification, and glorification was *mwalimu*, the Swahili word meaning teacher. He was always called mwalimu Nyerere. He thought he was the teacher to his people or something like a secular rabbi unlike Jesus Christ who had been a spiritual rabbi.

He translated Shakespeare's *Julius Caesar* into Swahili as *Juliasi Kaizari*. The word *Kaizari* is from the German word Kaiser which in German means emperor and is like the word Czar in Russia which was the title of the Russian

278

emperor. The German word and the Russian word have their origin in the name Caesar. So the Swahili word Kaizari indicates German influence on Tanzanian Swahili while in Kenya, Swahili the word for king or emperor is *mfalme*.

He also translated Shakespeare's *The Merchants of Venice* as *Mabepari WA Venisi*. The word *mabepari* in Swahili means capitalists. So the *Merchants of Venice* became the *Capitalists of Venice* in Nyerere's Swahili rendition.

Obviously, Nyerere decided to back the struggle for independence in Mozambique knowing what the dangers were and he had no illusions about it. The overwhelming Portuguese military strength in Mozambique could inflict a telling punishment on his country, if the Generals had received the green light they had sought from Lisbon to strike at his country. Luckily for him the Generals like the highly talented tactician Kaulza de Arriaga in the early 1970s, were not allowed to mount major raids into his country. Despite not having permission to raid his country, the Portuguese nevertheless intruded into his country's airspace day and night and with total impunity. Portuguese military aircraft roamed in the southern Tanzanian air space without any specific strategy and dropped bombs on civilians and pamphlets to discourage refugees from making common cause with "terrorists" meaning Frelimo guerrillas.

That was the Tanzania I was in after leaving dynamic Mozambique where there seemed to be no end to the transformation the Portuguese were effecting for their interests and benefits. But Tanzania lay stagnant despite having resources such as an ocean, woods, diamonds and precious stones and some of the best wildlife parks in the country which it could have used to promote tourism and generate foreign exchange as Kenya its next door neighbour was doing.

I had never really regarded Tanzania as a place where I wanted to live. I never stopped dreaming of going to France or in the worst case scenario, to Britain. America was never on the cards for me despite the fact that it succoured us with emergency food after the flood of 1958 in the lower Zambezi.

It was while I was at the Mozambican Institute in the Tanzanian capital that information about the situation not going well in Frelimo began to swamp me. On arrival I found that the students were already daggers drawn against the leaders. So the accusation that the leaders of Frelimo made, that it was I and other former seminarians who had joined the school and stirred the pot against them, was nonsensical to the best of my knowledge. They wanted to find a scapegoat for the generalized revolt they faced as a reaction to their misdeeds from militants not only at the school, but in the organization as a whole. I do not deny that I was one of those who entered the fray and in no time I was in the thick of things, and at the forefront of the rebellion after I had been fully apprised of the tyrannical nature of the leaders of the movement.

I amazed the students with my unmatchable command of Portuguese; most of the students we found there could not boast a good command of the language. Not even Eduardo Mondlane, the leader, knew much Portuguese, having only done his primary education in Portuguese and college and university in English in the United States where he obtained a PhD in Anthropology and Sociology. At confrontational meetings with the leaders, students would listen when I stood up and spoke. Because of that, my name was on top of the leaders' blacklist. And I do not regret what I did because I did it for the greater cause of freedom which I have always believed in even as a boy when confronting a group of foreign evildoers and capturing one of them so that they did not continue to disturb our freedom. I cherished freedom and was ready to make sacrifices for it. And for me there is nothing greater and more valuable than freedom from tyranny and totalitarianism, which were the hallmarks of Frelimo I came to know.

After the arrival of my group at the school in January of 1968, we had classes for only one month until the end of that month when the classes were suspended and confrontation including physical fights between students and leaders of Frelimo began to take place. At any rate, the school had ceased to function and had become a redundant place with many students leaving and going to Nairobi, Kenya, to resume their studies there peacefully without the ruckus of the constant warfare between them and the leaders of Frelimo.

From time to time, the leaders came to announce that they had decided to close the school and ordered us to go to the military base at Nachingwea. No one agreed to leave, as we knew that only humiliation and death at the hands of murderers awaited us out there in the bush and forest of Nachingwea or northern Mozambique where we would be taken to be killed, as had happened to countless other people before us. We stayed put and went to complain to the office of Rashid Kawawa who was the vice-president of Tanzania and who was also in charge of Home Affairs and refugees in Tanzania. Kawawa would countermand the decision of the leaders and say that the school should remain open. Remain open it did but with no classes and continuous clashes between the students and the leaders of Frelimo.

On the evening of 3rd March 1968, a boy by the name of Daniel Chatama who passed away from cancer in March 2015 at Santa Rosa in California, badly beat up another boy called Paulino Xadreque, who he accused of acting as an informant to the leaders. Shortly afterwards, a gang of leaders including Samora Machel, Joaquim Chissano, who became president of Mozambique after the death of Samora

Machel when his plane strayed to and crashed in South Africa on 19th October 1986; Aurelio Manave, and Luis Arrancatudo, stormed the school armed with pistols.

Luis Arrancatudo was later embroiled in a disagreement with Samora Machel and went over to the Portuguese, and he supplied them with information that enabled Portuguese planes to devastate guerrilla bases in Niassa where he had been a Frelimo commander against the Portuguese. Arrancatudo died when the Portuguese force he was commanding fell in a guerrilla ambush when it was returning to base after raiding a base of his former colleagues.

We students were saved just in time when Chatama, the boy who had beaten the other boy, broke the windows of his room, jumped out and ran to the police station which was close by, to tell them that the students were being attacked by their leaders. Armed policemen arrived and arrested Samora Machel and Joaquim Chissano who told them that they were leaders of Frelimo after which the police let them go. They disappeared from the scene as fast as their legs could carry them.

Luis Arrancatudo had left like lightning even before the police had arrived on the scene. But the plump, slow and ever sweaty late Manave, who was to distinguish himself after independence as the manager of the concentration camps Frelimo established under the misnomer of re-education camps, was unearthed from a clump of tall grass under a coconut tree where he was hiding, shaking with fear with a pistol in his hand after firing three bullets which did not hit or hurt any of the students. The police handcuffed him and marched him to their station with some of the students shouting insults at him while others rained punches and kicks on him as the police officers watched, apparently pleased to see students express their anger at the captive. The police officers never once asked the students to stop beating Manave and the beating only stopped after the captive had been marched to the front of the police station where students were not allowed to enter.

At the police station, Manave was divested and left only in his underwear before a police officer caned him mercilessly whilst the students screamed in anger urging the police officer to beat him without mercy. Manave sweated and grunted in pain, but never once screamed as he was being caned. Mucus flowed copiously from his nostrils. He was a sorry sight in a sorry state but we were happy to see the tyrant getting a dose of his own medicine. Before being thrown into a cell, one police officer checked the pistol he had after removing its magazine. He found out that three bullets were missing from the twelve-bullet pack. It seemed he had fired his pistol at nothing when gripped with fear while hiding in the grass under the coconut tree where we found and captured him, despite the fact that I and the other boys were unarmed. Despite being unarmed, I was fearless and brave because I was convinced that I was fighting the enemies of freedom and that no sacrifice would be too much in the struggle against their tyranny.

The invasion of the school which had initially terrorized us when the leaders kicked and beat us in our bedrooms before forcing us to go to the patio before the police intervened, ended in our victory and in defeat for the leaders. The following day students poured into the police station to make damning statements against the leaders.

Samora Machel was summoned to go and explain to the police why he had led others to storm the school. He used an interpreter as he could not speak Swahili and the interpreter told the police exactly the opposite of what he was stating in reply to their questions. The interpreter who was not a student, fled from Dar-Es-Salaam after the interview fearing that Machel could catch up with him and kill him, which he would have done without blinking an eyelid, for Machel was a very cruel man.

Aurelio Manave was released the following morning after Janet Mondlane, the leader's wife, gave a bribe of 11,000 Tanzanian shillings to the police. There ended the episode. Neither Manave nor Samora Machel was charged with criminal offences.

But that was not the end of the war between the students and the leaders, more was yet to come. One morning, Uria Simango, who was the vice-president of Mondlane, and Marcelino dos Santos, then the rebel minister for foreign affairs, called a meeting at the school to tell us that the school was to close and the students were to go to the Nachingwea base. A student who had appeared at the meeting with a sheathed dagger in a belt around his waist, prevented the two from leaving the meeting hall as he wielded his dagger in his hand, telling them that they should sit down so that we could talk as men. In no time we rushed to support him and surrounded the two leaders who were dragged out of the hall while being kicked and punched.

With a boy holding him by his long beard, Uria Simango held his hands on the shoulders of Jose Manhique, the student leader, and pleaded with him not to let us kill him. We had no intention of killing him or Marcelino dos Santos. We were not brutal and inhuman like they were. While that was happening, two boys were running here and there in search of gasoline and saying, in Portuguese, "*temos que queimar estes gajos vivos (we must burn these goons alive.)*" They did not find gasoline with which to burn them and I do not think the rest of us would have allowed them to commit such a dastardly act, although execution by fire was what Uria Simango met with after independence. After Mondlane's death, Uria Simango lost the power struggle to Samora Machel and after independence, Machel had Uria Simango executed by having him and a number of other detainees doused with gasoline and set alight at Mitelala in the northern province of Niassa on 24th June 1977.

As a group of students were beating Uria Simango, another group had surrounded Marcelino dos Santos and were also dragging in all directions and trashing him without mercy. I saw terror in the eyes of a leader who was himself a terrorist to people who fell into his hands. After we were pleased that we had disciplined the two leaders sufficiently, we let them go with a warning that should they return to cause more disturbance, they would face harsher and more resolute action and disciplinary measures than they had encountered on that day.

The following day we heard Radio Dar-Es-Salaam saying in Swahili that Vice-president Rashid Kawawa had decided that the school would remain open and students should stay put and go nowhere. We had won a major battle. We stayed defiant and ready for more battles against the leaders and their intentions.

On 11th May 1968, Dar Es Salaam was shaken after a daring invasion from a group of Mozambican Makonde men and women some with babies on their backs, armed with machetes, clubs and horns who mounted a daylight raid into Frelimo's headquarters in the Tanzania capital apparently with the intention of killing Mondlane, the leader, if they could find him there. Mondlane had gone out of Tanzania and the invaders did not find him there. There the invaders grabbed Joaquim Chissano, who was the security chief then. The KGB-trained security chief resisted and dodged blows from a machete aimed at him. He was able to get rid of his jacket from his body after all its buttons were ripped off before he was able to descend from the first floor of the building where the office was and run away downstairs and out into the street as furiously as he could to save his life. But a Mr Mateus Mutemba, an officer in charge of transmission and who was suspected of communicating information to the Portuguese, was not so lucky.

The invaders hacked him on the head with machetes and he later died at a hospital in the Tanzanian capital. The students to a man boycotted his burial and that angered Mondlane, the leader, because he felt that the students did not care and were not patriotic.

Sergio Vieira, an officer of Goan origin who headed the dreaded People's National Security Service or SNASP in short after independence, and who earned himself a place in a book that was published in Paris about the crimes of Communism worldwide, was able to get into the washroom in the office where he locked himself in and the invaders were unable to reach him. As they had no time for him because they had to leave as quickly as they had arrived, they went away. Thus, Sergio Vieira, the Stalinist ideologue of Frelimo, was lucky to have missed his date with the reaper, the same reaper of lives he himself later sent on dates to many unfortunate souls he did not like or regarded as enemies of the people or reactionaries.

The invaders withdrew before the police arrived. The following day newspapers in Dar-Es-Salaam were splashed on the front pages with the news of the event. Early that morning, I walked on the side of the road opposite the office in order to check things out for myself and laugh at what had happened to the tyrants. Everything was in chaos and the office was closed and the area cordoned off with a steel helmeted soldier armed with a British-made rifle grimly standing guard, and perhaps unable to understand what had taken place.

The Portuguese media rejoiced at the event and gleefully talked about a shootout between gangs of terrorists at the terrorist headquarters in Dar-Es-Salaam. Only that it was not a shootout but an invasion that took the leaders in the office completely by surprise and they were unable to react and use their weapons to fight off the invaders.

The students' war against the leaders continued unabated, but we were running out of luck without knowing it. We were to find out soon enough when the leaders came again to announce that they were going to close the school. We once again trooped to the office of the Tanzanian vice-president to complain about the decision. We were told to sit down and wait for a decision from the government. We waited silently for half an hour or so with some of us crouching, others sitting down and others standing before we saw police vans arriving, and out of the first van which stopped where we were, came a rather old, tall, slender and shrivelled police officer with a holstered pistol around his waist who began to vociferate orders to us.

"*Kaa chini. Kaa chini*," the police officer said in Swahili meaning "sit down. Sit down" before saying in English, "Sit down. Be quiet. "*Utapata tabu, mwanafunzi* (Student, you will be in trouble)," he added in Swahili as if speaking to just one person and not to all of us.

As more and more vans kept coming, he tacitly told us in Swahili about the situation we were in. "*Kutoka sasa wanafunzi mumekamatwa*," he said in Swahili meaning, "As of now, you students are under arrest." We were in no position to ask him questions, as he had not come for discussions with us but to detain us.

We knew that we were under arrest, but we were not handcuffed nor tied up with ropes. We were not manhandled or beaten. We quietly and in an orderly fashion filed into vans which took us to the cells in Dar-Es-Salaam's central prison, a place that was built in the colonial times either by the Germans or the British. I do not know. I never tried to find out. On arrival, they took our names and we were made to surrender anything we had—money and any tools before being shovelled into dirty cells without beds, blankets or water and without any explanation being given as to why we had been arrested. The cells were opened once or twice a day for us to go to the washrooms which had flooded with water and stinky shit floating in the hallway. It was a disgusting sight.

We were kept there for three days without being ill-treated or charged because we had committed no crime. But humour was never lacking amongst us. We told stories and laughed despite the uncertainty of what might happen to us. One day when policemen came to give us barely edible food, a boy from the seminary caused us to laugh when he told the police officers that he had trouble with his stomach. He said the word in a mixture of Swahili he could not speak then and his Mozambican language.

"*Nina mimba*," he said. There was trouble with the word *mimba* which in the boy's language meant stomach ache or pregnancy depending on the context but in Swahili, the word means "pregnancy" and nothing else.

"*Munanfanya nini huyu mtoto nyinyi?*" a police officer asked the boys in the cell where the boy was with a grave voice meaning "what are you guys doing to this kid?" The police officer had thought that the other boys were abusing him sexually to the point of making him pregnant, as if a boy could ever become pregnant. There was general laughter in all of the ground floor cells which we occupied.

On the upper cell, a police officer was talking to some sex workers they had arrested and a boy, another former seminarian, down below in my cell was calling him in a singing but mournful voice and telling him to leave the prostitutes alone and go to listen to him.

"*Askari wacha malaya, njoo usikilize. Mimi na tabu nyingi sana*," the boy was saying repeatedly in Swahili to mean "Oh police officer, please, leave the prostitutes alone. Come listen to me. I'm under heavy pressure." The boy needed to go to the washroom very badly.

After three days of imprisonment without explanation, charges, or trial and without being ill-treated or tortured, we were released, given our things back and marched out in single file to two big buses outside the prison waiting for us. We were ordered to get onto them. Each bus had one or two armed policemen with rather old rifles that had perhaps been left behind by the British. We were driven off without ever being told where they were taking us. The police officers were friendly though and we chatted with them. The buses stopped by the school to let us pick up some of our things with the police officers making sure that none of us escaped before the buses resumed their run due south. The buses stopped at one place late in the afternoon and we were taken in groups to go and eat at some roadside village restaurant where everyone ate a cooked tilapia fish with rice while the policemen watched over us and guarded us, as if we were criminals or prisoners. The government footed the bill for us.

Well into the night, the two buses stopped in the middle of nowhere because there was a truck that had allegedly broken down ahead of us. The policemen rushed to the truck with their guns cocked and drawn and we heard them shouting and hitting the truck with the butts of their guns before forcing it to leave, after which our buses resumed their run to our unknown destination. We later found out to our horror, that the truck that had forced the two buses with us inside to stop, had two Frelimo officers in it. Were they there to ambush us? How did they know that we students were being taken to some place or was it just a coincidence?

At around noon of the following day, the buses arrived at a UN refugee camp at Rutamba in the District of Lindi in the Province of Mtwara where the policemen handed us over to the UN personnel there and told us that we should inform the UN officials if we saw Frelimo leaders coming to try to harm us so that the Tanzanian government could take action against them. They also told us that the government had taken that action to protect us because it had known that the leaders of Frelimo had decided on an action to hurt us. They further said that our exile was temporary because the government wanted to sweep up and clean the mess in Frelimo before recalling us to go back to school.

That was not to be and all those good words were intended to distract us from the injustice that the Tanzanian government had done to us by imprisoning us without charge or trial. I was angry. I had committed no crime during the protest at the vice-president's office. Everything had been peaceful with none of us shouting, screaming, or acting in any disorderly manner at all. The government had violated our rights. But were we dealing with a government which respected the rights of its own citizens? No. We were not. Perhaps the government had taken that decision against us to stop us being a bad example to the Tanzanians who could take their cue from us and begin to challenge and rebel against their own government.

Vice-president Rashid Kawawa was, however, not amused by the leaders of Frelimo because the Tanzanian security agency had known about Mondlane's double dealing with the Portuguese and his links with the Central Intelligence Agency or the CIA and the Portuguese infiltration of Frelimo. He really did not like Mondlane at all, but he could not act against him or expel him from Tanzania because Julius Nyerere, his boss, admired Mondlane. He would not upset Nyerere, knowing that the latter could get rid of him. Nyerere, a practising Catholic who went to morning masses at St. Joseph's Cathedral in Dar-Es-Salaam every Sunday and Rashid Kawawa, a Moslem, were great colleagues, however. Christians, Moslems and animists lived peacefully in Tanzania where the Swahili Language was the universal language which united the people. But the Tanzanians had a defect though.

They did not take kindly to an African addressing them in English and they would disdainfully ask the person whether he thought he was a white man, whilst in Kenya, people speaking English were highly admired. And Kenyans had no problems being addressed in Swahili either.

It was while at Rutamba that I came to know Swahili which came to me in the twinkling of an eye and I was able to speak it without accent. In no time the language that had sounded like Greek to me, turned out to be a language I fell in love with. If there was anything positive about me having been exiled to Rutamba, it was that I came to know Swahili which enabled me to escape from there and later live in Nairobi with no language problems, before I came to learn English which is the language for the elite there.

As time passed and nothing happened to us to extricate from that situation, we began to understand that we had been dumped to be forgotten at the god-damned camp. We later decided to find our own way out after a small group of desperados amongst us decided to accept Mondlane's offer for us to return to Frelimo but to go to Nachingwea first before going back to the school in Dar-Es-Salaam. The desperados were taken to Nachingwea with the permission of the Tanzanian government and never went to the school in Dar-Es-Salaam which didn't open its door as a school again. One of them escaped later and joined us in Nairobi. After being trained at Nachingwea, he was sent to Cabo Delgado where he had a hard time surviving the large scale operation code named *Operaçao No Gordio* or *Operation Gordion knot* in which General Kaulza de Arriaga launched employing planes, helicopters, artillery, and infantry to wipe out Frelimo guerrillas, which he nearly achieved.

Frelimo only survived by refusing to engage his forces and by operating in tiny little groups after abandoning their bases which de Ariaga's troops took and destroyed before pursuing and hunting down the rebels in the bush. The guerrillas resorted to a diversionary operation from Zambia into Tete where the Portuguese had tied down huge numbers of troops to protect the construction site for the Cabora Bassa dam, the largest in Africa south of the Sahara, instead of using them in tactical operations against the guerrillas or in cross border operations into Zambia as they had done before. Kaulza who had sought permission from Lisbon to stage major operations against "terrorist bases in Tanzania and Zambia" was not happy about having his forces tied down at one spot, but he was a soldier and had to obey his civilian superiors in Lisbon.

I was in no doubt that my life was just one long adventure of survival. If the government would not get me out of that hole, I would get myself out of it. It was going to be as simple as that. I was set for another adventure, come what may.

Chapter 30

Initially all the students were bamboozled by the sweet words that the government had uttered to us when it dropped us off at the refugee camp. We believed that the decision the government had taken was temporary and that it would take us back to Dar-Es-Salaam. But where would it take us to in Dar-Es-Salaam? To the Mozambican Institute which was a Frelimo school run on CIA money Mondlane was able to access through the Ford Foundation in America? Surely, Tanzanians were not going to establish a new school for us, when they themselves could hardly build any new ones for their own youth.

As for Frelimo, for us it was an enemy as long as its leaders remained the same. Its leaders feared and hated us with a passion and we too feared and hated them with equal passion, as if measure for measure.

As months passed at that place which symbolized regression for our lives because there were no libraries, schools, or jobs for us and we had to depend on food handouts from the UN refugee agency, we began to realize that the government had got rid of us. We began to understand that unless we did something to get out of that place, it was going to be where we would die and be buried without pomp or circumstance.

What was worse still, we were under control because the government did not want us to leave there even for a day to go to anywhere else even if we were to return to there. Moving and travelling in Tanzania, particularly in southern Tanzania, was not an easy thing to do. The government and the people were edgy and the government asked the people to take precautions and be apprehensive of any planes they saw in the air and also of any strangers they met. Tanzania had thus been transformed into a Big Brother is watching you community.

During the time I was there, I became aware that the sprawling camp of grass huts that had been built tightly together, could become an inferno if a single Portuguese plane dropped NAPALM or incendiary bombs on any of the four villages of the camp which were called Cabo Delgado, Zambia, Mahuta and Chilala. It could be even worse if planes came in a group of four with each one of them dropping its bombs on a village assigned to it. The Portuguese knew them all. Those villages would burst into flames and become infernos which could kill hundreds of their residents and totally incinerate them. And when confronted by the international community, the Portuguese could claim that the camp harboured terrorists and would blame the civilians for having allowed terrorists into them. There would be a few noises and then the matter would have petered out like a storm that comes and vanishes.

While there from July 1968 to July 1969, I decided that I had stayed there longer than I should have, when Portuguese planes flew over it about three times or even more, mainly at night. They were not keen on attacking the camp as they noticed there were no soldiers when they flew daylight reconnaissance. The Portuguese knew that the camp was run by the UN refugee agency. So the planes only dropped leaflets close by asking refugees to return to Mozambique or to warn them against making common cause with terrorists.

Because of their nervousness and fear of attack, Tanzania, which had practically no air force worth the name to counter Portuguese air activity, did what it could. It turned its citizens into people who spied on one another and who were to arrest suspicious characters they saw. Huts in villages were organized into groups of ten, called in Swahili *nyumba kumi* or ten-hut security cells whose residents were to know one another and arrest any strangers they saw.

When I decided to leave, I knew that I would be violating the order that forbade me from leaving. I did not need to ask myself where I should go from there. There was only one direction: Nairobi, Kenya. The problem was how to do it without money. There was no way of getting money. I was to learn years later in Nairobi from father Robert Roesems, who had been my teacher of French at Zobue Seminary, that he had sent me money from Belgium while I was at Rutamba and that the money never reached me; the Tanzanians did not want me to get it as they suspected that I would use it to run away. So they pocketed it for themselves.

There was hope for me when I decided to get together with two boys called Manuel Njanje and Costa Magiga. I admired Manuel Njanje not for his intelligence but for his daring and mindlessness. As for Costa Magiga who was closer to me than Njanje, I liked him because he was my friend and we were together all the time. He was a good football player who was said to have gone to a witchdoctor to get juju so that he could perform even better in matches. The witchdoctor sent him to a cemetery to spend nights there, which I thought was a foolish thing to do just for the sake of becoming a great football player. Where did that happen—in East Africa? I never thought that East Africa had as powerful witchdoctors as those in Senaland. I would only do that to acquire invincibility and for general good luck, particularly to get money and acquire property. The boy seemed to attract luck though and girls easily fell in love with him. He probably had *n'nchena*, the juju to attract girls and make them lust for him. I always had wanted *mangolomera*, the magical medicine for fighting and defeating enemies or opponents. That would be the real thing for me in a world where I had many enemies who could easily bully me.

There was some entertainment in the air though while I was at Rutamba. As a result of the revolt against the leaders of Frelimo and our call for leadership change, the leaders called a congress, which came to be known as Frelimo's Second Congress; the first one having been held at the time of the foundation of the organization. Instead of holding the congress in Tanzania as we had wanted so that we could attend and vote for new leaders, the old leaders decided on a trick by deciding to hold the meeting in a wooded zone of northern Mozambique they regarded as a liberated zone. Obviously, the move prevented many people who had wanted to attend, for fear of being killed by the leaders who would use their armed men against the opposition at a place where they were armed and where the opposition would not be armed.

As they had wanted to make the world believe that they had liberated areas, they made a prior announcement that they would hold their congress inside Mozambique in that month of July without however indicating where specifically they were going to meet. The Portuguese were on the alert with constant reconnaissance flights. As soon as the meeting began, a reconnaissance plane spotted the gathering and the participants began to disperse as they knew that it would not be long before planes would be over them and began to bomb and strafe them. The reconnaissance plane, while still in flight, relayed the information to the High Command in Lourenço Marques. A few minutes later, attack planes were in the air while the High Command informed Lisbon that "the terrorist leaders will not leave the Portuguese territory alive."

The dense woodland did much to conceal the leaders who were carted away by experienced guerrillas to secure hiding places to be safe from the planes. Although the planes bombed the place with incendiary bombs, they were not able to kill the leaders. Mondlane, the tall, big-footed, and athletic leader, was able to run as fast as his legs could take him to the Rovuma River and cross it for the safety of Tanzania. The planes attacked the area for three consecutive days, using mainly incendiary bombs.

When we heard about the incident from fighters who were at the gathering, I and others had quite a laugh. We thought that the leaders got what they deserved, although they had not been hurt. The leaders did not disclose the event that had disgraced them. I was the first to report it in a newspaper in Maputo after the sixteen-year civil war ended in 1993 when some freedom was allowed in Mozambique. No one in Frelimo denied it. In order to counter what I wrote but without a verbal denial, the government in Maputo decided to visit the place they had not bothered to care about and declared it a historical site.

After enemy planes had dispersed the gathering, the leaders of Frelimo announced that the congress had been a great success and that all the leaders had been "re-elected" to retain their posts. The falsity of it made me laugh even more and scratch my head with incredulity at the sheer arrogance of the leaders of Frelimo to lie without their consciences ever bothering them. Lack of conscience had been the hallmark of their characters and personality.

The event which followed next was a sad one. I heard it first at around 8 p.m. from Radio Tanzania in Dar-Es-Salaam broadcasting in Swahili. The radio reported that Eduardo Mondlane, the leader of Frelimo, was killed in a bomb blast on that day, 3rd February, 1969. Unfortunately the hostility between us and Mondlane had run deep. We did not regret that it had happened and some students even expressed their joy. It was childish and stupid to laugh at someone's death. Someone told the Tanzanian official in charge of the refugee camp that the students were happy over Mondlane's death. The officer by the name of Kamtawa summoned some of us including myself to his office where he dressed us down.

"What you did is most reprehensible. This is the first time a bomb ever explodes and kills someone on Tanzanian soil and you guys dare express satisfaction over such a sad event?"

We did not argue with him nor did we apologize. For us the Mondlane chapter was over and closed. We had to continue with our lives which were more important to us than grieving his death. After all, he had been our enemy, had he not? If he had been able to lay his hands on us, we would all be dead.

Before continuing with my story, I must stop here to talk about Mondlane's death. Who killed him? Mondlane died at the residence of Betty King, an American woman then living in Dar Es-Salaam. It appeared that he had picked up a booby-trapped parcel from either the post office or from Frelimo's office, and took it to Betty King's house. King was not in her house when the parcel exploded as Mondlane attempted to open it, killing him and King's dog and extensively damaging her residence. In the evening of that day, Tanzanian police rounded up Joaquim Chissano, Frelimo's security chief, Marcelino dos Santos, the foreign affairs minister for the organization and Ms King who were subjected to intensive and extensive questioning and were mercilessly caned with sjamboks, a word of Afrikaans for whips made of hippopotamus skins known as kiboko in Swahili which is incidentally the Swahili word for the hippopotamus.

The cause of the death of Mondlane remains shrouded in mystery. After his death, the Tanzanians said that it had been caused by an explosive device from Germany, without stating whether from East or West Germany. East Germany would have done it on orders from Moscow because the Soviets did not like Mondlane who they regarded as an agent of the Americans. West Germany would simply not have done that. At any rate, it seemed that the Russians protested to Tanzania and the Tanzanians stopped spreading that version of the story. Another idea was that it must have been the Americans who were not very happy with Mondane's failure to stop or check the encroachment of communism in Frelimo. That too is doubtful. The Chinese who preferred Uria Simango to Mondlane, would not have done it because they were not in the habit of eliminating foreign leaders like the Americans and the Soviets were wont to do.

There were three other possibilities. One was that the Tanzanians did it because they found it easier to eliminate him than to expel him from their country after they had built him as the leader of Frelimo. One thing was certain though: the Tanzanians did not announce the findings of their investigations into Mondlane's death nor did they want Interpol to disclose its findings. Frelimo leaders were quick to blame the Portuguese. There was evidence that the Portuguese respected him and for them he was the devil they knew and they would not have liked to have a devil they did not know. They had not forgotten that in 1961 Mondlane on a visit to Lourenco Marques from the United States where he had gone to study on a Portuguese passport departing from Lisbon, he had publicly declared that he was proud to be a Portuguese as I myself had done earlier in Mozambique. There has been a strong suspicion that his death was the result of an internal conspiracy and that the pro-Soviet wing of the leadership got rid of him with or without KGB instigation or support.

After Manuel Njanje, Costa Magiga and I got some money from a former Belgian missionary in Mozambique who was then in Tanzania, with the promise that another priest at St. Joseph's Cathedral in Dar-Es-Salaam he had talked to would give us some more after arriving there to enable us to go to Nairobi, we began to plan our escape.

We had agreed not to talk about our plan to anyone else and none of us did because we did not want to be stopped dead in our tracks before even getting off the ground and be placed on permanent surveillance. The plan had a bad start right from the beginning. We were at a bus stop a mile to the north of the refugee camp to take the country bus that would arrive there at 6 a.m. It did not arrive at that time, but we decided to wait for it instead of calling our plan off. It arrived at around 8 when people were already out of bed and about Rutamba village. We boarded it. It stopped at Rutamba village where some permanent refugee residents going to Lindi also boarded it. Some of them knew us and we knew them. They suspected that we were running away but we decided to relax, talk and laugh with them and tell them that we were going to do some shopping in Lindi .

When we arrived in Lindi, the bus for Dar-Es-Salaam had left at 7, the time it was supposed to leave. We decided to be on the move so as to make it difficult for the Tanzanian security agents to spot us and question us about who we were and where we were going to, the two questions that had been drilled into Tanzanians to ask strangers so as to nab them as spies. We believed that being on the move was better than staying around Lindi and becoming sitting ducks.

It was a steaming hot morning, but we kept walking with the single purpose in mind: getting away from the hell we had been put in and making good our escape to be away to a land flowing with milk and honey and above all to be able to live in freedom. At around 4 p.m. we found ourselves walking through a sisal field when we heard a vehicle coming behind us. We ran and made for an anthill that was well covered with leafy short trees and got in there before the people in the Land Rover could see us. The leafy trees covered us so well that nobody could see us. The

300

vehicle went past us as we watched it and after a few minutes we saw it return to where it had come from. We did not know whether it was looking for us or it was on its own business. We left the hiding place after about twenty minutes had elapsed to make sure that it would not come back again.

We got back to the road and resumed our walk, talking, laughing and cursing about the people in the truck that had gone away. We had, by then, begun to feel hungry and thirsty. At some place, we ran into a senior citizen with a hoe on his shoulder going to his field. We supposed he was going to work in his field. When he saw us, he asked us the annoying security questions of where we were from and how near or far we were going. I was in pain because a few minutes before running into him, a bee had stung me on the arm.

"None of your business, you goof," Njanje said to him. "Go to your field. If you ask that question again, we'll beat you up." He advanced against the old man intending to beat him, if the old man started to swear at us. He did not dare. He folded his tail, placed it between his legs and continued on his way as we went on our way. We found ourselves at a place with tall grass when we heard and saw a lorry behind us. We waved it to a stop.

"Where are going to?" asked the driver who was with another man after he had stopped the truck.

"To Kilwa," I said. We had agreed not to say that we were going to Dar-Es-Salaam, if someone asked us, so as to prevent our enemies from tracking us up to the Tanzanian capital.

"We're not going to Kilwa but we can give you a lift and drop you on the road to Kilwa and Dar-Es-Salaam," the driver said.

"That's alright with us," I told the driver. We got behind the lorry without seats and where we remained standing as the truck roared on. The lorry drove for about thirty miles or so before it came to a stop where the one road became two, one went straight east which was the way they were going and another one went north to Dar-Es-Salaam.

"Here is as far as we can take you," said the driver. We got down and thanked him and his colleague before they drove off and we followed the road to distant Dar-Es-Salaam.

"Is there a village near here? We're angry and want to eat something," I said to him before he took off.

"Up ahead about half an hour or so walk, there is a village and a roadside restaurant there," said the good-natured driver.

"Thank you much," I said to him before my colleagues and I said *kwaheri*, Swahili for goodbye, smiled and waved to him and his colleague.

We again began to walk, it was fast becoming dark. It was pitch black when we reached the village with mango trees on both sides of the road. We recognized the shack on the left hand side of the road as the restaurant the driver had told us about. There was no life in there and the door was bolted, except for one senior citizen and a kerosene lamp illuminating the room. The village had no electricity which was a blessing in disguise for us. We knocked on the door and the old man opened it for us. We told him that we wanted something to eat.

"You're very late," he said. "We're closed, but sit down. I will see whether my cook can do something quick for you guys. I can see you are hungry." I was not convinced that he would order his cook to make food for us at that late hour, but we sat down instead of leaving and continuing on our way in that darkness.

The man went to the room behind after we had sat down. Njanje and I were awake and alert while Magiga had begun to doze off and fall asleep. After a few minutes the old man returned to tell us that he had ordered his cook to prepare something for us and that it would not be long before be brought us something for us to eat. We sort of believed him and continued to sit down instead of leaving the dirty place right away, to be as far away from it as possible, from the incoming danger.

We remained somehow unsuspecting, although there was no sound or noises of pots and pans in the kitchen. We continued to wait when two men came through the back door and kitchen and one of them began to harangue us. It was then that we realized that the old man had sent his cook to inform security agents about our presence in the village and that he had not told him at all to make some food for us.

"What you people are doing is inadmissible in Tanzania," said one of the two men in a dry and harsh voice which sent cold shivers down our spines as we realized that we had fallen in an ambush and we had to act tactically to defeat the enemy.

They both remained standing and did not sit down. "You know that when you arrive at a place you should go to report to the jumbe (chief) first before taking it easy and sitting down. You know that Tanzania is facing permanent danger of aggression from the *Wareno* (meaning the Portuguese) and the *Makaburu* (meaning the Boers or South Africans). At any rate, you can sleep here and go and report to the chief tomorrow morning." He and his companion left the way they had come without saying goodbye to us.

As soon as we heard the rear door close, I turned to my colleagues and spoke in Portuguese, which was the language the three of us spoke, if we had to communicate faster than in our mother tongue Sena. When it came to expressing complex ideas, we preferred to speak in Portuguese instead of Sena. As for Swahili, we could not speak it there because it was the language in which we had communicated with the old man, and in which the two security agents had spoken to us.

"Those two guys will be back in no time to arrest us," I said. "We must leave right away."

"Let's go," said Njanje as he stood up before I also did the same.

"Oh, let's just sleep," Magiga said. He was overwhelmed with sleep. "Nothing bad will happen. We can continue our journey tomorrow."

"You stay and sleep, if you want," Njanje told him as I was right behind him. On hearing the no nonsense words from Njanje, Magiga stood up after realizing that if he remained behind, he would be arrested and returned to the refugee camp alone. He lost his sleep, also stood, and followed us.

"Oh, boys, you can sleep here. There won't be a problem," the old man said. He was sitting with his legs parallel to the door, as if he had planned to prevent us from leaving.

"You stinking mother fucker," Njanje shouted to him as he kicked his legs hard and the old man fell on his back with a thud and a shriek, frightened like a monkey that had fallen from the branch of a tree and was afraid of the dangers on the ground. Njanje was out. I jumped over the old man while swearing at him with Magiga right behind me, whacking the man with his sack before coming out. We were on a war footing the old man had declared on us and we were ready to turn him and his colleagues into casualties with kicks, punches and any objects we could lay our hands on. Unfortunately, in that darkness there was no way and no time for us to look for or find tools to fight that war with.

As soon as we were on the road, we started to run as fast as we could. As all we had were sacks with our few possessions, as I had carried when escaping from Mozambique; we ran as fast as we could for about fifteen to twenty minutes before we stopped and began to walk. Darkness was our friend and protector. If it had been during day time with people around, we would have been chased and caught.

About twenty minutes after we had been walking, we heard a lorry coming behind us. We veered off the road and disappeared into a clump of mango trees with tall grass where we ducked down and laid down on our stomachs to let the vehicle pass. As if by extraordinary intuition, the lorry stopped right by the trees and we heard men talking and asking themselves where we had disappeared to. We guessed that they were probably militiamen and were armed with AK-47 rifles. We stayed put and were not tempted to stand up to rush deeper into the bush away from the road in a region we did not know, which might have revealed our position as they may have heard us.

After a few minutes, we heard another lorry coming from the opposite direction and going to the village we had left or beyond. That lorry stopped by the first lorry that had been pursuing us. Then we heard one of our pursuers ask the driver of the other truck whether he had seen three boys.

"I saw no three boys," said the other driver.

There was silence for a minute or so.

"Ah," said the pursuer. "I don't even think they're boys at all. They're *majini*," he said meaning evil spirits. Jinnis are believed to be evil spirits, witches in East Africa use to hurt people. They are the spirits of Arab mythology and the Koran talks of good jinnis who listen to and accept the Koran and of the bad jinnis in a state of revolt against Allah in the Chapter headed "The Jinn" (72.1-72.28). In the Chapter headed the "Merciful[1]," the Koran says, "He (Allah) created man from potter's clay, and the jinn from smokeless fire. Which of your Lord's blessings would you deny?" (55.12-14).

Before long, the pursuing lorry turned around and headed back to the village followed by the truck that was heading south. After five minutes or so, we returned to hit the road again. The talk of us being jinnis which we heard from our pursuers sounded like a joke to our ears, but what the three of us saw next after returning to the road was no laughing matter and no joke at all. It was quite haunting and we were agape in that dark night.

It was around 10 p.m. or so. Right in front of us, we saw a tall, slender and frail man with what seemed to be an incredibly large and long load of firewood on his head walking in the opposite direction to us. The three of us greeted him at the same time and with the same words.

"Jambo, mzee," we greeted him in Swahili, meaning "Hail, good old man."

He turned to us without replying and walked past us going where we were coming from. When we had thought that he must be way away behind us and continuing his walk home, we saw him again walking in front us going in the opposite direction with his load on his head. We again greeted him with the same words as before. He behaved in the same manner of turning to us without saying anything and continuing to walk in the opposite direction to us.

"As long as we keep greeting this man," said Magiga, the son of a witchdoctor mother in Caia, Sofala, "he'll keep showing up. Let's not greet him or say anything to him, if he appears again." Neither Njanje nor I took issue with anything our colleague had said or, in other words, we agreed with him.

He disappeared behind us and it was not long before we saw him for the third time in front of us going in the opposite direction. We did not greet him this time around and we never saw him again.

We did not talk about him after he failed to show up after not greeting him and he went on his way "home" for good. There was no doubt in our minds that what we saw was not an ordinary living person. It was inconceivable that an ordinary man would be out at that time gathering firewood in the bush, in a place known to have lions and other dangerous critters. And no person in African villages ever goes to collect firewood at night and firewood collection is usually done by women and not men.

A number of intriguing questions have remained unanswered to this day. Why was greeting him bad and made him reappear? Why did not greeting him make him disappear behind us and prevented him from showing up again in front of us? After he disappeared behind us each time, why was it that we did not see him hurrying up to go ahead of us before we saw him appearing in front of us again going in the opposite direction? How did he get to be in front of us after disappearing behind us twice?

What was that man? Was he a guardian angel? Probably, he was, but we saw no wings and a halo glowing around his head. We did not see him flying or floating in the air and declaring to us the glorious news of our approaching salvation and freedom. What we saw was his frail frame and the enormous load on his head that should have crushed his frail frame. Did he appear to help and protect us or was he hostile to us?

Everything seemed to indicate that he bore no malicious intent towards us, for, soon after the encounter, we ran into three life or death situations which we survived after which we faced no more serious situations on the way to Nairobi and our pursuers from the village never returned to look for us again that night or the following morning.

He seemed to be no agent of the security agents we had run away from or of the Portuguese, of the leaders of Frelimo or of the Tanzanian government. He seemed to be a good man from another dimension of existence.

The security agents were probably so scared of us being jinns.

The following morning the old restaurant owner, his cook, and the pursuers had probably rushed to consult a witchdoctor so that they could get an explanation about us and be cleansed from the ill luck our supposedly ghostly manifestation had cast upon them.

There is nothing that scares the Swahili-speaking people of the coast of East Africa more than jinnis. Fantastic stories are told in Mombasa, Kenya, of men following beautiful girls from night clubs and bars at night and finding themselves on tops of graves in a cemetery or on the tops of coconut trees the following morning without knowing how they got there. A rule of thumb in Mombasa is never to tease, laugh at, or provoke cats, as they may be jinnis instead of real cats. They say that jinnis like to manifest themselves as extremely beautiful girls or as cats or they can take many weird forms. I did not abide by that rule the first time I visited Mombasa. On the way to Fort Jesus that my ancestors the Lusitanians, (as we were told to refer to the Ancient Portuguese at schools in Mozambique), built from 1593-1596 to fight against the Arabs, I provoked cats to see what would happen to me and nothing untoward came my way. But I did not intend to be doing the same thing again thereafter to animals that had done me no wrong. But I think that such stories would make a good collection of African ghost stories because most of them have been invented or imagined.

Some years later while talking to the witchdoctor, who told me about missing children being eaten by Nubians in Nairobi, I recounted my encounter with the frail man with his load of firewood to him. But I did not ask him to check the incident by casting his divination cowries and bones. He simply said, "He was no man at all. He was an ancestral spirit of one of you appearing in the nick of time to help you survive or ward off dangers." He might have been an ancestral spirit, but I beg to remain sceptical. Regardless of whatever he might have been, one thing was clear: the apparition was certainly stranger than fiction.

Perhaps in his mind, in the world of his existence, he was also astounded to see us out there at that time of the night and was asking himself what we were doing out there at that time of night instead of being at home like normal beings of our kind should be. Were we ghosts to him as he appeared to be to us? It would be good to know what he thought of us. Were we stranger than fiction to him as he was to us?

One thing was true though. The three of us saw the apparition unlike the ghostly apparition of a dead mapanga which only Zefina, my cousin and lover, saw at Nakasero Forest when we were going to chief Jimo's village to visit the family of our great uncle Josias. The three of us greeted him twice in unison and we decided not to greet him anymore after which he stopped showing up.

After we got rid of that apparition, we kept marching along the road with cotton fields on both sides until we came to a place where the road went through one of the densest forest in southern Tanzania. Just the cacophony of the diverse sounds of animals coming from the edge of the forest intimidated us. We decided to enter a cotton field and sit down somewhere there but mosquitoes biting us ferociously chased us away. We decided to approach a shack by the edge of the field and rest by its wall. What we did was quite a gamble as the owners could come out with spears and kill us if they knew we were there. But they did not hear us because they were sleeping very soundly and we made no noise or sound whatsoever. Njanje and I were awake while Magiga snoozed, as if he were not in a situation of emergency. When I heard voices and people talking inside, I whispered to my colleagues that we should leave. We left quietly and quickly before they came out and saw us leaving and hurled their spears at us to kill us, as they would not be cocky enough as to chase us in the dark.

We left quietly and quickly before they came out.

I guessed that they wanted to come out to answer the call of nature. In places with dangerous animals, people living in huts without latrines come out of their huts together at night and armed with spears. I knew that in parts of Mozambique people did that in areas with dangerous wild animals, and it would not be surprising if people in that area with many dangerous critters did the same thing.

Back on the road, we decided to enter the forest. We took out our torches, some matches, and old newspapers from our sacks which we could light to produce flames to wave at and scare off any wild animals we might encounter. We were not afraid of anything at all like I was the night I entered Malawi from Mozambique. Being with other people had a consoling effect and lightened the oppressive burden of fear and loneliness. It lifted the fear I would have felt, if I were alone. Frankly speaking, I do not see how I would have coped and survived on that long journey, if I were alone. Even over the short run from Zobue to Mwanza, it was a nightmare for me and I felt that I had died and was reincarnated after surviving the ordeal of darkness, forms and shapes. Fear might have killed me this time around if I were alone.

We decided not to switch the torches on, except in an emergency or in reaction to some danger because we did not want to give away our position to anyone on that dark night. After walking for two hours or so along the road with walls of grass and trees on both sides, we heard a herd of wild pigs squealing and coming towards us and the pigs almost crashed into us. After seeing us, they panicked even more because they were caught between two dangers or between a wall and a sword as the Portuguese say. They veered off the road and entered the forest to our left after which we came face to face with what they were running away from: four lions, one male with a huge mane and three females. We stopped and they stopped with their fire eyes on us. The three of us switched on our torches at about the same time and began to wave the lights at them, producing a spectre they might never have seen before other than perhaps the occasional lights from motor cars they may have seen along the road at night. The lights rather blinded them in that darkness and they remained rooted where they had stopped and were unable to spring on us and maul us.

We lighted the old newspapers which produced good flames which we waved at them whilst screaming. The combination of light from our torches and the flames from the newspapers was too much for the cats. They panicked and jumped, with earth-shaking roars, to the side of the forest the pigs had taken. Their roars had shaken our bodies but not our spirits and the forest echoed with them. We had won a victory against them. As they disappeared, we heard the pigs squealing in the distance. I was so sorry for the stupid things. Instead of continuing to flee silently as we had done after bolting from the restaurant in the village behind us, they were actually making noises that gave away the direction they were taking to the hunting cats.

We continued flashing out torches in the direction the cats had taken to let them know that we were still there as a danger. I had actually thought of putting my flaming newspapers to the grass by the road to start a forest fire. On a second thought, I decided against the idea, as a roaring fire could force forest services, if there were any in that god-damned place, to rush to the scene of the fire. We could run into them and be arrested and shot dead that night without the formality of a trial in a kangaroo court.

Having won the confrontation, like Don Quixote with a caged lion he taunted with his sword and dared to come out to confront him, we also felt victorious like him, if not more victorious than him because we had confronted four free brutes in their own territory. We resumed our march after conquering the lions and putting them to flight and shame. As we walked with our torches on, we constantly turned behind us to flash the lights to ward off the cats in case they failed to catch up with the pigs and decided to come after us instead.

After a forced march of five hours or so with a stony and spooky silence greeting us as we walked without encountering more lions or seeing other animals, or seeing people or hearing cars coming from ahead of us or behind us which would have forced us to dash into the forest to hide and to let them pass, darkness beginning to give way to light, we emerged out of the forest to a deep stream with a bridge straddling it and the forest looming as menacing on the other side of the river as it did behind us. The grass area close to the stream and adjacent to the road had been cut and cleared, and there was a grass shack to the right of the road we suspected to be the lodge of policemen or security agents or forest service men.

"Boys, "I said to my colleagues, "we should stop here. Let us rest. If we cross the bridge and continue to walk this early, we will encounter hungry cats hunting or elephants sallying forth in search of food, and we will be in big trouble, bigger than the one we went through last night."

Neither of my colleagues argued as they saw sense in what I said. We also needed to rest, even if for a couple of minutes. Because of the tribulations we had faced and conquered behind us, we were no longer hungry. At any rate, hunger or no hunger, there was nothing for us to eat. We decided to go to a place at a corner by the edge of the grass from which people emerging from the hut could not see us. We had actually wanted to walk into the grass and sit concealed down under it, but the grass was dewy. We did not want to make ourselves wet. We sat down at the place we had chosen where we stayed for about half an hour. While we were there, a big bus full of people zoomed past us, shaking the ground as it went on its way. It was probably from Dar-Es-Salaam going to Lindi.

As we did not want to be sitting ducks for long and sitting still when people in the grass structure came out, if indeed there were people in it, we decided to resume our march. We entered the road once again, crossed the bridge before washing our faces on the other side of the stream and drinking voraciously to fill up our empty stomachs before continuing our march.

Soon after, we saw enormous fresh mounds of elephant dung with steam still coming from them and we knew that the pachyderms were not far away. In the late 1990s, an exile of the Shangaan tribe from southern Mozambique told me in Nairobi, Kenya, as I recounted to him this episode of my flight with Njanje and Magiga, that it was a good thing for someone escaping from pursuers to see elephant dung, as it acts as a potent magic to prevent the pursuers from following him if the fugitive picks up a bit of the dung and carries it with him,

We did not know that simple Shangaan magic then. Now that I know it, I would not hesitate to do it, if I ever find myself bolting for it from pursuers and chanced upon elephant dung. So we did not pick up a bit from the dung and wrap it in bits of newspapers as potent charms against other would be pursuers during our flight or against our pursuers of the previous evening who had already been discouraged from returning to look for us because they had suspected that we were jinns and they could not chase jinns! After encountering jinns, people usually go to see sheiks to have them pray from the Koran in order to cleanse them of them curse and protect them. That is what people usually do along the coast of East Africa from Sofala in Mozambique to well the way northern Somalia.

It is a fact though that Africans have a lot of little magical tricks to deal with difficult situations. But there are no common superstitions to all Africans. Each region or tribe has its own peculiar beliefs which are unknown to other regions or tribes.

We just continued to march and ran into the herd of between ten to twenty elephants to the left side of the road. They did not see us, but they had smelled us or sensed our presence. We watched them disappear, but a bull turned around and saw us. It got nervous and made straight for us, to charge at us with its head lowered and its trunk raised while grunting threats. In that nick of time, we moved to behind the trunks of huge trees opposite it and it could no longer see us. Not wanting to be left alone and perhaps face some kind of danger alone, it turned around and trotted off to join its colleagues, thudding the ground as the enormous brute ran to catch up with its friends and relatives. I cursed and wished it ill-luck and imminent death for having been a nuisance to us.

After the danger had passed, we once again resumed our walk with the forest on both sides of the road, as if nothing had been the matter after dodging the monstrous bull, which would have crushed us to pulp with its feet or bashed us against trees with its trunk, if it had caught or seized us.

We were about 70 kilometres from Lindi and we had been on the move for over twenty-four hours without food or sleep. We walked on, full of energy with all sensation of hunger gone as we thought only of survival and not of eating or filling our stomachs with food. After one hour or so, we heard the thunder of a motor car engine droning and drawing ever closer. It was a big bus from Lindi. I told my colleagues that I was going to stop it. They were not sure whether it would be wise to do so. They feared that our pursuers of the previous evening could be in it looking for us. I did it all the same. I waved it to a stop and it halted. We got in and the driver resumed the run without saying anything.

A conductor came to us. He was friendly. He asked us where we were going to. We told him we were going to Kilwa Kivinji for the funeral of an uncle of ours who had passed away there, adding that we might actually go to Dar-Es-Salaam first before going to Kilwa on our way back home. There are actually two Kilwas: Kilwa Kivinji and Kilwa Masoko which had been known for their trade in slaves. Arabs and the Portuguese left vestiges of their past presence there. In 1587, Zimba cannibals from the Zambezi captured it and killed 3,000 of its residents, which was something like genocide, if we take into account the small populations of those days.

We wanted to pay him, but he said that he would collect our fares when we signalled to him that we had made our decision on where we would go to first. His decision was working in our favour. We decided not to signal to him until he came to us, as he would for his money. During the trip, the three of us only spoke in the Swahili we had mastered while at Rutamba and referred to each other with false Swahili names of Rashid for Njanje, Abdul for Magiga and Saidi for me.

When the conductor finally came to us, the bus was approaching the place where a road to Kilwa branched off the main road to Dar-Es-Salaam. We did even not know that we were approaching the spot until he came to us.

"Fellows," he said. "Have you decided where to go first?"

"Dar," I said.

"Your fares please," he said. "Since you're good guys and in mourning and need money, I will charge you 30 shillings instead of the usual 40."

Each one of us paid the 30 shillings that was due to him after which we thanked him.

The bus rambled on until it reached a field of oranges where it stopped for a break of an hour or so. There was also a Land Rover full of soldiers of the Tanzania People's Defence Force going in the same direction as our bus. We even got out of the bus for some fresh air. Before the bus resumed its run, the conductor shouted to people who had been in the bus to return to it. The bus then took off and reached the Rufiji River which we crossed in a barge after which the bus trundled on with an increased speed.

While I now recall crossing the Rufiji on our way to Dar-Es-Salaam, I do not remember us crossing it on our way to the refugee camp. It is possible that I do not remember crossing it on our way to Rutamba because I was tired and angry with what was happening to us. The Rufiji region became important to me five or six years later when studying African History at schools in Nairobi. It was the epicentre of an African uprising against German colonial rule which had oppressed the natives with taxation, forced labour the natives had to do while supervised by fuming Germans or by their askaris or native policemen who liked to crack their sjamboks on their backs for allegedly being lazy, and had required them to grow cotton instead of grain that was important for the natives and forced them to build roads for European occupiers.

The uprising came to be known as the *Maji Maji* revolt. It was led by a witchdoctor called Kinjikitile Ngwale of Ngarambe in the Rufiji area. The healer inspired the rebellion by assuring the rebels that the medicine mixed with water, maji in Swahili, he gave them to douse themselves with before fighting the Germans would render them immune from them, or that it would turn enemy bullets into water.

The uprising which was planned in secrecy and in Swahili as the language of communication for ten tribes from Dar Es Salaam to the Mozambique border, was apparently successful at the beginning as it took German administrators, their Arab collaborators and missionaries, by complete surprise before the Germans then counter-attacked and killed more than 75,000 natives and resorted to a scorched-earth policy, which resulted in the death of over 200,000 natives. The uprising, which began in 1905, ended in 1907 with Kinjikitile Ngwale himself having been captured and hanged early at the outbreak of the uprising. This historical event was being celebrated under the rule of the late President Julius Nyerere, who saw everything in terms of leftist ideology, as a Revolution against imperialism, colonialism and capitalism.

Back in Dar, we had no time to waste. We were in a race against time. We went to the Afro-American Institute at Kurasini, a school the Americans had established as a secondary school for refugees from southern Africa. Some Mozambicans were studying there. As they were our comrades in spirit against the dictatorship of the Frelimo leadership, they proved to be of great help to us. They took us to eat in the cafeteria with them and no one objected to the fact that we were eating there as we were not students at the school.

As we were in a hurry, we discussed our plan with one of the Mozambican students who got paper with the school's letterhead and typed three letters stating the name of each of us on each sheet and that we were students at the school going on vacation to Nairobi before signing them. They looked very official and he gave each one of us this letter. We went to St. Joseph's cathedral where the priest who had been instructed by the former missionary in Mozambique gave us 60 shillings each, which was the exact fare from Dar-Es-Salaam to Nairobi. From there we went to the bus depot to purchase the tickets for our trip three days after that. We wanted to hang around a bit longer because we wanted to be in the city for a little mischief.

We were able to track the ultra-secret *Baraza la Wazee*, Swahili *Council of Elders* who had worked ceaselessly against the leaders of Frelimo. The members of the Council of Elders regarded the leaders of Frelimo as sell outs to or agents of the Portuguese. Not all of them were agents of the Portuguese while some were indeed infiltrated agents of the Portuguese. They even gave us a place where we could sleep and asked us to attend one of their meetings, which we did. They were well organized. They collected funds from friends and sympathizers for their activities and helped people from Mozambique in dire need of assistance. We thanked their secretary for the help before we left the Tanzanian capital. We were eager to liberate ourselves from oppression and attain freedom.

The bus for Nairobi left Dar at 7 p.m. We were at the bus depot before the departure. The bus travelled the whole night over Tanzanian territory. We saw nothing of the Tanzanian countryside in the night. When day broke the following morning, we had little interest in looking out of the window to see the landscape we wanted to get away from. We arrived in Arusha town at about 10 a.m. the following morning. From there we could see the snow-peaked Mount Kilimanjaro, the highest mountain in Africa. From Arusha, the bus drove through the territory of the Maasai people who are regarded as the fiercest tribe in Africa. Some pretty much naked Maasai warriors known as *moran* with sharp spears and women kept boarding the bus as if they were entering their *manyatta*, their huts of cow dung, without paying any fares at all, as if they owned the bus. The driver who spoke Maasai did not ask them to pay or he did not dare ask them to pay. It is always better not to fool around with the Maasai.

In his book *The Lunatic Express: an Entertainment in Imperialism* about the building of the railway from Mombasa to Uganda at the end of the nineteenth century, when the British engaged Indian railway builders from India because they had built a vast network of railways in India which had given Indians the expertise of building

318

railways while the Africans knew nothing about railway building, Miller Charles talks about the Maasai warriors as men who could run from sunrise to sunset without stopping anywhere on the way. According to the author, their activities could range from their homeland all the way to Mombasa on a single day. They struck terror into the hearts of Arab slavers who feared them so much that they kept clear of what is now Kenya in the heyday of the slave trade, thus sparing the area of the scourge and ravages of slavery. Even German and British explorers at first feared to venture into Maasai country. Maasai country sits astride the Tanzania-Kenya border and extends as far into Kenya as Nairobi, which is a Maasai word meaning "A place of cold water." It is the name of the Nairobi River, rather a stream, known to the Maasai as Enkare Nairobi.

The Maasai are pastoralists and nomads which explains why they have been at war with lions principally. In the 1980s, I met a Maasai man in Nairobi and I chatted with him quite a bit. His name was Samora, which was the name of the Mozambican dictator who came to power in Frelimo before independence and consolidated his power after independence, until he died in 1986. I asked him whether his name was Samora because he admired the Mozambican leader; he was surprised that I asked that question. He did not even seem to know who Samora Machel was. He said that Samora was a very Maasai name. I also asked him why the Maasai did not fear lions. He hissed his contempt for the felines before telling me that there was a simple magic the Maasai did on encountering lions. "To us a lion is nothing," he said. "If you see a lion, pick up sand or some earth from the ground and throw that towards it. That robs it of its strength and renders it powerless."

Wow! I was intrigued, amazed, and also amused without scoffing at what he had told me. I was just too happy to learn a new trick from the Maasai, as I had learnt from the Swahili people at Mombasa the simple magic of holding one wrist with the palm of the other hand to paralyze snakes and prevent them from moving away and escaping so that other people could kill them.

The Maasai are a very interesting people. In Maasai concept, all cattle in the world belong to them. If other people have cattle, it is because they stole the cattle from them in the past and they have the right to go and get them back. At the beginning of the colonization of Kenya, British settlers had at first a hard time understanding why the Maasai would enter their farms and carry away their cattle. With time they understood what the Maasai thought and they learnt a new thing about the Maasai.

The bus went full steam to the border of Namanga where upon arrival the driver left us in the bus either for fresh air or to find something to eat. We were a bit apprehensive about going through the Immigration but I urged my colleagues that it would be better if we went to present our papers than if we were later seen in the bus and stopped and asked why we had not reported to Immigration in the first place. We walked into the Immigration and told the man there that we were students going on vacation to Nairobi and would return to Dar-Es-Salaam after a week. The man read our forged papers and was pleased with them and with us. He gave them back to us without stamping them and wished us good luck and a good stay in Nairobi.

We got back onto the bus and rubbed our palms with satisfaction. I felt like I was dreaming when the bus began to roll on and go past the border and entered Kenya. Once it was in Kenya, the three of us exploded into a joyous celebration with uncontrollable laughter, handshakes, and hugs while speaking in Portuguese. We had attained liberation from the bonds of hate, stupidity and slavery we had left behind us, and we were walking on the path to freedom. We brought out the bottles of Fanta we had bought in Dar-Es-Salaam from our sacks and began to drink to each other's health. The people who did not know why we had exploded into a sudden rowdy celebration, thought that we had gone crazy. We had indeed gone crazy, but with joy.

We reached Nairobi at around 7 p.m. that evening. We were able to find the residence of some of our former colleagues who had left Tanzania earlier on. They sheltered us and helped us in the first few days.

If this were a fictional story, I would end it here with the goal of freedom having been attained. Although there were also challenges in Kenya, they were rather minor and were more concerned with overcoming the difficulties of life; having to learn English without which I could not continue to study and later work; my inability to use my time according to priorities and falling prey to sensual pleasures I had suppressed during my adolescence. There is also something I must say about the seventeen years in Kenya, with two of them lived in Swaziland, even if not in detail. And the story of my early life would be incomplete without that part of my life in Kenya.

Chapter 31

I arrived in Nairobi in August 1969. The place lived up to its reputation as a cold place as attributed to it by its Maasai name. Situated 5,000 feet at the foot of Mount Kenya, Nairobi was indeed a cold place for someone like me from the then steaming hot areas of Tanzania. Only the cold weather of the Zobue highlands of Mozambique could rival that of Nairobi. Generally speaking, Nairobi has perhaps the most moderate weather in the world or "the best weather in the world," according to a lady I met in Victoria, Canada. She told me that she had arrived in Nairobi from Austria when she was three, grew up and went to school there until Kenya became independent in 1963. She was one of the whites who felt she would have no future in Kenya under an African government. Her feeling was understandable because Kenya was about to emerge from the turbulent years of the Emergency which the colonial government had imposed on the colony in order to fight the Mau Mau uprising against British rule. The white settlers had generally sided with the colonial government and the prospect of them finding a niche in a country about to be ruled by the natives whose desire to become independent they had opposed, looked rather dim for some of them, if not damned and damning.

Also some of the settlers had entertained the idea of transforming Kenya into a white country like their counterparts were to do in Rhodesia where under the leadership of Ian Smith, they unilaterally declared independence for the British colony in an act of open rebellion against the British crown. In the case of Kenya, that idea had been killed when the British government had declared that if the interests of white and Indian settlers conflicted with those of the native people, the interests of the natives were to prevail. The decision taken in 1923 known as the Devonshire White Paper came about when a delegation of Indians went to London to complain that the whites in the colony were discriminating against them and treating them as second class individuals. Although the decision of the British Government favoured the Africans whose plight London deplored, nothing much happened or was done to improve their lot.

I would not dismiss as figments of imagination the fear of those whites who panicked. Unlike some African countries like the Congo and much later Mozambique, which slid into chaos before and after independence, Kenya under Jomo Kenyatta, who became the prime minister at independence in 1963 before becoming president of independent Kenya later, proved them wrong. No acts of revenge against the former settlers who stayed took place, nor were their lives disturbed in any way because the wise Kenyatta had decided to place his country on a path to harmony and freedom for its citizens regardless of their race and ethnic background. His philosophy was based on forgiving and not forgetting. That was the sticking point. He would be asking too much, if he had asked his people to forget the past. Why would anyone ask people to forget their past or history anyway?

Kenyatta's greatness also stemmed from the fact that he had personally suffered during the Emergency from 1952 and in 1959 when he was detained, tried in a court of law by a judge who had decided to find him guilty on the charge that he was the leader of the Mau Mau rebels. Kenyatta denied the charges and went as far as condemning the Mau Mau as terrorists for their ignoble behaviour and acts. He was incarcerated at the remote desert region of Malalal for seven years before being released and allowed to lead his country's struggle for independence.

As people may want to know what the Mau Mau was, what the name means and what they stood for, I must say that no one really knows what the acronym Mau Mau stands for. According to the School of Education, Makerere University of Uganda and the Open Learning University of Britain, "Mau is an abbreviation which stands for 'Mzungu Arudi Ulaya, Mwafirika Apate Uhuru" (which is Swahili meaning: Let the white man go back to Europe and the Africans regain Independence). It has also been said that it stands for Mwingereza arudi Uingereza, Mwafirika Apate Uhuru (also Swahili for "Let the Englishman or the Britishman return to England or Britain so that the African can become independent").

But the article falsely states that Kenyatta, a Kikuyu tribesman, and Tom Mboya from the Luo tribe of Lake Victoria, were leaders of the Mau Mau. Nothing is further removed from the truth than this. The article fails to approach the topic of the uprising academically by doing pro-Mau Mau propaganda in a discussion that should instruct future teachers of History. Like in any war, the British and the Mau Mau violated human rights. But just deploring British vices and presenting the Mau Mau as benign and ignoring their ignominious acts of violence against their own people who they killed for breaking oaths taken under duress while at times drinking human blood, falls short of academic seriousness.

The main reason for the Mau Mau uprising was land and not independence as such; they wanted their land back from the settlers who had taken it from them and the rebellion was mainly in the lands of Kikuyu and tribes related to them such as the Embu and the Meru, the

324

Akamba in central Kenya were also involved. But it was the British who attributed a nationalist dimension to the Mau Mau uprising. They gave the impression that the rebellion was the coming together of Kenyans of all tribes against colonial rule while in fact its activities were limited to the area the British called the Abardare Mountains and the Kikuyu called Nyandarwa where British Forces suppressed the rebels before granting independence to Kenya, which explains why the Mau Mau were ignored and were not included in the post-independence leadership of Kenya. After independence, Jomo Kenyatta himself used British forces to suppress those of the Mau Mau who did not want to give up the bush and return to normal civilian life.

Jomo Kenyatta knew the British and respected their democratic system and concepts better than anyone else did, although the system was applied only in Britain and not in the Kenyan colony. He had lived in Britain for twenty years where he married a lady from one of the foremost aristocratic families before returning home to lead his country's struggle for independence. Unlike the leaders of other African countries who shouted with hoarse voices against the West and lived in a utopian fantasyland wanting to change what the colonial rulers had left behind, Kenyatta was a realist who combined African wisdom and British pragmatism to help his country prosper. He continued to build from where the British left off rather than demolish what they had done, as other leaders had done in other African countries.

As other countries around Kenya stagnated with impractical policies and ideologies, Kenya forged ahead with its aggressive capitalist policies, although they created, and with time, widened the gap between the rich and the poor. While the neighbouring countries were ruled with an iron first, Kenyatta, although not quite a democrat towards those who challenged his power, left his people largely free.

I witnessed the freedom during my stay in Kenya for seventeen years. In Kenya I never worried or looked over my shoulder to see who was around me or who was trying to spy on me. Never did strangers ever ask me who I was and, while travelling no one asked me where I was from, and how near or how far I was going, unlike the Tanzanians who would have pestered me before arresting me. At school, some classmates of mine asked me to go on holiday to their villages. Upon arrival in their villages, I never had to go and report to the local police station or to the chief of their villages to announce my presence in the village, and never did policemen or security agents ever come to the homes of my friends to try to find out who I was and what I was up to. I never had to carry identification papers on me and no one ever asked me for identification papers.

In Kenya there was no Big Brother watching me as had happened in Tanzania. I lived respecting rules and the law, as I had done in Tanzania where Big Brother hounded me all the same, unjustly imprisoned me before sending me on an internal exile like the Soviets used to do with their dissidents. I did not leave Mozambique after breaking any rules or laws. I did not leave it to become a rebel to fight in a war of liberation under leaders who dreamed of exploiting my sacrifice in order to liberate the country and impose their own despotic rule and who, even before independence, were violating the rights of the rank and file of the organization and killing those who did not agree with them. I would have made the ultimate sacrifice of fighting for Mozambique's independence and freedom, which would have been a glorious undertaking, but not for despotic rule by and under anyone after Mozambique's independence.

Settling in Kenya did not mean arriving there and beginning to get everything at the wave of a magic wand. It involved a slow process of struggling to get services in order to begin life afresh. The first thing I did was to legalize my stay and find a place where I could live in a city with the most acute shortage of housing for its residents. The morning of the day after my arrival, I went to the Immigration office. I was issued with a P. I. (prohibited immigrant) paper which I had to renew once every month. And when it pleased an immigration officer or when officers got to know me, I would sometimes get three months or even six months before I would have to go back to renew it. Like all other foreigners in my category, I was never asked to quit even when I failed to go back to have it renewed after the date when I should have done so. It was always renewed with no questions asked or warnings given that next time if I were late, I would be thrown out of the country.

Despite its intimidating name, the P. I. was like a permanent residence paper. With it I was able to apply for a scholarship, find admission to a school and study. After beginning to study, I got a letter from my school to the Immigration which issued me with an educational permit which did not need to be renewed for the duration of time that I was at the school. The government later decided to issue permanent residential permits to refugees. The permits did allow people holding them to work without work permits which were not difficult to obtain as it was usually the employers who filed the application for persons they wanted to employ.

Luck did not take long before smiling on me. I got a scholarship from United Nations Development Programme or the UNDP as soon as I applied for one. To top it all, the UNDP office in Nairobi received a letter from the government saying that it had reserved a number of places at some state run schools for Mozambican refugees. And the UNDP sent me and two other boys to Eastleigh Secondary School which was regarded as one of the best secondary schools for boys in Nairobi. The school, which in colonial times was a school for Asian boys which really meant students of Indian and Pakistani origin because there were no other Asians there apart from those two nationalities, was also proud that it was getting refugee students from Mozambique for the first time. It already had two south Sudanese students who were remarkably dark, as charcoal-dark as the Nilotic people of southern Sudan can be.

Our presence at the school generated its own kind of humour. As soon as other boys came to know that my two colleagues and I were from Mozambique, they did not even bother to find out our names. They began to call us Portuguese like the Malawians were wont to call us. Only the watchman Muiruri, a fat and no nonsense Kikuyu tribesman who patrolled the perimeter of the school in the evening with a sharp machete in his hand, had a different sense of humour towards me. I was going to the office at lunch time one day when I saw him sitting with the cute young secretary on chairs outside the office. I thought the secretary had a crash on me and I definitely had an eye for her, but neither of us knew how to start the ball rolling. I thought it unwise to start an adventure that could end up badly with me becoming a laughing stock, if the girl later turned against me. In those days there was no such thing as sexual harassment as we have today. She also had her own reasons for leaving the ball in my court for me to start kicking it instead of her doing so. Generally African girls are shy and will not confess their love to men they do not know well enough for fear of being branded prostitutes and being humiliated.

As I walked past them, Muruiri greeted me before turning to the secretary and drawing her attention. "You see this boy here. His name is *Agora-Mozambique*," he said to her in Swahili. He combined the names of the two African territories of Angola and Mozambique then still under

Portuguese rule, saying the names with the affectations of his Kikuyu tongue which appears to have problems with the letters n, m, and does not have the letter l. The Kikuyu and people who speak languages related to Kikuyu, are usually unable to pronounce the letters n and m before consonants and they pronounce l as r. "He had to run fast from his country because the Portuguese are no joke. They're really merciless. They flogged him. They even flog small kids like him who have to flee as far as Nairobi in order for us to protect them. What would he have done, if we were not here? The Portuguese would have killed him like a worthless dog."

I was not a kid at that time otherwise that young secretary, though older than me, might not have been attracted to me. The secretary did not comment on what Muiruri said. Perhaps she did not quite understand what the watchman said in all seriousness, but which I understood and regarded as a joke. I was amused and laughed it off before continuing to the office.

I was very happy about being at Eastleigh Secondary School and felt blessed that I was attending a good school after leaving my beloved Zobue Seminary in Mozambique. The beginning at the school was rather stormy because of my lack of English. I was in the same class with boys who had done nursery and primary education up to grade 8 in English. It was not that they knew much English, but compared to me, they were better off because they could understand and follow what the teachers were saying while I did not understand a thing apart from a few words here and there.

Although I was in the second year or Form II of secondary education when I left Mozambique, when I resumed education in Kenya, I was placed in Form I. And it was the right move. Even this move was not initially helpful to me and the other two boys who were sent to that school with me. Not being able to understand what teachers said in the early days had a detrimental effect on future classes, particularly in mathematics where rules were hammered out to students in those first days. Fortunately, I had studied and known some of them in Mozambique and that helped me a bit later on.

Things came to a head in the English class after the teacher had asked us to write our first composition. As I could not write in English, I wrote my composition in Portuguese and translated it into English with the help of a bilingual dictionary. The outcome was disastrous. As the French would put it: "c'*était* c*atastrophique*." The teacher was not pleased with the general standard of everyone's English and not at all amused with mine and that of my two Mozambican colleagues. She called out our names and we stood up.

"What was that you wrote?" she asked us.

I was silent, so were my two colleagues because we could not answer her in English.

"Where do you come from?"

I at least thought I understood what she was asking.

"Mozambique," I said and fell silent. I could not say more to her in English.

Obviously the lady had no idea of the problems facing Mozambique then. She exploded with anger.

"You should have stayed in Mozambique instead of coming here," she screamed, before ordering us to sit down. None of the boys laughed at us because their own essays were not good either and they had received much flak from her for them. I sat down feeling totally humiliated and sad because I was unable to explain to her what my problem was. But I was not to remain totally behind the others.

I later learnt after reading *The Memoirs of Field-Marshal Montgomery* that the teething problem I had with

English had not just been unique to me or mine alone. Montgomery who was born in London and, as a young boy, lived in Tasmania where his father was a missionary, faced the same humiliation with his first compositions. He was laughed at and told by his teacher that what he wrote made no sense. Montgomery who wrote humorously said later that he hoped that people understood what he was writing after his initial difficulties with writing essays in English. For Montgomery, English was his first language which he spoke from his infancy and not his fifth as was, and still is, the case with me, and yet he had serious teething problems writing essays to the point of leaving his English teacher completely flabbergasted with him.

I admired Montgomery for his humility. He hardly bragged about anything in his memoirs. He was steadfast even under pressure as demonstrated by his refusal to interrupt his plans for a big offensive against the Germans at Alamein in order to counter attack the Germans who were about to attack his forces. He took counter measures against them while working on his plan. When the Germans attacked, they were checked by his counter measures and the action of the Royal Air Force which bombed the Germans from the rear after which he unleashed his plan against them with the infernal fire of 700 artillery guns opening up on the enemy. He inflicted the first biggest defeat Hitler's troops in Africa had ever suffered, thereby signalling the end of the Nazis' victories in the Second World War and their rolling back to ultimate defeat in 1945. His book was one amongst the many that instilled the spirit of defiance and steadfastness in me. It convinced me that setbacks are not necessarily defeats.

I was also inspired by *Panzer Leader* of Heinz Guderian, the German theoretician of mobile warfare and the use of tanks in war to produce a blitzkrieg effect. Guderian wrote as a military thinker and not as a warmonger. He was critical of Hitler for unleashing a big war and never easily accepted his *Fürher's* orders which led Hitler to dismiss him from commanding armies and to appoint him to head the armaments' procurement sector. He was perhaps the only one who could stand up to Hitler, argue, and quarrel with, and defy him. He helped defy and sabotage Hitler's order for the destruction of "all factories, water and electrical installations, railways and bridges before they should fall into enemy hands" (Guderian, *Panzer Leader*, 422) because for him, "If the war should be lost, then the nation, too, will be lost" (423). Guderian argued against the plan with the German dictator who thought that the loss of the war would mean that the strong would have perished, leaving the weak to lead a primitive life (423).

I have always thought that the world needed exceptional people like General Guderian to stand up to and confront tyranny and tyrants. I have done my little bit against the despots of Mozambican politics and I don't regret having done so, and I feel proud for what I have done. And I will do it again for freedom, if need be.

I recognized my failures and worked to address my weaknesses in order to triumph. Despite having been a brilliant student while studying in Portuguese, I did not grasp the idea that I should have started to read the books that had been prescribed for my first class at Eastleigh Secondary School; these were usually abridged forms of much bigger works on the lives of Mahatma Gandhi, Abraham Lincoln, Florence Nightingale, Marie Curie, and Albert Schweitzer, *The Murder of Roger Ackroyd* by Agatha Christie and some other books. Notwithstanding that, English came to me with lightning speed and I cannot even say how. After three months, my English was on a par with that of the Kenyan boys. I was soon to surpass them, which was no small achievement for me because English was a fifth language after my own tribal Sena language, Portuguese, French, and Swahili I learnt in Tanzania.

After the initial failure of realizing the importance of reading, I began to take pleasure in reading. I found that reading was the best teacher of any language because it enriches vocabulary, exposes the reader to various writing styles, expressions, idioms, and educates him. My essays improved greatly and no teacher ever spoke thereafter of the low standard of my English, not even when a teacher when I was in Form 2, gave a zero for my essay with the words "Dirty Mind" for the content rather than for style or the standard of my English.

I thought that it was unfair that the teacher should have given me zero because it was not my fault but rather his fault that I wrote what I had decided to write on. For that particular essay, he had told us to write on whatever topic we wanted to write about because it was free composition. I later saw his point and thought that it was silly of me to have written about a scandalous incident without actually giving any details. I thought that by telling us to write on whatever we wanted to, he had given us freedom with no holds barred on what to write. I was wrong.

The old conservative teacher in a secular school was different from Mr. Francis Xavier, the deputy headmaster, who wanted to see everybody reading and admired boys he saw with books in their hands or reading. He would stop, look at the titles of the books, shake his head with satisfaction, and commend the boys for doing the good job of reading. One day he walked into our class where we were rowdy because our teacher had walked away for some brief business in the office.

"Why aren't you studying or reading instead of making noise and disturbing the entire school?" he asked. No one answered him. We were all silent because our behaviour had been manifestly wrong. "I want to see you reading, no matter what you read. It can be the dirtiest sex stuff. You won't be in trouble with me for that, but you will if I find you not reading." After admonishing us, he walked away and we began to read silently with no one talking or goofing until the teacher returned.

For that free composition I thought it would be amusing to write about an incident I had heard while holidaying with a friend of mine in a village in Western Kenya. Their next door neighbour was a tall and hefty man by the name of Kephas who had been a soldier with the King's African Rifles in the British Army. He still looked every bit like an active soldier. He stood bolt upright and walked with his body firmly together as if on a drill march. He had a daughter who had her own cottage in his compound. Unknown to him, a boy from his next door neighbours used to sneak into his compound and sleep with her.

The boy would leave very early in the morning but one day, he saw him leaving his daughter's cottage. He stalked him and pounced on him and gave him a good beating before tying him up against a mango tree in his compound which he usually left his bicycle leaning against, after returning home from a trip out. He left the boy tied up against the tree for the greater part of the day for people in the village to see him, punishing the trespasser of his residence and transgressor of morals. At one point the boy was somehow able to untie himself and disengage from the ropes and grab the old man's bicycle, jump onto it and ride off as fast as he could to another village where he hid and missed school for three months before returning to the village with Kephas' bicycle, surrendering it, and apologizing to him before paying the old man some money as compensation for the humiliation he had inflicted on him. By then the old man's anger had cooled down and he had forgiven the sinner, but he did not force him to marry his daughter as Senas would have done. Morals here were different from those of the Senas and attitudes about sex were lax. Boys and girls made love all the time without marriage in mind. And more often than not, girls became

334

pregnant and single mothers and would later get married to other men. That was unacceptable to Senas who were obsessed with the purity and virginity of girls.

Kephas who got to know me while I was in the village, had some funny ideas about me. He thought I was a fitting match for his daughter, she of low morals, but my traditional Sena mind regarded the girl as having been desecrated and would not accept his idea. Besides, I was still young and at school. In Nairobi, I was jumping into bed and tumbling with school girls all the time, which in a way affected my academic performance. If I had wanted a girl for the serious business of marriage, I would get myself one in Nairobi and not his daughter. He talked about his idea to my friend's mother, who had two nubile daughters of her own. She told me about Kephas' idea. I ignored it after laughing it off. She also informed me that some women in the village had remarked about how handsome I was. I felt flattered, but I was not going to fall prey to traps that would interfere with my education and my decision at that time, of not ever wanting to get married.

The surprise that showed that I had overcome my difficulties with English did not take long to come along. While I was in Form 2 in 1971, there was an essay writing competition on "Tree Planting." It is an event that is taken seriously in Kenya once a year for afforestation is deemed important to arrest the desertification of the country which was two thirds desert or semi-desert.

The essay was divided into a junior section for Forms 1 and 2 and a senior section for Forms 3 and 4. I was surprised when I heard Mr. Sharma, the headmaster, announce at the morning assembly after we had sung the Kenyan national anthem in English and Swahili, that I had won the junior prize while a senior boy called Narendra Singh won the senior prize. It was hard for me to believe that I had achieved such a feat against about 400 junior boys who had been studying in English for close to ten or eleven years. The school had a population of 700 students.

I received my prize, a book of short stories by African writers with the title of *Drums of Africa,* from the hand of Mr. Charles Rubia, who was the deputy minister of education in Kenya then. He was the guest of honour at the school's prize-giving day that year. My photo in uniform receiving the prize and shaking hands with the minister appeared on a page of *The Eastleighan,* the school magazine that was published at the end of every academic year.

I was to repeat the feat on a much grander scale in 1975 when, in another essay competition in English, I won the senior prize for Forms 4, 5 and 6 whilst at the Aga Khan Academy in Nairobi where I did my A-Levels. The essay competition with the title of "The Ideal Headmaster" was for all Aga Khan Schools in Kenya. The winner of the junior prize for Forms 1, 2 and 3 was an Asian girl from an Aga Khan school in Mombasa. She travelled all the way from Mombasa to join me at a big dinner party held in our honour in Nairobi during which we received certificates to go to bookstores to pick up books. The 300 shillings I was awarded allowed me to buy many books, a whole basket full of books, mainly literature books in English.

The year 1975 was an eventful year in a good and bad way. Leftist junior officers of the Portuguese armed forces who were tired fighting unwinnable wars against guerrilla movements in Mozambique, Angola and Guinea-Bissau, staged a coup d'état in Portugal in 1974 and ended the old Salazar dictatorship which had been in power for about 48 years, to install democracy in their country. The leftists precipitately handed over power to the former guerrilla movements after negotiations with them and without prior elections and safety guarantees for the former enemies of the guerrilla movements. That hasty decolonization set the stage for bloody civil wars in all the three territories after they became independent. The post-independence wars were more ferocious and bloodier than the wars against colonial rule in all of those three countries.

That event saw the leaders of Frelimo with whom I was at daggers drawn, ascend to power as the new leaders of independent Mozambique with no prior elections at all because they regarded elections as a bourgeois luxury and a reactionary tradition of the Western countries. The first thing the new leaders did against us was to sabotage the education of those in diaspora who had earlier disagreed with them like me. They asked the scholarship organizations not to grant us new scholarships without the recommendation of the ministry of education in their new capital of Maputo. And none of us went so far as to apply for scholarships and seek the recommendation from our enemies in Maputo. The new regime went as far as asking the scholarship organizations to give it the scholarships so that they could administer these themselves.

These unsuspecting organizations which did not know of the quarrels between us and those now in power in Maputo, agreed to stop giving us their scholarships but they did not hand them over to Maputo. They thought that the new authorities had our best interests at heart. Those organizations did not even bother to listen to us. They just stopped supporting us. We were stranded and unable to continue with our studies. I found myself unable to pursue my education, at least not immediately. I never lacked the talent to explore new ways however. I was convinced that the setback was temporary before I found different means on my own to pursue my education.

A Mr. Kader, perhaps not the correct spelling of his name as I no longer remember how it was spelt, was a man from Iraq. He was the representative of the United Nations High Commissioner for refugees in Nairobi. He acted in a typically dictatorial manner, which was rather a reflection of the cultural and political background of the country he was from and which had never had a history of experimentation with democracy and freedom. He informed us that we should just pack up and return to Mozambique because our country was independent. And it was also possible that he was an ideological sympathizer of the new regime in Mozambique.

We told him that we were not going to Mozambique because those in power were our enemies who were after our blood and we had arrived in Kenya after fleeing from them, having run away from the Portuguese first. The man was such a pathetic and pitiful figure. He did not want to understand us. He did not want to listen to us. We held meetings with him several times until we told him to sod off and go to Mozambique himself, if he wanted to do so.

In my opinion, a man like Kader should never have been placed in a position or in a situation to deal with refugees. Dealing with refugees is a very complex humanitarian business and requires patience and the ability to listen, scrutinize and learn about complicated situations. Placing a man like him from the backyard of tyrants, was a major failure on the part of the UNHCR, but I also understood that the UN has to deal with all the countries of the world and with individuals who are the protégés of unsavoury tyrants, and who can only forge ahead in life with the blessing of their dictators. I do not think that Kader would have been allowed to work for the UN without being a protégé of the dictators of Iraq or even without being from a family that grovelled to the dictators of that country.

We defied Kader and stayed put, even after he announced the termination of our refugee status. Most of us, if not all of us, could survive without the help of his office, and we had done so for a long time because we had over the years found things to do to generate income in order to keep us alive in Kenya. Some of the refugees were businessmen.

Only those who had to travel found it difficult because the man would not allow his men to sign immigration papers to enable refugees to get travel documents from the Kenyan Immigration office. I remember a boy who could not go to study in Britain where he had admission to a college and a scholarship, simply because the UNHCR's representative's office in Nairobi callously refused to sign his papers to get a UN Travel document so that he could go to Britain. People who were supposed to support stateless individuals who had reasons to fear going to Mozambique had become evil incarnate, as evil incarnate as any of the other tyrants. Instead of protecting people with genuine fear of being executed, those good for nothing UNHCR's employees became the new persecutors and oppressors.

The authorities of Kenya did not interfere even when we entered and staged a rowdy demonstration in his office and forced him to flee panic-stricken. The police came and we talked with them amicably before they asked us to leave. The newspapers in Nairobi picked up the story and reported our demonstration and the world media echoed the news. And that must have been quite a humiliation for the new potentates in Maputo who were being hailed as liberators, which was true but they were not men of freedom. Their liberation struggle had never been a struggle for freedom.

I learnt years later that many people in Mozambique had hailed our courageous act because they understood our decision and courage because they themselves were already chafing under the tyranny of the new regime. They knew that if we had returned to Mozambique, the Frelimo regime would have killed us all, as it did in fact do to those who had gone back from other countries, even people who had not even quarrelled with them like we had.

As years passed, the UNHCR office in Nairobi became ashamed and embarrassed as none of us ever went to them to ask to be repatriated to Mozambique; instead, individuals arrived in Nairobi in the most degraded conditions after escaping from concentration camps that the post-independence regime in Mozambique had established all over the country, mainly in the woodlands of the northern region of the country which they euphemistically called re-education camps. I had to help some of these people before they could settle down in Nairobi.

The UNHCR's representative stuck to his guns and we stuck to ours. He could not force us to leave Kenya because the host country was not an admirer of Frelimo for a number of reasons. The Maoist Frelimo had made comments condemning Kenya's capitalist system and the Tanzanian regime had condemned Kenya for keeping us in its territory. And Kenya was dead set against Maoist ideology and anyone caught with Chinese writings from Beijing could be sent to prison, although Kenya had full diplomatic relations at ambassadorial level with Mao's People's Republic of China. One Mozambican refugee was sent to prison for a half a year after being found in possession of Maoist writings. And why was the refugee displaying Chinese literature knowing that it was illegal in Kenya? It is bad to challenge the rules of a host country that is giving you protection.

Any other writings were accepted in Kenya except the inflammatory Maoist writings which were sold in the streets of Dar-Es-Salaam, Tanzania, and were also freely distributed in the streets of Kampala, Uganda, which was then under the presidency of Milton Obote, a protégé of Julius Nyerere of Tanzania. Two Mozambican boys and I went to Kampala in 1970 to meet father Robert Roesems who had been our teacher at Zobue Seminary in Mozambique. He was in Uganda to attend a three-month seminar of Catholic prelates on the theme of Liberation and the Catholic Church, an aspect that was vexing the Catholic Church especially in Latin America where priests were becoming increasingly militant by siding with the peasants and sometimes with guerrilla movements that were fighting rightist regimes there.

While there we collected much Maoist literature from the streets and read it voraciously because we were amused by its highly inflammatory language against the Americans and the Soviets, but we did not dare take it with us on our return to Kenya. It would be too dangerous. We wanted to be at school and not in prison for such a frivolous reason as possessing childish Maoist writings. Obote was overthrown in 1971 by Idi Amin Dada, the army commander who later made himself quite a name with his erratic behaviour and strange outbursts.

I saw Idi Amin Dada from close quarters in Nairobi in 1973. He was a very huge and tall man, ebullient and charismatic with a tendency to make bizarre statements that amused people in general as they demonstrated his unstable mind and offended the people he directed his statements to like when he told Julius Nyerere of Tanzania that he would marry him, if Nyerere did not have white hair or challenging Nyerere to settle their differences in a boxing contest in course of which he would fight only with one arm with the other arm tied to his waist. During British rule, Idi Amin had once been a boxing champion of Uganda. He dwarfed Jomo Kenyatta and the rather smallish Emperor Haile Selassie of Ethiopia who was also in Nairobi for the All Africa Trade Fair. Wherever he went, people wanted to see him and cheered him because he cut a funny figure as a grotesque buffoon. Idi Amin joined the King's African Rifles of the British Army in 1946 and served in Burma, Somalia and Kenya during the suppression of the Mau Mau uprising. He was known to have committed many atrocities against Mau Mau detainees and there were calls for him to be arrested and court-martialled. He also excelled in brutalities when he was sent to deal with cattle rustlers in northern Uganda after the independence of Uganda in 1962.

Faced with our intransigence, the UNHCR representative's office in Nairobi later decided on who amongst us should still be considered genuine refugees and who should not before the government of Kenya later decided to restore the refugee status to all of us after the civil war in Mozambique had raged for close to six years. The decision to restore our refugee status happened while I was working for the American government in Swaziland. I missed the boat. I had relentlessly worked for it, but I was to all intents and purposes a refugee as I had a UN Refugee Convention travel document to work in Swaziland from 1983 to 1985 as a Mozambican refugee in Kenya. In 1982, the BBC Monitoring Service had forced the UNHCR to recommend the renewal of my travel document to the Government of Kenya so that I could travel to England. The fellows at the UNHCR were very reluctant but they felt intimidated by the sheer ponderous name of the BBC.

With no means to continue with my studies, I had to make do with what I could do. I began looking for jobs. I first taught English and History as an untrained teacher at a secondary school in Nairobi before landing the job with the BBC Monitoring Service at its unit in the Kenyan capital in 1976. I worked with the monitoring service until 1983 when I went to Swaziland. I regard the job with the BBC as one of the greatest jobs I have had because of the prestigious name of BBC. The pay was good and I was able to save money and live very comfortably in Nairobi even with a domestic worker who took care of cleaning my flat, washing my clothes and cooking my food, which left me with much time to read, particularly on the days when I was off duty.

The money I saved was never enough for the amount I would require to study at the University College of Buckingham, the only private university in Britain that was about to open its doors and to which I had gained admission after passing a tough entrance and scholarship exam under the supervision of the office of the British Council in Nairobi. But in the end, I missed the boat to go and study History and English Literature in Britain due to lack of financial means, as the assistance I would get from the University at Buckingham and my own finances combined, was never going to be enough to amount to the more than 3,000 pounds I would require annually for three years.

Although going to France had been my dream because I had learnt and known French while in Mozambique, I had begun to admire everything about Britain after learning English and liking it as much as I adored French. I read more in English than in French because Kenya is an English speaking country and every way I turned there was English and there were books in English and I spoke English with the members of educated elite reserving Swahili for the common people. English and Swahili are the two national and official languages of Kenya. I never neglected French. I later studied for a BA and MA in Canada at the prestigious University of Victoria in British Columbia, where I also attained a BA in History for which I studied in English. I regard myself as a very lucky person because I received my education in Portuguese from primary to junior secondary level. I did my secondary education at ordinary and Advanced levels in English in Kenya before doing further college and university education in English in Canada, where I also did my college and university education in French.

I regard my knowledge of three European and two African languages as my cultural heritage and I am very proud of this; I am able to think in each of the five languages I know and can speak fluently.

It was ironically not to France that I went when I travelled to Europe for the first time in 1982, but to Britain. The previous year had been a very good year for me at the monitoring unit. I was the only employee who got a double pay raise for outstanding performance whilst everyone else

343

got a single pay hike. The job sharpened my knowledge of Portuguese, French, and English. At times I also dealt with news in Swahili, translating into English. News monitoring is quite a challenging and intellectual job. Translating keeps you on your toes and you have to think fast, but once mastered, it becomes easy.

On top of the double pay hike, the BBC also sponsored me for a familiarization tour of some BBC installations in England. I went to England in March 1982 and from England I went to Portugal to reconnect with the former colonial power, a power which no longer recognized me as its citizen because I had fled from Mozambique and the regime change there also meant that everything else changed. I would not have gone there without being arrested for desertion if the old Salazar regime were still in power. The BBC paid all my expenses including my visit to Portugal.

In England I went to Caversham Park in Reading, Berkshire, where the Monitoring Service has its headquarters. There I was able to renew my acquaintance with John Bamber who had worked as an editor with me in Nairobi after his time in Malawi where he had heard those stories of children disappearing and being eaten. He took me to his house so that I should not be alone in the evenings in a room at Caversham Park. Staff worked there but did not live there. So when someone arrived there as a visitor, he would be quite alone with everything at his or her disposal but no other people for company in the evenings.

Although he lived in this house in Reading Bamber, whose family had special links with Kenya as his two daughters were born in Nairobi, was no longer with the monitoring service. He had become an editor with the World Service at the BBC at Bush House in London. I travelled to London with him once by train and on another occasion, by car. While he worked at Bush house, I went gallivanting in the city. My most memorable foray was by bus from Paddington Railway Station to Oxford Street where I went to buy clothes for myself seeing en route, St. Mary's Hospital where Dr Alexander Fleming discovered penicillin. From there I went around and about on my own before joining up with John again in the evening at Bush House.

There I watched the news going out to the world from the newsroom followed by a newsreel when correspondents gave accounts of what was going on in the countries they were reporting from. I had always listened to BBC news and newsreels which was different from actually seeing it leave the newsroom at Bush House. Later that evening we returned to Reading.

The second time I went to London with him, I had my most memorable walks from Strand to Trafalgar Square and from there to Buckingham Palace, a place that is mentioned in Alexandre Dumas' *The Three Musketeers*, which I read in French and also in the English translation.

The road to Buckingham Palace from Trafalgar Square was teeming with people. While at Buckingham Palace, I saw the unmistakable Westminster Parliament to the north-west. I had to go there to see the place that is regarded as the birth place of modern representative democracy. I walked around and about and found my way there. Before reaching it, I discovered Westminster Abbey; I went inside to see the place I had read so much about, the scene of coronations and the burial place of British monarchs and of some famous British individuals. I could not see much at that time because most of it had been sealed off for repairs and renovations.

The Parliament on the Thames and the statue of Oliver Cromwell outside Parliament, were remarkable sights. Seeing Cromwell, who in his time suppressed freedom in England, honoured appeared to be the genius of the British people. They honour even a man like Oliver Cromwell who had been instrumental in the execution of a king. The monarchy was reinstated; the new king was not amused even though Cromwell was already dead. His body was disinterred for trial in death, and was symbolically hanged. By having his statue there, Parliament was making the point of honouring a man who had fought for the rights of Parliament against the usurpation of powers by the king. There were illustrations of history I had studied every way I turned.

To see more of London in a very short space of time, I should have taken a trolley or a sight-seeing bus from Trafalgar Square to the most prominent places in London, but unfortunately I did not do so. I did not figure out then how huge London was. John Bamber told me that there were people who had lived for40 years in London and yet they did not know the entire city. In the 1980s, I read a book whose title and author I do not remember which said that London was the largest city in the West and was even bigger than New York.

Tell it to the French, someone in Paris will pooh-pooh it and say that Paris is larger than London with a statement like: *Bigre! Les Anglais, eux, peuvent dire n'importe quoi, tout ce qu'ils veulent dire et cela ne changera en rien la vérité que c'est Paris, et pas Londres, qui est la plus grande ville en Occident. Voyons alors, Paris est plus grand que Londres, n'est-ce pas? Il doit être ainsi pour la plus grande gloire de la France.*

Gosh! The British can say anything, whatever they want and it will not change the truth not even a bit that it's Paris, and not London, which is the largest city in the West. Let's face it; Paris is bigger than London, isn't it? That's how it must be for the greatest glory of France.

From London, I flew to Lisbon and had a hard time getting an entry visa at the airport. I later found out that the UN travel document was a curse and not a blessing. Countries fear to admit people with such a document that allows them entry and then they might refuse to leave. I was finally given a seven day visa to Portugal. That was too bad for a former Portuguese citizen. The city was still in the grips of the 1974 revolution which overthrew the old Salazar regime and brought democracy to Portugal, while Mozambique was chained to the tyranny of men who became the hirelings of the Soviet Union, although it was the Chinese who had helped the guerrillas in the war of liberation more than the Soviet Union. The new rulers of Mozambique thought that the country would get more modern weapons from the Soviet Union than from China. The change was also because the pro-Soviet wing in the upper echelon of the Frelimo leadership was much stronger than the Maoist group.

The Portuguese had hastily abandoned Mozambique in 1975 and it was plunged into chaos and a devastating civil war that broke out in 1977 because its new leaders, unlike Jomo Kenyatta who had worked for reconciliation in Kenya, decided to establish a reign of terror and unleash a revolution with mass detentions of real and imaginary opponents, and internal exiling of people who could not justify why they were in cities and towns, to concentration camps or the re-education camps which were Frelimo's own version of a Gulag.

I had a good time in Lisbon where I went to see Os Jeronimos which is the Portuguese equivalent of Westminster Abbey where I saw two big tombs, supposedly where Vasco da Gama, the fifteenth century Portuguese explorer who was the first European to voyage from Europe to India, and Luis de Camoes, the poet who celebrated da Gama's voyages of discovery to India in his *The Lusiads* epic, are entombed. The Portuguese were as loud, friendly and as jocular as I had known them in Mozambique.

By 1982, I had a family after marrying a Kenyan girl in 1980. As I did not know her maternal tongue and she did not know mine of far flung Mozambique, we communicated in English right from the time we knew each other and English became our language and is the language of our family. She was pregnant by the time we got married. Our first born was a girl I gave the name of Albertina after my healer aunt Albertina who was the mother of my beloved cousin Zefina. Two years later we got our second born, a boy to whom I gave the name of Moises after my paternal grandfather. That was the best I could do to honour some of my family members I had loved so much, most of whom are no longer still alive. I had loved them all, but, unfortunately, I could not honour them all in the same way. I honour them all in my memory.

Swaziland I had feared to go to for being close to the enemy territory of Mozambique, turned out to be a good distraction and a lot of fun. It is a very beautiful little country with exceptionally beautiful women and good people, and a language that has clicks like the Bushmen's languages. It is one of the southern Bantu languages which have clicks while Sena of central Mozambique and southern Malawi, also a Bantu language, has no clicks whatsoever. Swaziland is mired in old traditions and no woman there can object to her husband taking another wife or multiple wives.

Before my family joined me there in September 1983 - I had been there from March of that year, I made the acquaintance of a princess Spiwe Dlamini of the Royal House of Swaziland, who was a granddaughter of the late King Sobhuza II who was known to have had 66 official wives and about 500 wives unofficially, and to have fathered about 1,000 children. The Dlaminis are the royal clan of Swaziland and they are very proud and regal.

The princess was always dressed royally with hats with feathers and all. She told me that she would like to become my second wife. Much as I, a commoner, might have wanted that beautiful, pale-complexioned and soft girl to be my wife, I did not think I could have her as a wife without upsetting my family and causing myself many problems. Home for me and my family was Kenya. Swaziland would not do for being so close to the hostile territory of Mozambique.

I had gone to Swaziland after the American Government hired me from the BBC in 1983 to go and work at the monitoring station they had established in Mbabane, the capital of Swaziland, because the Americans were going to take away the monitoring of the broadcasts from Radio Maputo in Mozambique and Radio Luanda in Angola from the BBC in Nairobi. While in Swaziland, I registered with the University of London to study law by correspondence. I later gave up studying law because I simply felt that law was not for me. I got to know quite a bit about the English Common Law.

In 1985, my family returned to Nairobi where we stayed for two years before applying to immigrate to Canada which has been home to us as permanent residents and Canadian citizens since 1987. Here we have done well and have done our bit for the greatness of Kanata, which is known as Canada because it is the way Jacques Cartier wrote it after hearing the word Kanata from Iroquois natives, and the governments of Canada thereafter adopted Cartier's transliteration of the word as the official name of the country.

End

Bibliography and Notes

Boddy-Evans, Alistair. "Biography: Idi Amin Dada: Despotic President of Uganda in the 1970s." www.google.com.

Bwana is Swahili word for mister, master or lord or sir.

Ç cedilha in Portuguese or cedilla as in French cedille like in François has the sound of s in Portuguese like in Moçambique read: Mozambique. Operaçao: Operasao

Charles, Miller. *The Lunatic Express: An Entertainment in Imperialism*, London: MacMillan Publishing, 2010.

Chico (pronounce as sheeko) short or diminutive form of name Francisco

Corbett, Jim. *The Man-eaters of Kumaon* (A history of the man-eating tigers and leopards of Kumaon, India). Oxford: Oxford Paperbacks, reprint Feb 18, 2003.

Curandeiros (from Portuguese word curar: to heal) healers or witchdoctors in Brazil.

Devji, Faisal Fatehali. *Subject to Translation*: *Shakespeare, Swahili, Socialism*. Postcolonial Studies, Vol. 3, No. 2, pp 181-189.

"Devonshire White Paper: Africa (1923)." Encyclopedia Britannica, 2005.

"Fort Jesus, Mombasa." Nairobi: African World Heritage, 2011.

Guderian, Heinz. *Panzer Leader*. Foreword by B. H. Liddel Hart, introduction by Kenneth John Macksey. (Boston): Da Capo Press, 1952. pp. 422, 423.

"How Kanata Became Canada." Language Portal of Canada. www.ourlanguages.gc.ca. Date modified: 2014.04.17. www.google.com

Hyslop, Leah. "Baobab: the 'Superfood' for 2015?" (London): The Telegraph, 07 Jan 2015. www.google.com

"Leopard of Rudraprayag (India)." Wikipedia, the free encyclopaedia, www.google.com.

"Le Tiers-Monde: Afrocommunisme: Éthiopie, Angola, Mozambique." *Le livre noir du communisme : Crimes, terreur, répression.* Stéphane Courtois, Nicolas Werth, Jean-Louis Panné et al. Avec la collaboration de Rémi Kauffer, Pierre Rigoulot, Pascal Fontaine et al. Paris: Robert Laffont, 1997. pp 810, 812-813, 818-823.

"Life in England under Oliver Cromwell." History/Learning. Site.co.uk. 2014. Web.

"L.S.B. Leaky: Kenyan archaeologist and anthropologist." Written by editors of Encyclopedia Britannica. Last updated 9-10-2013. www.google.com.

Macumba (Portuguese pronunciation: [maˈkũᵐbɐ]) is a word meaning both "a musical instrument" and "magic". It was the name used for all non-Abrahamic religious practices in Brazil during the 19th century. In the 20th century, these practices re-aligned themselves into what are now called Umbanda and Quimbanda. (www.google.com).

Maji Maji (1905-1907): Arrows and Spears." Contributor(s) Beverton, Alys. University of Sussex. www.google.com.

Majini (jinni in singular) in Swahili are evil spirits to the coastal people of East Africa. The Koran has a chapter on the subject of Jinns mentioned in this Bibliography.

Menon, Ramesh. *The Ramayana: A Modern Retelling of the Great Indian Epic.* New York: North Potnt Press, 2001, 2003.

Mondlane, Solomon. *A Clown in a President Samora Moises Machel: A Comedian and a Dictator*. Text in English on macua.blogs.com/files-in-a-president-1pdf. www.google.com

Montgomery, Bernard Law. *The Memoirs of Field-Marshal Montgomery*. Pen and Sword, 2005.

Mzee (pronounced as mzé) is a term of respect for elders in Swahili.

Mzungu (white man or white person), Wazungu (white men or white people) in Swahili.

Ngerezi (an Englishman or a British man) and Angerezi in plural in Sena.

Nairobi National Museum, Kenya.

Nzungu (white man or white person), Azungu (white men or white people) in Sena.

Obeah (sometimes spelled Obi, Obea, or Obia), is a term used in the West Indies to refer to folk magic, sorcery, and religious practices developed among West African slaves, specifically of Igbo origin. Obeah is similar to other Afro-American religions including Palo, Vodou, Santería, and Hoodoo (www.google.com)

On Cannibalism by Sudanic tribes. Turnbull, Colin M. *The Forest People: a Study of the Pygmies of the Congo*. New York: Simon and Schuster, 1961, 1962. pp. 19, 235.

On Zimba Cannibals of the Zambezi Valley. "The Portuguese Empire (1498-1698). " Kenyalogy, www.google.com, 2000-2012.

PIDE (Policia Internacional para a Defesa do Estato. In English: International Police for the Defence of the State) was Salazar regime's secret agency.

Purdah defined as "(of women) segregation or seclusion, wearing veil" in Glossary of *I am Malala: the Girl Who Stood up for Education and Was Shot by the Taliban*. p.317.

Reference to the mysterious stone at Sena in the article in Portuguese "Renasce Fortaleza de Sena," Moçambique para Todos, www.google.com.

"St. Francis Xavier." Catholic Online, www.google.com.

Senhor (pronounced as senyore) Portuguese for mister, sir, lord.

Shona Customs: Essays by African Writers edited by Clive and Peggy Kileff. Illustrations by E. Lee. Harare: Mambo Press, 1970, 1972, 1974, 1976, 1980, 1982, 1983.

Swahili comes from a word of the Arabic meaning coast or coastal and it's the name of a language from Bantu languages with heavy Arabic influences and words from Portuguese, German and English and also Indian languages.

The Bible. The New and the Old Testaments.

"The Emergence of Modern East African Nations 1900-1963: the Mau Mau Uprising 1954." Elate: E-Learning and Teacher Education, School of Education, Makerere University; The Open Learning University. http://www.elateafrica.org/elate/history/maumau/maumauin tro.html

"The Jinn (72.1-72.28)." *The Koran*. Translated with notes by N. J. Dawood. London: Penguin Books, 1956. Revised editions in 1956, 1959, 1966, 1968, 1974, 1990, 1993, 1997, 1999. pp 408-409.

The Nubians. www.google.com.

Tse-Tung, Mao (Mao Ze Dong). *Quotations from Chairman Mao Tse-Tung*. Foreword by Lin Piao (Lin Biao). Peking (Beijing): Foreign Language Press, 1966.

Thompson, Amy. "The Maji Maji Rebellion: German East Africa." African History Blog, May 14, 2013.

Wareno Swahili word to mean the Portuguese with mreno (singular). The Swahili word for Portugal comes from the Portuguese "O Reino (pronounce oo rayno) meaning the Kingdom and "O Reino de Portugal" meaning the Kingdom of Portugal. In interaction with the Swahili people during the 200 years of the Portuguese presence in the coast of East Africa, the Swahilis got hold of the words *O Reino* in the *O Reino de Portugal* and transformed them into URENO as the word for Portugal.

Yousafzai, Malala with Christina Lamb. *I am Malala: The Girl who stood for Education and Was Shot by the Taliban*. New York, London: Little, Brown and Company, 2013.